THE DOUBLE E

Percival Goodman is an architect and town planner who began at age thirteen as apprentice to his architect uncle. He was awarded the Prix de Paris to study at the École des Beaux Arts in 1925, and remained in Paris until 1929. On his return to the United States, he started an architectural office which is known for its religious and educational buildings throughout the country. Although his primary interest has been in the practice and teaching of architecture and town planning, he is a furniture designer, book illustrator, sculptor, and painter. He has taught at New York University, the New School for Social Research, and for twenty-five years at Columbia University. He has written on art and architecture, and, in 1947, wrote *Communitas* with his brother Paul, the social critic, novelist, and poet. During the last ten years, Mr. Goodman has been increasingly concerned with ecology and the human environment, and has taught and lectured on these problems here and abroad. He is a Fellow of the American Institute of Architects and Professor Emeritus of the Columbia University School of Architecture and Planning.

THE DOUBLE E

Percival Goodman

ANCHOR BOOKS
ANCHOR PRESS/DOUBLEDAY
GARDEN CITY, NEW YORK *1977*

I gratefully acknowledge the work of John Morris in preparing the following charts and diagrams: figures 2, 3, 12, 13, 14, 15, 17, 18, 19, 20, 24, 26, 28, 31, 33, 46, 47, 48, 49, 50, 51, 56, 57, 59, and 60.

I have no words to express my thanks to Naomi Goodman for her aid . . . and patience.

Grateful acknowledgment is made for permission to include excerpts from the following copyrighted publications:

"Town Plan for Tokyo," by Noriaki Kurokawa. Originally published in *Stadtstrukturen für Morgen*, by Justus Dahinden. Reprinted by permission of Verlag Gerd Hatje, Stuttgart (1977).

Drawing of "Broadacre City" from *When Democracy Builds*, by Frank Lloyd Wright. Copyright © 1945, 1973 by The Frank Lloyd Wright Foundation. Reprinted by permission of the copyright owner.

Craft Horizons of the American Crafts Council for permission to reprint material that first appeared in the June 1976 issue of that publication in an article entitled "Reflections from the Post-Industrial Society." Copyright © 1976 by *Craft Horizons* of the American Crafts Council.

Portions of this book are based on material presented in lectures and reprinted in the *Journal of the Royal Institute of British Architects* Vol. 80, No. 7 (July 1973).

Library of Congress Cataloging in Publication Data

Goodman, Percival.
　　The double E.

　　Includes index.
　　1. City planning.　2. Architecture—Environmental aspects.　3. Human ecology.　I. Title.
HT166.G638　　　309.2′62

ISBN: 0-385-12868-1
Library of Congress Catalog Card Number 76-50873

For *Paul*
in the presence of his absence

Contents

PART ONE

CHAPTER I

Introduction

Since global resources will soon be inadequate to support us in the style to which we have become accustomed and since radical transformations are occurring in our attitudes toward work and domestic life, we must expect and plan for large-scale changes in the way we build our houses and our towns. In this book I examine these coming changes, assume optimistically that if we select rightly among the alternative possibilities, and plan well, the shift in our ways will be for the better. The problems will be not problems, but opportunities.

Years ago my brother Paul and I wrote *Communitas*, an examination and analysis of representative town plans built or proposed in modern times, in order to discover how they reflected the way people lived and earned their livelihood, how they reflected the technological, economic, and political forces that formed them. From this study emerged a set of proposals (or paradigms as we called them) for the future man-made environment. It was, we presumed, feasible to recommend many possibilities since "for the first time in history, spectacularly, we have in the United States, a surplus technology, a technology of free choice that allows for the most widely various community arrangements and ways of life."

The presumption was correct, but who could have guessed how quickly our appetites would grow, how quickly our surplus would diminish, and how badly we would choose? Only thirty-five years later what had seemed an ever-brimming cornucopia threatens to run dry. Limits, not free choice; scarcity, not surplus, are now the facts that will condition our future.

PLANNING

Planning has a built-in contradiction. It is, as Gunnar Myrdal said, "an exercise in a non-deterministic conception of history" permitting a freedom of choice which may turn the course of future development. On the other hand, planning even on its simplest level tends to be inimical to future freedom of choice, since to plan requires the fixing of boundaries, the channeling of actions, and the fixing of goals. The contradiction cannot be resolved by not planning; as a decision, not to plan is also a plan. We cannot help but plan—a shopping list is an instance. It is based on a simple assumption: X will purchase Y. Here we presume that X can purchase Y. But what if the truck broke down and supplies didn't get to the supermarket? What if the price jumped beyond our means? What if the supermarket disappeared? Then, no matter how carefully thought out, our plan is useless. Inherent, then, in planning is a further trouble—it is hypothetical, for its subject is the future.

In history there have been long periods of stability, periods when the past was like the present and no circumstance forecast a different future. But even in such times who could say they knew the future until it had arrived; was not the prophet Jonah himself wrong when, on the highest authority, he predicted Ninevah's fall?

Times of change are hard times not only for prophets but for planners as well. Prediction becomes sheer guesswork, and the most solidly based research may lead to absurd conclusions. Nevertheless, the planner cannot be fainthearted. He must have the courage to interpret what he sees in the light of his own vision and have the daring to make assumptions even when they are contrary to the wisdom of his peers and the past. It is just such times that call for speculation on the future, for who pays much attention to it in periods of stability, who thinks on the need for alternatives except when there is the need for change?

We have made the transition. New things have happened calling for change. And what has happened is not only technical, it is total; and so drastic as to suggest mutation rather than evolution. We live in a world of improbabilities come true—a world not so solid, earthy, and dependable as we thought, a world suddenly seen as a fragile network of interlocking, interdependent systems in imminent danger of overburden and disruption.

In such a time it would be expected that such words as "ecology" and "economy" would haunt all discussions of planning. Not so. Architects and planners, like businessmen and even statesmen, are fixated on a science and technology, an ideology and an economics closer to 1900 than 2000. With few exceptions, they seem incapable of realizing that there has been a change in quantity—like the ultimate straw breaking the camel's back—making the qualitative change to which we must address ourselves.

"Ecology" and "economy" are two powerful words linked by the Greek *oikos*, meaning house. The root meaning of *ecology* is a knowledge of the house; *economy* means management of the house. Modern usage doubles the impact: *ecology* being the study of mutual relations between organism and environment, *economy* the management of expenditures. Are not these the operative concepts in planning for a world with diminishing resources and increasing populations?

THE BUILT ENVIRONMENT

Like a poem, the built environment has always been more than the sum of its parts, but unlike a poem—which may be achieved by an individual out of his own psyche—it is a collective work calling for many skills, using solid chunks of the planet in its making and subtly or overtly conditioning our movements. Throughout history these sticks and stones have been a crystallization of the technical, social, and moral qualities of the society that did the building, a crystallization of its way of life showing how it spent its substance, what it revered, admired, loved, and cherished as well as to what it paid no heed.

The built environment of the late twentieth century differs from the past not merely because it uses greater chunks of material to make it, not merely because the whole thing is more complicated and needs more fuel to keep it going, but because it no longer evolves from the climate, geography, or history of the place where it is, nor is it the collective work of the people who inhabit it; instead, the new environment is conceived at conference tables and pieced together on drawing boards in distant capitals, its design aspiring to be the result of computerized decision-making suitable to the printed circuits of a society transformed into technology. Parts of the obsolete old cities are torn down or new land is found to serve as sites for the architecture of filing cabinets—impersonal, abstract, and elegant— the difference between one and another shown only on their modishly lit labels. Offices and apartments, law courts and concert halls, are wrapped in glass blankly reflecting the onlooker, concealing all expression like the mirrored shades worn by Haitian gangsters. All is hidden within the climate-controlled, floodlit modules, hard-edged against the evening sky. The semeiologist looking for symbols finds but the letters of the alphabet, informing, exhorting, advising in the special language of advertising copy writers.

During most of the twentieth century the future has been projected as just such an artificial, urbanized world in which human muscle long ago replaced by machine is now preparing the next stage—the human brain replaced by machine, the human brain redun-

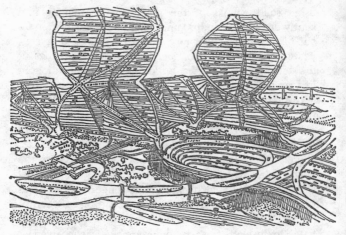

Town plan for Tokyo by Norioki Kurokawa (1961).

dant. The world is conceived as a colony of vast termi-
taries run by agencies, conglomerates, and cartels who
are in turn directed by a queen computer buried in the
air-conditioned depths.

How fortunate it is that such a simple fact as the
need to live within our means precludes such a future
and rids us of all those boring discussions on the moral
and social implications of life in such a world. What a
pleasure it will be to consign to the Museum of Architectural Curiosities all those schemes calling for cities
built on top of cities, cities under the earth or under
the sea, on man-made islands floating on the Atlantic or
Pacific, under domes in Antarctica or on the moon, in
the stratosphere. . . . How interesting it will be for future historians to see renderings and models of those
mile-high, miles-long megastructures in which dwelling
places are plugged in, clipped on, or otherwise arranged for ready removal to suit the latest fashion.

Since the world cannot afford such schemes, what

can it afford? What are the ways of creating more feasible man-made environments? What are the form-making elements and how should we use them? In a general way, what would the routine of daily life be like in such a future habitat and what would it look like?

Since the technical solutions offered have proved to be no solutions, we may ask whether we need new technologies or different solutions. My answer is categorical: It is not new technologies or inventions that are needed; to the contrary, we have more than we can conveniently use, thanks to talents and skills nourished by the Industrial Revolution.

It is useful to remember that by the end of the nineteenth century all the inventions commonplace today such as the telephone, the automobile, the typewriter, even the electric chair, had already been devised; by the first half of the twentieth century the task of refining the products, increasing the speed and scale of production and distribution, was completed along with the developments in nuclear power, electronics, and the life sciences. Yet, as I write, new devices are touted, new "needs" generated, including the need to build humanity-extinguishing implements on a scale previously unknown.

The time has come to rid ourselves of useless gadgetry, simplify and limit the devices we use, reduce our dependence on them, revaluate our technology. At the same time we must reconsider our customs and our manners in order to learn how to live, gracefully, within our means. By living within our means, I refer not only to whether we can afford a thing economically and ecologically but whether what it affords us is good, needed, a contribution to the ease, beauty, and wholeness of life. To live within our means does not require that we dismantle our machines, burn our cities, and return to the cave, but it does mean, especially among the high technology nations, a reorganization that must take account of the effects of mass urbanization, the need to humanize work processes and provide meaningful occupations, the effects of sexual symmetry on the dwelling unit, the degradation of the environment. . . .

Such diverse concerns entered this book often against my will, since my aim was to explain in simple ways why our present towns and cities are obsolete, as is most planning practice, then to propose a planning theory more appropriate to our time and, as an example and a test of the theory, delineate and describe a populated area, a town within it, and even a house on one of its streets.

The facts, figures, opinions, and forecasts I gathered will be familiar to all who follow this kind of literature. My reason for including them in a series of supporting papers is threefold: They bolster conclusions that most planning agencies and some planners will consider outré; they, I believe, will serve as a convenient reference; and finally I trust my comments help relate these disparate matters to my subject.

The focus of my criticism, the examples and proposals, almost without exception, relate to the United States. As it is my country, I know a fair amount about it, and because it is so big, so powerful, and so technically advanced, it is unhappily a major, although not the only, threat to world survival. In somewhat the same way I use New York as my city example, since this is where I was born, where I've lived most of my life, and where I find exemplified the fate of all huge urban agglomerations.

We now know at what a disquieting rate the machines have been using up mines, oil deposits, and forests; how much they pollute in the course of their producing and what they produce is also a pollutant. Quite suddenly we've come to realize what mismanagement and ignorance of nature's symbiotic ways has done or threatens to do to our planet. Neil Armstrong, our first man to walk on the moon, voiced this new understanding: "Earth is an oasis of life in space that must be protected against its population."

Few nowadays think it cranky to say such things; to say that there is an immediate cause for worry not only as to the quality of life on earth but even as to its continuance. Nevertheless, I realize that when I conclude there can be no acceptable future, perhaps no future at all, without the dismantling of the war machine, population control by humane means, and a curbing of appetites by democratic process, and when I assume these things will come about, I have no facts, only hope. What keeps hope alive is my belief that our species is life-, not death-, directed.

A viable future assumes users inclined toward modesty and a certain frugality who favor a physical environment designed for people, not things, and who will support plans based on the scale of humankind in its symbiotic relationship with nature. My conclusions are based on these optimistic assumptions.

CHAPTER II

Cities and Other Settlements

The city form is a creature of technology: Cannons made city walls obsolete, steam engines expanded city to metropolis. Now airplanes and electronic devices shrink space so that center, periphery, and hinterland become equally convenient locations for city work—the manufacture and distribution of goods, administration, and services. From structures contained in tight grids of streets, cities become amorphous masses loosely connected by highways, enmeshed in invisible webs, networks of pulsing signals. Cities as we knew them are no longer needed for city functions.

The city form is also a creature of polity: There have been cities shaped to memorialize gods, serve the whims of kings, or the needs of war, but it took the Industrial Revolution to shape cities whose every part was considered marketable. Land and buildings were commodities, the inhabitants a labor force to exploit. In such a system any effort to make the city more salubrious or add to its amenity was bitterly fought, concessions such as parks or even a decent water supply had to be squeezed out of political parties whose chief function was to protect the money machine. These are the cities we have inherited.

Throughout history, the city depended on the countryside for food and the replenishment of its population. Some rustics came willingly like Dick Whittington, or unwillingly like those dispossessed by the English Enclosure Acts. In our time, the mechanization of agriculture and the inordinate growth of populations have driven ever-increasing numbers of the rural poor into the world's great cities where they do not supplement the established population as in other times but replace it, for the old population is outward bound, taking with them their city culture, city skills, and, increasingly, not only the purchasing power derived from city-held jobs but the jobs themselves.

Newcomers with no city skills were once welcome; they manned sweatshops and mills. Now the employers find the city impractical: Taxes are high, energy often two or three times more costly than elsewhere, land is so expensive that efficient, large, horizontal factory space is unavailable, the cost of transporting goods is excessive, unions are strong, and because living costs are high, a higher wage must be paid. There are increasing numbers of job seekers, but city jobs diminish as production moves to suburb and hinterland. Nor do factory jobs merely move from the city; there are fewer of them everywhere. The promise of industrial society comes true: As new technology increases productivity, the number of people required to produce goods shrinks, in 1973 to only a third of all national employment. In the cities the proportion of factory jobs is even lower. For instance, New York, where in 1970 only 24 per cent of its employed were in manufacturing and, like most American cities, the decline continues in all work, with blue-collar jobs disappearing fastest. Such trends spell disaster especially when the growing part of its population are poor blacks and Puerto Ricans—13 per cent of the city's population in 1950 and 33 per cent in 1970 (in those twenty years, the white population of the city declined by 1.5 million while the "ethnics" increased by 1.6 million). For a majority there is no way of becoming a productive part of the city's economy, since the traditional way of gaining a foothold—easily learned blue-collar work—is in short supply, manufacturing jobs having dropped from 1 million in 1950 to 650,000 by 1974.

In that same year New York City's economic administrator said: "It's true we are in the post-industrial era, but the city cannot go on indefinitely losing manufac-

EMPLOYMENT CHANGE IN SOME
CITIES & THEIR SUBURBS - 1965-72

	City	Suburb
New York	-0.1	+21.9
Philadelphia	-2.7	+24.6
Baltimore	+3.6	+32.1
St. Louis	-1.9	+26.8
San Francisco	+9.9	+24.3

turing jobs . . ." while the New York Urban Coalition "argued strongly for urban industrial development as a basis for building job opportunities for male adults not likely to be adaptable to training for clerical or office positions. Only through adequate jobs for these men can we hope to reduce the level of aid to dependent children—the major welfare burden in New York City." It was true, all too true. But what of the facts, especially if to the disheartening statistics we add that three out of every four new jobs during the 1960s were in the public sector (tax eating, not tax paying), and the forecast is for 8 per cent fewer jobs in 1980 than in 1970. We can only conclude that New York, like most of our central cities, is sick. Treating the obvious troubles must prove fruitless, since chronic unemployment, income dependency, crime, pollution, crowding, and all the other physical, social, and fiscal troubles are but symptoms of a terminal complaint which might be likened to senile dementia whose syndrome is "a progressive, abnormally accelerated deterioration of the faculties."

Newark, New Jersey, is a case study, a city of 375,000—61 per cent black, 11 per cent Puerto Rican. In 1970 an unemployment rate of 25 per cent resulted in a third of the population getting some form of public assistance. Newark has the highest crime rate in the nation, the highest rate of venereal disease, TB cases, and maternal mortality, and is second in infant mortality. The guess is that there are 20,000 drug addicts, only 7 per cent treated. Mayor Kenneth Gibson said, "Wherever the central cities of America are going, Newark is going to get there first."

Those who know Mexico City, the world's third largest metropolis, would not agree. They claim it is one of the least habitable areas on earth, where three quarters of the population live in slums, where 2 million people are without drinking water, 2 million vehicles pollute the air trapped between the surrounding mountains, where the dried-up lake on which the city sits slowly sinks, cracking buildings and pipes, where a swelling population of peasant migrants adds to the million now unemployed . . . 12 million people growing by 500,000 every year, 18 million by mid-1980s, 30 million by the end of the century.

The great cities of the world increasingly become traps for the poor, their obsolete grandeur a surrealist background for tourists and slum dwellers. By night, only prowl cars, junkies, and muggers are on the golden-lit streets. The millions of daytime inhabitants are safe in the suburbs or relatively safe huddled behind their double-padlocked doors. By day and night there are short periods of comparative quiet—a pervading hum of air-conditioners and smooth-flowing traffic—suddenly broken by the wild bleating of an ambulance or police car, the shriek of fire engines, the roar of tractor-trailers, buses, or low-flying jets. Somewhere is the continuous despairing wail of a burglar alarm or a klaxon gone wrong.

In such an ambience, what becomes of a city like New York with its monuments to man's ingenuity, pride, and art, fantastic and beautiful, its impersonal rectangles of glass reflecting the sun and outshining the starry skies at night? What becomes of those vertical filing cabinets, symbols of greed rising in the polluted air, reflected in contaminated waters? What becomes of a city where packs of wild dogs run in the garbage-strewn streets of one of its boroughs while in another mannequins are showing off furs costing the yearly welfare checks of entire families? And what becomes of a city whose expense budget increased at a rate of 10 to 15 per cent annually since 1965 (while public services—streets, transit, water and sewer facilities—progressively decayed or became obsolete) and in fact, if not in law, has been bankrupt since 1975?

URBANIZATION

U. S. Census: Between 1860 and 1900 the United States urban population quadrupled, the rural population merely doubled. In 1900 not more than 35 per cent of the population lived in cities. Now it is 75 per cent, and soon only 10 per cent of the population will live outside of metropolitan areas.

Such statistics are misleading, for what the Census calls "urban" is population densities that any city dweller would consider country: 2,800 people to the square mile is *not* an urban density, since almost ten times that number (25,000) is the typical population of older towns, older city centers having densities in the range of 100,000 to 250,000 to the square mile.

These statistics are misleading for a more important reason. Urbanization is not simply the physical herding together of a large population; it has a wider meaning. To be urbanized means accepting city culture, emulating city customs and style. Easy communication urbanizes. As technology and its networks expand, so does the urbanizing process. The railroads and cheap postal service were early urbanizers, bringing news from the city, store-bought bread, and flush toilets to the hinterland. Each new artificial satellite furthers the process, beaming endless streams of chitchat, commercials, and even useful information to countless households, hamlets, villages, towns, and cities in its orbit. Local dialects soon are found only in city-inspired country and western music, while denim pants and cowboy boots styled in New York are worn in Palm Beach and Malibu.

Life on the farm has come a long way from the time described by John Dewey when "instead of pressing a button and flooding the house with light, the whole process of illumination was followed in its toilsome length from the killing of the animal and trying of the fat to the making of wicks and dipping of candles. So it was with all things, the entire way of producng goods stood revealed from raw material to end product." With all its benefits the great penalty exacted by urbanization is the loss of this direct relation between means and ends and the self-sufficiency made possible because of it.

Seventy-five years ago, Robert Park wrote of "life [in Chicago] becoming constantly more complex. In place of simple, spontaneous modes of behavior which enable the lower animals to live without education or anxiety, men are compelled to supplement original nature with special training and with more and more elaborate machinery, until life losing all its spontaneity seems in danger of losing all its joy." Yet these complex and expensive systems, developed to satisfy the complex programs supposedly needed to "supplement original nature," aim at satisfactions not so different from those sought by the "lower animals"—an adequate diet, a satisfying life.

It is no longer escape from the city that leads to more spontaneity or less elaborate machinery, to a more direct relationship of means to ends, for outside is just another urbanized place. Dependent as they are on vast and remotely controlled organizations for every survival need and every comfort, the urbanized become the epitome of the helpless when faced with any break

in the routine and panic when faced with any unto-
ward circumstance, for self-sufficiency is all but obsolete.

THE FUTURE OF GREAT CITIES

Urbanized though we have become, the American attitude is not pro-city. To the contrary. The average middle-class American believes with Thomas Jefferson that
the city is ". . . pestilential to the morals, the health
and liberties of man," while the more thoughtful find,
as did John Dewey, that "neither face-to-face relationships nor even social intelligence can thrive in megalopolis, where there is no place for cooperative activity,
natural division of labor, spontaneity, or closeness to
nature."

The poor don't know these things—led by 5.5 million black farm workers, a huge population of rural
poor flooded our large cities in the single decade
1950–60. Coincidentally (or was it a coincidence?),
highways were vastly improved and the automobile
business flourished as never before. Common wisdom
has it that the exodus of the middle class from the
city was a running away from the poor. It is an odd
explanation, for since when have the strong and entrenched run from the foot-loose weak? Other explana-
tions are more likely—a people brought up to believe in
technical efficiency will discard, when they can, out-
moded machines such as cities had become. Or, could
this migration be the result of a vague desire to escape
the complications altogether, a yearning to be part of
a simple community in a more natural place?

Two decades of flight are over, the die is cast. It is
clear that the population projections made by the National Commission on Urban Problems in 1960 were, if
anything, underestimates. The forecast was that by
1985, 70 per cent of metropolitan area whites will be
living in the suburbs and 75 per cent of metropolitan
area blacks and Hispanics in the cities. Each year this
economic absurdity grows, since "city nonwhite" in our

time means poor, yet every study (e. g., the Advisory Committee on Intergovernmental Relations) tells us that the larger the city, the greater the cost for public services and for families to maintain acceptable living standards. Yet these are the places the impoverished are led to by the hope of jobs or the bait of larger welfare payments. The future? For the people, poverty and failure in slums where discontent and frustration feed on each other. For the city budget, a population needing housing, schools, hospitals, and social services with no means to pay for them. What were once the advantages—centralization of resources, variety of choice, and a large producing and consuming population—turn into a sink of human and vehicular congestion and pollution, physically unmanageable and financially bankrupt.

METRO AREAS

Demographers' forecasts and population trends suggest that most of future United States population growth will be in metropolitan areas. The Commission on Population Growth in 1973 estimated that in the year 2000, 85 per cent of our population would be "metropolitan," that is, part of a "Standard Statistical Metropolitan Area" (a city of 50,000 and its surrounding area) as compared to the 71 per cent in 1970. The assumption has been that these metropolitan areas would grow and join, becoming continuous cities—Boston to Washington, San Francisco to Los Angeles, etc.—and among planners, who are fond of such inventions, we hear "Bowash" and "Sanange" used to describe these agglomerations. If this comes to pass, Jerome Pickard warned in a 1968 Urban Land Institute study, we shall "place great strain upon the regional resources: water supply, air, and the land itself. The pollutants generated in such large-scale urban and industrial concentrations may threaten a large segment of the environment, inhabited by a large majority of U.S. population. . . ."

As we have seen, these urban "concentrations" are not so concentrated. What makes them ecological disaster areas lies elsewhere, in sprawl and spread, in the highways and the traffic required by sprawl and spread, in the industries and their wastes, in the people's garbage, end product of a society where artificially generated cravings are taken for healthy appetites.

BACK TO NATURE

More than half of all urban dwellers in the United States prefer to live and work in rural places, or so they told Gallup pollsters in 1973. The truth of such a preference is dubious, for people in general don't think very seriously of variant ways of living, and surely the typical urban dweller has but the vaguest and most rose-tinted notion of what he means by a rural place. Nevertheless, it certainly shows a lot of dissatisfaction with the existing environment, lending credence to the notion that the mass move to the suburbs could be the beginning of a search for a simpler society and a more human scale. Some further reinforcement is given by census statistics indicating that in the 1960s non-metro areas stopped losing population and since 1970, the growth rate in these areas was higher than in metro areas, a major change from the pattern of twentieth-century population movement in the United States.

Perhaps, then, there is a trend toward country life. Is it toward a simpler society?

In the past, rural people were believers in the virtues of self-reliance, Jeffersonian democracy, local autonomy, and homespun wisdom. The job of government was to keep law and order and protect property rights, welfare was something for the church to provide, or if need be, the county poorhouse, and a decent austerity was a way of life. Electricity came in, roads got improved, children got bused to school; public services for some, including medical care and welfare aid, and, for others, farm subsidies, became part of life. *Urbs in rure*, the "urbanized rural" people sought the same kind of public services given city folks, and the more astute got the same conveniences, then the same comforts and the same luxuries. The elimination of the difference between the city and the country (not quite as dreamed of by Karl Marx) became a reality as did the environmental degradation of the countryside.

The penalty paid by the small rural producers for their urban-oriented culture is dependence on a cash crop which places them at the mercy of agribusiness and makes them dependent for all things—even bread— on store-bought goods. Predictably, they ultimately quit (it's a hard life) or go broke (big farm machinery needs big investments), their land goes to further enlarge the big farm (which has gotten the subsidy), and they become part of the "crisis in our cities."

The countryside becomes the place where the second home, the resort hotel, and the retirement village are found as well as the fields and factories of agribusiness whose labor force is called "migrant worker," the serfs of our time. What shall we say of such a system except that a quarter of this agricultural labor force in 1970 were children who started working from the time they could walk, that 15 per cent suffered from pesticide poisoning, that government spent only twelve dollars a year on the health of each as compared to the two hundred dollars spent on the average American, that less than a tenth of the families received any welfare assistance yet their wages rarely equaled the wage law's minimum. Housing? It rarely approached what planners from places like Karachi and Bangladesh called the minimum essential for decent habitation: "access to pure water and sanitary waste disposal."[1]

[1] United Nations Seminar, London, 1973.

SIZE AND SPREAD

Cities grew at fantastic rates during the Industrial Revolution. A hundred years ago, only 5 cities had a population of more than a million; today, there are 115 such cities. Tokyo and its environs have passed the 20 million mark and New York's metropolitan population is around 16 million. Los Angeles in 1880 had 10,000 inhabitants; now there are 7 million *and* 3 million private cars. Such sizes are staggering when we recall that in 1500, Paris, the largest city in Europe, had a population of 200,000. Changan at the height of the Chinese Empire (seventh to tenth centuries) and Rome at the height of its empire numbered about 1 million while Athens in the age of Pericles counted 110,000 freemen, and Florence when Leonardo and Michelangelo were citizens counted 245,000 souls. We may conclude that the cultural greatness or spiritual grandeur of cities never depended on huge populations. On the other hand, smaller size in itself proves nothing, since the majority of American city dwellers live in towns of under 50,000 people, of which few are paradigms of civic delight.

While size cannot be equated with quality, it may have a great deal to do with convenience. In modern democratic societies whose avowed aim is to provide satisfaction for all people, the ease with which they can carry out their daily chores and find their pleasures should be basic to good planning. It is surprising, then, to find in modern town planning theory no serious study and in practice no common agreement on such a basic element as size. In British new town planning a population of around 80,000 was once a magic figure which gradually was revised upward to 150,000, yet Cumbernauld (near Glasgow), a comparatively recent town, is planned for 70,000. In the Soviet Union the "ideal communist city" is designed for 100,000. In the United States, Reston, Virginia, is planned for 75,000 while Columbia, Maryland, is planned for 125,000. The much admired Tapiola (outside Helsinki) houses 18,000, and if we hark back to Ebenezer Howard, we see his magic number was 32,000 for his subcenters and 58,000 for his central city. Still further back, Robert Owen (like Charles Fourier) proposed a population of 1,000 to 2,000 for his ideal community while Plato considered 5,000 the suitable number. In 1947 my brother and I proposed 4 million people as the required population for a city in a consumer-oriented society while only 300,000 was desirable for an econ-

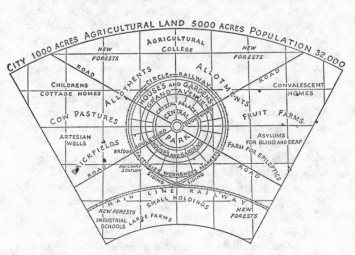

Ebenezer Howard's plan (1898).
Agricultural land = 5,000 acres
Town = 1,000 acres
Population = 32,000

omy of communal production and use. Then there are those who deny the possibility of establishing population size and see the city as indefinitely expanding and still others, like Frank Lloyd Wright, who claimed that

cities as geographical entities had lost their reason of
being, hence his Broadacre City, whose population is
Usonia[2] itself.

Obviously, at least in man-made things such as
human settlements, it is reasonable to assume size
should have some rational relationship to function. We
should be able to assume that a country proud of its
pragmatism and mechanical efficiency could tell the
cost of providing public services to towns of various
sizes. Surprisingly, there is no solid information, as substantial research has not been done on what K. D.
Rainey calls the *J curve,* a graph "which indicates that
it is more expensive on a unit basis to provide certain
kinds of public services in low population areas or
small communities" and as "we go along to larger communities, the cost becomes less until we hit the trough
of maximum efficiencies. Then as we move into even
larger communities, the cost begins to increase again."
Studies by George Sternlieb, of Rutgers University, indicate that a town of 10,000 may be the place where
efficiencies really begin and are maintained in cities up
to 50,000. Other studies tend to indicate that inefficien-
cies begin somewhere between 500,000 and 1 million.
It is my guess that most present cities of over 500,000
cost more to run than smaller cities and it requires no
stretch of credulity to believe that from the viewpoint
of conservation economics the future belongs to compact cities in the 50,000 to 150,000 population range.

Another calculation deals with density. In 1974 an
analysis was made for several federal agencies called
The Cost of Sprawl, describing the cost penalties or
benefits resulting from various uses of residential land.
The study is hypothetical using characteristic American
housing types—single-family, town houses, two- and
six-story apartment houses—arranged in different ways.
At one end of the scale was a pattern called *low density sprawl* modeled on the typical suburban single-

[2] Frank Lloyd Wright's name for the United States.

family development although slightly improved, since only three quarters of the houses were on standard lots, the balance being clustered. This pattern proved economically the most costly as well as ecologically disastrous, which hardly suggests that the mass middle-class exodus to the suburbs was a search for a more efficient environment. At the other end is a scheme called *high density planned*, a misnomer, since it assumes but fifteen households to the residential acre. Here there is a sprinkling of single-family dwellings and town houses; two- and six-story apartment houses predominate. Although the density is low by any city standard, it is surprisingly beneficial when compared to suburban sprawl—50 per cent less energy is used, 52 per cent less automobile travel time is required (the low density pattern needs about three hours per day per household), air pollution is reduced by 50 per cent, etc. Calculations such as these are quantitatively pretty crude and qualitatively worthless, since they give no hint as to what the city is really about—its place, its work, and its folk, as old Patrick Geddes put it. But for the moment let us postpone discussion of these essentials and continue thinking of the city as machine, as a technical creation whose form changes as technology dictates.

We have seen the city atomized by decentralized energy sources, the automobile and electronic communication. We now enter a new period, a time when conservation economics become better understood and the need for thrift more urgent. To conserve resources all mechanical transportation will have to be stringently curtailed; therefore the distance people travel in their daily round must be reduced. City distances become preindustrial, scaled to the pedestrian. Buildings also: The heights in most cases must be limited by the stair-climbing ability of the inhabitants, the plan depending on windows for light and air instead of fluorescent tubes and air ducts. A town planned to meet such requirements will be relatively small and tight-knit.

How tight-knit? As tight-knit as a building technology that depends on sun for winter heating and breeze for summer cooling will permit, as closely knit as the need for close-by green areas will allow.

With such constraints there is no place for the huge cities of the nineteenth century, nor much place for those sprawling nonentities dubbed by the Census Bureau "cities of 500,000 or under" in which 85 per cent of our people now live.

DO WE NEED NEW TOWNS NOW?

At the end of the sixties, the National Urban Coalition concluded that if present trends continued "most cities by 1980 will be predominantly black or brown and totally bankrupt." At about the same time, a prestigious committee[3] asked national, state, and local help to establish before the year 2000, 100 new towns averaging 100,000 population plus 10 cities of at least 1 million each, while Jerome Pickard urged Congress to back 272 new towns for 30 million persons.

Using the dollar value at that period, it was estimated that to build a new town would cost about $20,000 per inhabitant; thus a town of 50,000 would cost a billion, a city of a million, 20 billion. It was said such huge expenditures were required: (a) to offer better living conditions with less damage to nature, (b) to accommodate spill-overs of population from congested central cities, (c) to provide working and living space for new industries, (d) to bring back industry and commerce to areas whose economic base was eroded, (e) to aid low-income people by providing more tolerable environments.

Six years later a program which promised 110 new communities accommodating 30 million resulted in the

[3] Sponsored by the League of Cities, Conference of Mayors, Urban America, Inc., and the National Association of Counties.

start of 16 new towns designed for an eventual population of less than 1 million and plenty of financial difficulties. The government's principal contribution, aside from talk, was to guarantee new-town capital borrowing totaling about $336 million, "a drop," as the developers said, "in the bucket."

Considering the fondness American business has for the huge project, one would have assumed instant city would have been appealing. To the contrary; from 1947 to 1970 only 63 so-called towns were built with but 35 designed for future populations of 50,000 or more people. What people? Robert Weaver judged, "The vast majority appear destined to become country club communities for upper income families."

Even before Ebenezer Howard, new towns were urged as instruments of social reform, yet there is not a shred of evidence to support the belief that an improvement in the physical environment is *by itself* an adequate solution or even an early priority in overcoming the troubles of the poor (or rich!). However, as René Dubos wrote, "since human beings are as much the product of their total environment as of their genetic endowment, it is theoretically possible to improve the lot of man on earth by manipulating the environmental factors that shape his nature and condition his destiny. In the modern world urbanization and technology are certainly among the most important of these factors and for this reason it is deplorable that so little is done to study their effects on human life."

Dubos is right, we should attempt the studies he suggests and make our hypotheses, and then as we adjust our lives to new priorities, come to grips with our ecological problems, and re-examine our technology, we can begin to dream of new towns. For it is out of this dreaming that new towns will evolve.

The time for building them is not now—there is no great shortage of built space and there is adequate unused land in our built areas to accommodate the growth of our population for a decade or two if we use land and buildings less wastefully. There is no emergency, and the simple truth is that *we don't know enough to build a town for the postindustrial society.*

REPATTERNING

Instead of gigantic bulldozing and billion-dollar schemes based on obsolete ideas, we have a more difficult and larger task: the gradual repatterning of our existing built environment. In this process we may learn by trial and error to sketch the shape of the future.

It would be absurd to believe a beneficial repatterning will occur simply because a fraction of the people see the urgent need for repairing and renewing the symbiotic relationship between man and nature. What makes the prospect of change believable is the hard times ahead, the shortages and general restiveness, the uneasiness and dissatisfaction among us. We are beginning to find that there isn't enough and must soon learn to make do with what we have, preserving and improving as best we can, rather than, as in the past, destroying and moving on. Ten years ago this would have been wishful thinking.

Times change. To conserve land many towns are limiting growth by restricting connections to water and sewage systems, imposing moratoriums on new subdivisions, rationing building permits, and sequestering open lands.[4] These restrictions may not always be for such a laudable purpose (as civil rights workers have been quick to point out); nevertheless, the destructive leapfrogging of the speculators is slowed and ways are opened to repattern, instead of condemn through neglect, our older towns.

[4] Federal Housing and Development Administration (1974): 226 cities are using such devices to preserve their ecology and character or to match ability to finance public services with population.

Since these smaller places are potentially the most effective units of habitation, they must be rejuvenated, again becoming the pleasant habitats they were before strip development, parking lots, and regional shopping centers sapped them. Suburbia will, of course, strive to retain suburbia, but in the end scarcity and high costs will open the way for bargaining. A legal device, the "transfer of Development Rights,"[5] may aid, as it suggests, a way of gathering together pieces of land and of creating compact and convenient towns separated by green belts instead of urban sprawl.

These green belts, which allow close-by space for sports fields and nature trails, may serve an equally important function as sites for fruit orchards, berry patches, and vegetable gardens. Once again Americans, in spite of themselves, may be eating fresh foods in season, as the energy cost of freezing, processing, and shipping produce over vast distances puts today's omniseasonal diet back in the luxury class.

Earlier we asked what shall we do with those extraordinary monuments, our great cities, for we must assume that as they lose their ability to provide livelihoods for their citizens, the citizens will leave. Ultimately, we may suppose, the population will reach a level functional to the new needs and goals. A large part of these vast investments of resource and wit may then be abandoned, drifted over with sand like the Sphinx or swallowed in the jungle like Angkor Vat. The skyscrapers may become mines from which the next generation will extract its needed metals as the Colosseum served as quarry for the palace builders of Renaissance Rome. The downtowns may become museum cities like Venice or Carcassonne.

Up to now the history of modern cities has been to

[5] A municipality designates an area of open space and prohibits development on it. The development potential is transferred to other districts where development is desired. Landowners in the preserved area may sell their development rights to those who wish to build where development is permitted.

expand by tearing down and rebuilding. The future history will be the opposite—tearing down and *not* rebuilding. The reel, though, will not be played backward, for history does not repeat but moves as a great helix showing no change in its plan view but in side view each turn is seen to reach another level.

The might of great cities is ephemeral: "Who in 4th century Rome," a historian once asked, "would have thought that in the 5th century goats would be grazing in the Forum?"

THE FUTURE CITY IN RETROSPECT

*To prophesy is a hard task—
especially in regard to future
events*

—Anon.

In Italy only sixty years ago, Marinetti pointed out a new way of life in the first futurist manifesto: "Futurism has as a principle a complete renewing of the human sensibility under the action of the great scientific discoveries. Almost everyone who today uses the telegraph, the telephone, the gramophone, the train, the bicycle, the motorcycle, the automobile, the transatlantic liner, the dirigible, the airplane, the cinema, and the great newspapers, does not dream that all of these exercise on his spirit a decisive influence." New ways are opened by the new technology; even the provincial can escape by train or if not, the newspapers will tell him of strange and wonderful things, "Japanese athletes, Negro boxers, American jugglers who have tricks Parisian elegance cannot match." But to grasp the new, one must develop a new awareness, since "these extraordinary images awaken no curiosity in superficial minds incapable of plumbing the depths; like Arabs who regarded with indifference the first airplanes over the sky of Tripoli." Subtle forces are modi-

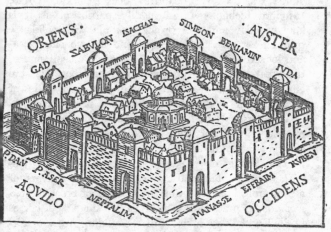

The Future City: Jerusalem promised to the tribes of Israel by
Ezekiel (woodcut by Hans Holbein).

fying our sensibilities; our lives are being accelerated; a
horror of the old and known, a love for the new and
unexpected, a hatred of convention, an infatuation with
danger is being engendered. Futurism is for the individual who wants to live his own life, who believes not
only that human desires and ambitions are limitless but
that they can be multiplied, for now an exact knowledge of the previously inaccessible and unrealizable is
made possible by the new technology.

"The world splendor," Marinetti declares, "has been
enriched by a new beauty, the beauty of speed, a racing motor car, its frame adorned with great pipes like
snakes with explosive breath. A roaring motor, which
looks as though running on shrapnel, is more beautiful
than the Victory of Samothrace" and he adds, "We
shall sing of the man at the steering wheel whose ideal
stem transfixes the earth rushing over the circuit of her
orbit." In 1911, three years before the outbreak of
World War I, Marinetti, who had once cried, "We

glorify war . . . the beautiful ideas that kill," wrote,
"Modern technology will modify patriotism as it is
known today and will provide people with solidarity
through commercial, industrial and artistic enterprise"
and looked forward to the time when "we shall sing of
the great crowds in the excitement of labor, pleasure
and rebellion, of the multi-colored, polyphonic tides of
revolutions in modern capital cities, of nocturnal vibra-
tions of arsenals and workshops beneath their violent
electric moons, of the greedy stallions swallowing
smoking snakes of factories suspended from the clouds
by their strings of smoke, of bridges leaping like gym-
nasts over the diabolical cutlery of sun-bathed rivers, of
adventurous liners scenting the horizon, of broadchested
locomotives prancing on the rails like huge steel horses
bridled with long tubes, and the gliding flight of airplanes, the sound of whose screws are like the flapping
of flags and the applause of an enthusiastic crowd."

Einstein, Freud, Rutherford, Edison, Marconi, Ford,
Blériot, the Wright brothers, Kropotkin and Lenin,
Picasso and Matisse: These are among the names of the
first decade of the century; from these men the century
took its form. This was a time of excitement and dis-
covery, a time of confidence, broken by World War I
which ended the old ways, many believed, and with
the Russian Revolution began (as many thought) the
new—"I have seen the future and it works." The time
had come to destroy the remnants of the past, the
slums, the ancient libraries, the dusty museums, the
barnacled philosophies; to air the rooms, burn up the
mildew in the bright sun of a new world.

To build cities for speed and efficiency; to free men
and women from their slavery! This was to be done
through the application of those scientific discoveries
praised by Marinetti, through technology and five-year
plans. There were to be belt lines where the machine
worked, and the men, wreathed in cigar smoke and
flowers, danced with their perfumed girls to endlessly

turning gramophone records, *à nous,* as the song went in the René Clair film, *la liberté.*

The new shape for the city was sketched by the Italian Antonio Sant'Elia in 1914. "Houses," he said, "will not last as long as us," for every generation should build its own city. "We must invent and remake the future city to be like a huge tumultuous shipyard, agile and mobile, dynamic in all its parts." Building for obsolescence was a necessary premise for continued creativity (in the 1960s the Archigram group in England and the Metabolists in Japan repeated the same slogan—not for the sake of creativity, but because life changed so rapidly). The futurist house will be a gigantic machine, said Sant'Elia (ten years later Le Corbusier announced the house as a machine for living). The drawings of Sant'Elia suggest the shape of things to come—elevators riding up the outsides of buildings, many-layered levels of streets, buildings of concrete, glass, and steel displaying mechanical and structural functions as their main mode of decoration.

In 1922 Le Corbusier exhibited his Ville Contemporaine, a proposal for the rebuilding of cities. His manifesto (those were times of manifestoes) announced: "The great city determines the life of a country; if the great city is stifled, the country goes under" (just the opposite of Balzac, who found Paris destroying the provinces). In order to transform our cities, we must discover the fundamental principle of modern city planning. What is this principle? "The means of transport is the basis of all modern activity." Although the city is the spiritual workshop in which the work of the world is done, Le Corbusier agrees with Sant'Elia, it is but a tool: "Towns that don't want to fulfill their function, that are ineffectual, use up our bodies, destroy our souls so must be gotten rid of."

In the last quarter of the twentieth century, it is touching to read Le Corbusier writing of Paris in 1922: "Then there came the autumn season. In the early eve-

After Sant'Elia, Città Nuova: "Not nature the inspiration but mechanics . . . the city should be like a huge shipyard . . . the future house a gigantic machine."

ning twilight on the Champs Élysées, it was as though the world had suddenly gone mad. After the heat of the summer, the traffic seemed more furious than ever. Day by day the fury of traffic grew. . . . I think back just twenty years when I was a student, the road belonged to us then, we sang in it and we argued in it while the horse bus swept calmly along. Now motors in all directions going at all speeds. I am overwhelmed, enthusiastic rapture filled me, not because of the shiny coachwork under the gleaming lights but the rapture of power; the simple and ingenious pleasure of being in the center of so much power, so much speed. We are a part of it, part of that race whose dawn is just beginning! We have confidence in this new society which will in the end arrive at a magnificent expression of power, we believe in it!" It was with this confidence, Le Corbusier said, that he designed his city for 3 million; *nevertheless*, one must rely "only on the sure paths of reason. Having absorbed the past I felt able to give myself up to our own age, which I love. My friends astonished to see me so deliberately passing over immediate considerations said, but all this is for the year 2000. Everywhere the journalists wrote of it as the city of the future yet I had called it a contemporary city, contemporary because tomorrow belongs to nobody. I felt and knew that the solution was at hand." We must, Le Corbusier said, "burn our bridges and break with the past. . . . create a theoretically watertight formula to arrive at the fundamental principles of modern planning, everything proven scientifically. . . ."

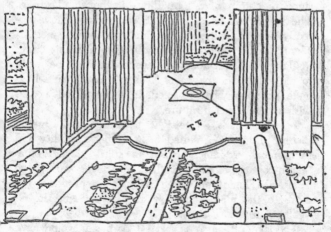

La Ville Contemporaine by Le Corbusier.

The city site must be level to avoid exceptions but there is a river. It flows away from the city, since a river after all is but a "liquid railway, a goods station, a sorting house." "In a decent house, the servant's stairs do not go through the living room even if the maid is charming." Like the river are the streets. The modern street is a new type of organism, a stretched-out workshop, a home for many complicated and delicate organs such as gas, water, and electric mains. "It's not a place for wandering, it's not a boulevard to be built by navvies, it is a piece of civil engineering." The essence of a modern city is speed; "the city which can achieve speed will achieve success." So what is the good of regretting the golden age? Work today is more intense and is carried on at a quicker rate so it will be gotten through with quicker, then perhaps the working day may finish even at noon. "The city will empty as though by a great breath," and then the garden cities come in to play their part.

The cities of today, Le Corbusier finds, are dying through lack of geometry; "the true geometrical layout lies in repetition and this is the cities' only salvation," since repetition allows buildings to be standardized. The people are housed in cells responding "most perfectly to their physiological and sentimental needs." The idea of home disappears with its local architecture, for labor will shift about as needed and must be ready to move bag and baggage. "The words bag and baggage describe what is needed: standardized houses with standardized furniture."

Le Corbusier's "watertight formulas" and "fundamental principles" resulted in a primitive rigidity and mechanical orderliness closer in spirit to late nineteenth-century technology than to today's world, the "Cartesian logic" of which he was so proud owing more to the utopias of Edward Bellamy and H. G. Wells than to Descartes.

The joke, of course, is that Le Corbusier would have

been an early dropout from his city as Plato would have been from his.

Broadacre City. Why did Frank Lloyd Wright, the anti-city man, design a dream city? Certainly the times suggested it: the period of the Great Depression with its talk of planning, including town planning. Perhaps it was a belated response to La Ville Contemporaine, for Wright heartily detested everything Le Corbusier admired: the metropolis, the machine aesthetic, European ideas, especially French ones.

The difference in ideas between these two great architects was not simply one of age (Le Corbusier designed his city at thirty-six while Wright designed his at sixty-seven), but one of total viewpoint: the European rationalist with a penchant for Louis XIV and the great city; the American romantic, Jeffersonian, with the ruralism of the country gentleman. It could be guessed that Le Corbusier would quote Descartes, and Wright, Walt Whitman. It was Le Corbusier who praises the "captains of industry" and speaks scathingly "of the mason pounding away with feet and hammer, smashing up everything around him and what he does soon falls to pieces," while Wright, though he appreciates the machine and designed houses for mass production, opposed the "pressers of buttons and pullers of levers" as well as those trades of the citified man, "broker, vendor of gadgetry, salesmen dealing for profit in human frailty, speculator in the ideas and inventions of others."

Frank Lloyd Wright found that the mechanical roar of the city, so filled with hope when heard by Sant'Elia, "has turned the citified head and filled the citified ears," so he can no longer understand or enjoy as he once did "the songs of birds, wind in the trees." To Wright "The value of earth as man's heritage has gone from him in the cities which centralization has built," adding, "centralization has over-built them all." The skyscraper "casts its shadow and that shadow falls

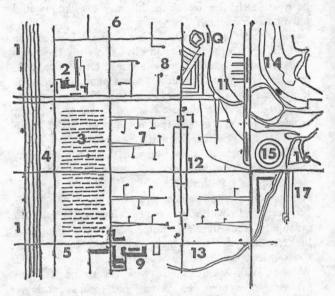

Broadacre City by Wright: (1) main highway, (2) small industry, (3) vineyards and orchards, (4) industry, (5) tourist camp, (6) small farms, (7) medium houses, (8) minimum houses, (9) markets, (10) church, (11) university, zoo, aquarium, (12) schools, (13) recreation, (14) larger houses, (15) arena, (16) county seat, (17) airport.

in utterly selfish exploitation" and must be done away with. "No more overpowering concrete shelves," says Wright, "pigeonholes for human occupancy, no more submission to landlords expedients." A tall building though has an advantage—you ride up high in the air and see how far away you can get. The broad horizon calls, mobility is provided by the automobile. Thus "we are going to call our legacy from the past, this great city for the individual, Broadacre City simply because it is broadly based upon the minimum spacing of an acre or several to an individual. But more important because when a democracy builds it will build this—the city of democracy."

Wright is for spread and Le Corbusier for high density but both consider transportation the key. "Now," says Wright, "we have the Usonian vision. Imagine spacious landscaped highways, grade crossing of a new kind bypassing, over and underpassing, all cultivated and all living areas. All these great highways have no ugly scaffolding of telegraph, telephone poles and wires. They are free from glaring billboards, especially free from ugly fencing; ditching and hedging now taking its place. Imagine these great highways of generous size with an always easy grade, bright with wayside flowers and cooled by shaded trees joining at intervals with modern air rota fields from which safe noiseless transport planes, radio controlled, take off from convenient stations and land anywhere." Along these roads are found service stations, "no longer eyesores but good architecture expanded to include all kinds of service with charm and comfort. . . . These great roads unite and separate, separate and unite in endless series of diversified units passing by roadside markets, garden schools, dwelling places each on its acres of individually adorned and cultivated ground; all placed for pleasure in work or leisure."

Le Corbusier's ideal site is level. Not so, says Wright, "the ideal architectural features of this great democratic ground freedom would rise naturally from topography which means that its features would all take on the natural character of the ground in which an endless variety would be a component part."

It is all very Usonian, very democratic. A glance at the plan shows, as one might expect (from the man who once said, "In my youth, I had to choose between honest arrogance and false humility—I chose the former"), neighborhoods of "minimum houses," of "medium houses," and of "larger houses." There are "tourist [trailer?] camps" as well, located along the highway between the zone of small industries and that of the vineyards and orchards. Are these perhaps for migrant workers? All extends indefinitely, for Broadacre City is "everywhere and nowhere" linked by "automobility" and "electric communication."

CONSUMER ARCHITECTURE

Inspired in part by La Ville Contemporaine and in part by a more skeptical view of modern society, I designed a City for Efficient Consumption in 1938 when it seemed clear that the drift in the United States was overwhelmingly in the direction of increasing consumerism and artificiality. The problem as I saw it was to design a physical environment efficient for the mass production of goods and the mass delivery of these goods to a clientele conditioned to want more and more of them.

"We must," my brother and I said later, "have a big community. For it is mass production that provides the maximum quantity of goods and we need a big population for efficient distribution of them." We agree with Le Corbusier on the dense center but we find his technology not very modern. We can provide much greater densities and more ideal conditions in the City of Efficient Consumption than those he and others had envisioned by simply gathering all the area of all the buildings and pouring it into the artificial climate of a single huge multileveled container. At its base are the ground transport terminals for goods and people, on the roof the airport. Within, all the light manufacturing, shopping, office, entertainment, and hotel activities are carried on. The population moves up and down, diagonally and horizontally, through the perfumed air and under the golden lights controlled by experts in the city's Department of Physiological and Psychological Welfare. The city is a department store.

City of Efficient Consumption by Goodman.

"The goods must be on display . . . the chief motivation to get those goods for oneself is not individual . . . it is social. It is imitation and emulation, and these produce a lively demand."

Somewhere, unstated, are the gears and pinions, generators and power lines, that heat and cool the air driving it through the ducts into remote orifices, that light with artificial suns the darkest corners, that push the elevators through their cylinders and sweep the floors at night. We are back to the "nocturnal vibration of arsenals and workshops beneath their violent electric moons."

* * *

Since 1940 many projects such as these prototypes have been proposed—Rush City, Instant City, Regional City, Mobile City, Motopia, etc.—to be built in Antarctica, on the moon, or actually built in Brazil. A 1960 plan for the expansion of Tokyo, a proposal by a brilliant architect, follows the same now typical path: "Let us construct a huge new city in Tokyo Bay which will have a multi-storied orbital road net work, two airports built on artificially made islands linked by underground tube service, huge terraced housing each large enough to be a self contained neighborhood."

But enough, the reader can complete the catalogue of Kenzo Tange's scheme and add the plug-ins and pull-outs, the nodes and the spines, the capsules, the tubes, and the stacks of the thousand and one dreams and nightmares. Common to all such schemes was a dependence on vast stores of energy for the creation of artificial climates and the daily moving of huge populations from place to place. Common to all of them was a belief that physical plans of the vastest scope are possible if we could think them up, that our planetary resources were not only adequate to build but also maintain these gigantic machines.

In retrospect, it is amazing that so many bright and concerned people paid absolutely no attention to the ecological changes, the depletions, despoliations, and pollutions that would result from their constructs, since each one was recommended by the authors for its economic, social, and technical feasibility. Alas for a Broadacre City when it turns out to be smog-enveloped Los Angeles, alas for La Ville Contemporaine when the office building windows must be broken to let in air and brown-outs stop elevators in mid-flight. Alas for us now that Marinetti's roaring engines and Sant'Elia's tumultuous shipyards and obsolescibles have become realities.

CHAPTER III

Ways of Life

Although the city's form may have been conceived to suit its founder's dream or some notion of utility, its ultimate form and essence results from the way in which it functions as an environment fostering a social and economic life for a gregarious species. Whatever the original intention, the people's needs and aspirations

The Selim Mosque. *Chairman of Building Committee:* "Architect Sinan, will your design make better Moslems?" *Architect:* "? ? ?"

St. Peter's. *Chairman of Building Committee:* "Maestro, will your design appeal to the faithful?" *Michelangelo:* "? ? ?"

alter the built form, erode or add to it, unconsciously creating the basis for new styles.

Up to the nineteenth century architects working in the tradition of their craft had no difficulty designing streets, squares, and houses in tune with their time; the pace was slow, changes were almost imperceptible, the built forms like the common language easily accommodated evolving needs and visions. The vocabulary of the architecture, the meaning of the forms, seemed self-evident so deeply were they engrained in a culture and accepted, if not understood, by all. Who in Rome, whether priest or prince, would have felt the need for Bernini to consult the Pope on the probable effect of his colonnade on the faithful, and no one, I am sure, in the Continental Congress questioned the dome as a fitting symbol for the capitol building of a budding republic.

Since 1850 the rate of change has been accelerating, until now the speed puts all in doubt, skewing the old relationship between us and our past, us and the planet. Programs and projections that yesterday seemed sound, even inevitable, today are obsolete.

We are baffled not only by the rate of change and its magnitude but by contradictory views held by the most esteemed people on the direction in which the society will or should move. Opinion and belief, forecast and prediction, shift with the wind.

Nevertheless, each day the line between those who support economic expansion as the sole road to the good life and those who find it the sure way to catastrophe becomes sharper. The former view is of course dominant, being entrenched both in corporate board room and in union hall. The opposition, poorly organized and relatively powerless, calls for restraint, a moving forward (or back) to less exploitive ways. Let us consider these opposing views.

MORE IS BETTER, OR THAT WHICH DOES NOT GROW DIES

The basic precept is put succinctly by Mustapha Mond: ". . . but industrial civilization is only possible where there is no self denial. Self indulgence up to the limits imposed by hygiene and economics. Otherwise the wheels stop turning."[1]

Who will deny this is the aim of Western society? Production must be increased, goods must be sold, the market must expand, more consumers are needed, or, more accurately, more goods must be consumed. In the

[1] In Aldous Huxley, *Brave New World*.

ideal world of brokerage houses and advertising agencies, there is no logical limit to growth. That which does
not grow dies—it is an axiom, the lesson nature teaches
us! The less euphoric agree there are limits but we have
not reached them. *This* is not the time to spoke the
wheels of progress—not now, not yet, and not in the
foreseeable future, for plethora, scarcity, and breakdown
are, at the moment, portents, not of impending trouble,
but—as in the past—of opportunities for new financing
schemes, new technological "break-throughs" which will
postpone payday.

The economy is organized and run by administrators
whose goals are limited to short term, quick turnover,
high profit. Such goals, exploitive and heedless of consequences, inadvertently cause economic inflation, destruction of the environment, and depersonalization of
the individual. Management seeks power and efficiency
through the creation of multinational conglomerates,
cartels, and other centralizing devices and finds itself,
instead, saddled with bureaucracies—unwieldy, unre-
sponsive, and vulnerable. It is trapped in the machine
of its own devising. As the organizations become larger
and more complex, it depends more and more on the
answers given by computers and less and less on what
is fed into them. Chains of command, buck passing,
and protocol take the place of individual responsibility
or merit. People under such a setup tend to become
personnel and "those whom the system does not need
as personnel have no productive life at all so inevitably
becoming out-caste."[2]

Unfortunately, many in the system do not seem to
fare better, for if we judge by their dissatisfactions,
they too have no productive life. A large-scale government study[3] described the "blue collar blues" of bored,
alienated assembly line workers as well as widespread
"white collar woes," of dissatisfaction and even despair

[2] Paul Goodman, *People or Personnel.*

[3] *Work in America,* Department of Health, Education, and
Welfare, 1972.

at all occupational levels up to and including managers.
The study provides a curious commentary on the inhu-
manity of an economic system where only 24 per cent
of the factory workers and 43 per cent of the office
workers found satisfaction in their work, a curious commentary on the inefficiency of the system when "about
8% of the workers would quit each month. This
meant that 4,800 workers had to be hired each year to
maintain a work force of 5,000."[4] As Paul Maine, of
Case Western Reserve University, put it, "We may
have created too many dumb jobs for the number of
dumb people to fill them."[5]

Since the real business of business is to show a profit,
companies making profits should be reluctant to tamper
with proven methods. For instance, it would be fool-
hardy for an industry with a great capital investment in
plant and machinery to undertake costly and difficult
changes in work patterns to satisfy such ephemeral notions as the supposed hang-ups of its labor force. From
the point of view of Taylorism (still the dominant
training method in American business) if a worker is
dissatisfied with his job, management's first question
must not be "How shall we improve his lot?" but "Can
the job be automated?" Even if a company finds it desirable to enrich or humanize the job, chances are the
Engineering Department will come up with a machine,
for that's *their* job. An example: During a period at
AT&T small teams were given the responsibility for
producing whole telephone books. Morale immediately
went up as did production, errors and sabotage down.
IBM came along with a new machine that did the job
cheaper.

At home and on the job, social attitudes develop that

[4] The Wixom Plant outside Detroit, New York *Times*,
April 4, 1972.
[5] It is interesting to note the Bureau of Labor Statistics
estimated that only one out of five jobs would need college
training in 1970 yet college enrollment went from 2.75 million in 1955 to 8.5 million in 1970.

are opposite faces of the same coin, one side aggressive, the other passive, but common to both are non-co-operation, frustration, and alienation.

As discontent spreads in office and factory, production declines and absenteeism increases. There is much viewing with alarm, government committees make studies, social engineers and behaviorists are employed to instill loyalty to the firm, propose ways of adjusting jobs to the workers or workers to the jobs. As the discontent grows, extending to home and family, the studies are enlarged to include ways of creating "community" and family stability. It's an uphill struggle, since the fundamental difficulty is that most people are normal and normal people don't want to be converted to suit the needs of an abnormal system.

How dismaying it is to discover what limited, uninventive, and faked-up solutions the Establishment's medicine men concoct to cope with basic problems. Job redesign can mean repainting the drab gray vats and machinery in psychedelic colors[6] or, ". . . on summer Fridays at McDonald's, all work ends at 1:00 P.M. to give employees an extra afternoon. Furthermore they also receive free coffee and nickel soft drinks."[7] Eighteen thousand employees perform monotonous filing chores in a government agency. To make the work less boring, music is piped through the building with occasional interruptions—the weather, union meeting times, features at the cafeteria.[8] But what then is expected? Surely not the subordination of production and economic norms to less measurable benefits?

"Designing for community" is on the same level. In the (now not so) new town of Reston such features were introduced as a "nature center," a "rathskeller for teen-agers," six express commuter buses serving drinks going home, and a "blanket of discussion groups and

[6] At the Baltimore Kennecott Refining Corporation plant.
[7] McDonald's hamburger headquarters, Oak Brook, Illinois.
[8] Social Security Administration Headquarters, at Woodlawn, Maryland.

classes to build a sense of community." Columbia, Reston's neighbor, has "group mail boxes at the curb, there's one for every 16 families. It's meant to encourage casual friendships." There are also ballet lessons for children aged five to eight on Wednesdays and some dance classes for adults, also judo, Chinese cooking, macramé, sculpture, and squash. Columbia's developer called it "a garden for growing people."

On the most fashionable street in the most fashionable neighborhood of New York City, opposite St. Patrick's Cathedral, stands a fifty-some story building called Olympic Towers, a name probably selected by the Greek shipping magnate who put up the money to remind us of the old country and point up the fact that it is intended as a place for the modern gods and goddesses to dwell. What a thought—a tower on Mount Olympus itself! The building is zoned as a layer cake; above, elaborate residential quarters, in the middle, palatial offices, and below, exclusive shops. It is advertised as a building one need not leave from morn to night (perhaps never?), for "within its walls are contained every convenience, comfort and luxury needed for modern working and living." Such a building provides an architectural framework for a selected group of people sharing elements common to the historical community we shall shortly describe.

These examples verge on the absurd, yet they are typical. It seems a fact that within the system it is hard to avoid the deadening jobs and dehumanizing environments that tempt increasing numbers to drug abuse and alcohol addiction and lead to mental and physical breakdowns. "Our contemporary western civilization," as Erich Fromm once said, "is increasingly less conducive to mental health and tends to undermine the inner security, happiness, reason and capacity for love in the individual."

The Household

Once the three- or even four-generation family was the focus of loyalties, mutual aid, and love where all worked together unified around common economic tasks of farm and handicrafts. The Industrial Revolution through the central drive shaft of the factory changed this ancient grouping, eliminating home production, enticing or forcing the men (and often the women and children) into wage labor. The household shrank, becoming a unit of consumption instead of production, dependent on impersonal organizations for every need. Supermarket, school system, clinic, housing agency, and nursing home replaced mutual aid and the personal exchange of goods and services between people.

With the family reduced and dispersed, mothers received less family aid than did their mothers and certainly less than their grandmothers. Nurses and baby-sitters, sewing and diaper washing, had to be paid for, no surprise then to find more and more women (even those with no aptitude or desire for careers but real aptitudes for domestic life) fighting for the available jobs. Being personnel may not be enchanting but it is often less lonesome and boring than housework and does pay off in hard cash as well as freedom from the domination of the rooster at home. By 1976, 48 per cent of American females over the age of sixteen were working for wages or seeking a job.

Divorce, once the privilege of the rich, and infidelity, once the custom of the very rich and the very poor, become common to all, while single-person and women-headed households increase. By 1974 women-headed families made up 9.6 per cent of all white families and a third of all black families. Fourteen per cent of all children under age eighteen were being raised by their mothers only (compared to *8 per cent* in 1970!) while 12.8 per cent of these mothers had never been married. Naturally statistics such as these, which coyly assume that unless a marriage license is prominently displayed no man is around the house, are to be taken with a grain of salt, since without doubt there is no box on the census taker's form marked *Living in Sin*. Nevertheless, with the parents' role diminished, and the children in day-care centers and schools, a projection of present trends suggests the next step will not be the "dual career family" or the "symmetrical family" as described in recent books.

Perhaps, as has been said, marriage for most people has outlived its usefulness and is doing more harm than good. Perhaps an even more drastic change than abolishing marriage should be considered—something more suited to the *Weltanschauung* of an advanced industrial society. It can be urged, it has been urged, that coition as a way of continuing the race is slipshod, inconvenient, and puts women at a disadvantage in the job market. If our aim is zero population growth, selective breeding seems indicated. Since the pleasures of sexual intercourse and the science of eugenics have nothing in common, the obvious answer is the test-tube baby properly processed after decanting.[9]

If, as Paul Goodman wrote, "*1984* is the terminus of being personnel," then is *Brave New World* the terminus of family?

Community and Society

As usually understood, a natural community is a group of limited size living in geographical proximity, having common interests and a way of life conditioned by the traditions, tools, and the environment in which they live. Individually and as a body they act to protect and enhance the commonly held values. Kinship, loyalty, and a common faith are essentials to belonging. Co-

[9] Diderot and Huxley.

operation and mutual aid are generally among its virtues; exclusivity, distrust of outsiders, and blind adher-
ence to tradition among its vices. History has shown
how vulnerable such communities are, for almost none
have absorbed or withstood the impact of rapid change
—a square-rigger destroyed Polynesia, a rifle the Es-
kimo.

In contradistinction, the aim of modern society is to
be rational, ecumenical, and inclusive. Mobility, social
and physical, fosters shifting sets of relationships between people. Loyalty is conditioned by value received, so the society depends for its continuance and
stability on how well it performs as a market. When
it performs erratically as it has for half a century,
there is a nostalgic search for other values—for the
old times of kinship, loyalty, and a common faith.
The rhetoric of blood and soil begins spewing up the
worst aspects of the historical · community to confuse
the simple issue—the people are dissatisfied because the
system is not delivering the goods as promised. The
contradictory demands of nationalism in politics, inter-
nationalism in trade, competitive individualism and bureaucracy, expansion of production and declining resources, all lead to the disequilibrium of expedient
planning and stop-gap solutions in economics and unadulterated hypocrisy in politics.

In such an ambiguous world there are no fixed
places, only roads not always leading to the destina-
tions pointed out by the signposts, sometimes not leading anywhere. The plan symbol is not the village green
or public square but the throughway and airway. The
town plan is a standardized mobile home park with its
drive-in theater, drive-in bank, and shopping center all
air-conditioned (for the smog is pervasive). Not too
close but too close for comfort are the vertical office
buildings and the horizontal factories. The architecture
is a modish packaging of mass-produced wares designed for early obsolescence. The residential style is
kitsch adapted to the plug-in, clip-on machine for liv-

ing, the ideal "dwelling unit" for a community of strangers united by car models they admire, the deodorants they use, and the mental and physical rootlessness they share.

The bother is the increasing cost and difficulty in finding the resources needed to build and run such physical plants. A second bother is an increasing need for multiplying controls to keep the great creaking machine on the rails. This is not surprising considering how jerrybuilt it is, but what is surprising is how few overt controls are needed to keep the machine tenders from running amok. As fewer and fewer are needed for the job, a vast amount of free time (a major by-product of automation) accumulates. What with longer years of schooling at one end, enforced early retirement at the other, and shorter work hours as well as extended vacations in the middle, plus periodic spells of unemployment, there would seem to be long, empty periods that the dissatisfied two thirds of the work force would use to figure out why they are dissatisfied and even plan for change. Instead there is some boozing, some drug addiction, a bit of grumbling along with a lot of gold-bricking accompanied by social and political conservatism. It's quite unlike the old radical belief that once the masses gained a living wage and some leisure, they would learn to think for themselves, sweep away the privileged few, and the millennium in the form of the classless society would be on us.

That old reactionary Gertrude Stein saw things more clearly than the old radicals. In 1936 she wrote: "Just the other day I was reading a Footner detective story and the crooks who were being held together under order under awful conditions said when somebody tried to free them sure you got to be organized these days, you got to have somebody do your thinking for you. And also the other day a very able young man, you would not expect he would feel that way about it, wrote to me and said after all we are glad to have Roosevelt do our thinking for us.

"That is the logical end of organization and that is where the world is today, the beginning of the eighteenth century went in for freedom and ended with the beginning of the nineteenth century that went for organization."

In the past those blessed with time freed from the compulsion of labor were called the leisure class, who spent their time in gambling, drinking, sports, and such. They were known for their political and social conservatism. It seems absurd to compare 66 per cent of the American work force with such people, yet when you come to think of it . . .

THE OTHER SIDE, OR MORE IS NOT BETTER

Within the accepted framework there are few controls in the democracies. We are open and pluralistic, allowing a great variety of religious and social expression, of economic and sexual experimentation. The limits, however, are there, blurred and shadowy but real enough once you overstep them. There are restrictions but those of Iron Curtain countries are of one sort, those of lace curtain countries another.

Other nations may need midnight raids and book burnings, surveillance of their citizens, and censorship of what they say, read, and do. We have no such need. Although incidents such as Palmer raids, McCarthyism, Kent State, even large-scale CIA surveillance and the like do occur, they are rare enough to be listed—quite unlike the antics of the totalitarians, where such happenings are a daily way of life (and death).

Disaffection, dissatisfaction, and dissent are no new things with us; they were the midwives of our Revolution. The nineteenth century is filled with prophets and preachers who cried out against injustice seeking a universal brotherhood where not only black slaves and wage slaves but women as well were emancipated.

Schemes for a golden age proliferated and even respectable folk dreamed them. But sooner or later the voices were stilled, more often by stuffing the mouths with pork chops than by the gags of our less civilized neighbors. Nevertheless, now as then there are those who would not be still.

In 1959 Paul Goodman summed up the modern dissatisfaction in what we called his *J'accuse* style: ". . . our abundant society is at present simply deficient in many of the most elementary objective opportunities and worth-while goals that could make growing up possible. It is lacking in enough man's work. It is lacking in honest public speech, and people are not taken seriously. It is lacking in the opportunity to be useful. It thwarts aptitude and creates stupidity. It corrupts ingenuous patriotism. It corrupts the fine arts. It discourages the religious convictions of Justification and Vocation and it dims the sense that there is a Creation. It has no Honor. It has no Community."[10]

The nineteenth-century rhetoric was different but the complaint is not. More than a hundred years before, George Ripley[11] wrote: "We cannot believe that the selfishness, the cold-heartedness, the indifference to truth, the insane devotion to wealth, the fierce antagonisms, the painted hypocrisies, the inward weariness, discontent, apathy, which are everywhere characteristic of the present order of society, have any permanent basis in the nature of man; they are the poisonous weeds that a false system of culture has produced; change the system and you will see the riches of the soil, a golden fruitage will rejoice your eyes."

Yet even if the complaints are the same there is a difference between the time of the Reverend Ripley and Dr. Goodman. The quantitative changes engendered by the Industrial Revolution are now qualitative, the once outlandish ideas of the utopians are no longer so outlandish. We now see the failures of Owen,

[10] *Growing Up Absurd.*
[11] Founder of Brook Farm.

Fourier, and John Noyes as due not so much to wrongheadedness but rather to conceptions that were out of phase with their time.

There Is a Time Propitious to Each Thing

In this century we have seen no small proportion of the people become cynical or disenchanted with the ways of the established order whether in religion, economics, or politics. We have seen the tumultuous times of the 1960s when the universities in Europe, Great Britain, and America erupted calling for peace, social and political decentralization, sexual freedom, and women's liberation. Suddenly youth announced it was fed up wth the ways of their elders, their beliefs and their political parties.

The anti-organizational sentiment of the times was voiced in what might well be the slogan of the counterculture: "A Free Society cannot be the substitution of a 'New Order' for the old order; it is the extension of spheres of free action until they make up most of social life."[12]

With such a definition it is not surprising that there is no clearly defined program, no heroes marching in cadence, simply people of different ages and conditions ranging from those who seek in small ways accommodations outside an unsatisfactory system to those who find the system utterly revolting and drop out or drop bombs. In short there is no movement, just "an extension of spheres of free action." The extension is multidimensional and the various inputs manifest themselves in different ways—religious, political, and sexual—none exclusive, all searching for community.

Communes and Collectives

Though ideologies and opinions, geographical locations, and life styles may differ, what binds them is the

[12] Paul Goodman.

youth of the members and their opposition to a society they find technologically too complex; impersonal, too centralized, large, and bureaucratic; materialistic and consumer-oriented; and ecologically unsound.

Against this they seek voluntary association, decision-making diffused through the entire population, mutual aid, small-scale enterprises, and an altogether simpler life, aims right out of Bakunin, Kropotkin, and Gandhi. Aims also vaguely Tolstoyan such as were put into the mouths of "some young architects" by Simone de Beauvoir:

> Socialist or Communist, in every country man is crushed by technology, alienated from his work, chained and stultified. This has come about because man has multiplied his needs when he should have limited them; instead of aiming for an abundance which never existed and probably will never exist he should have contented himself with a subsistence minimum as still happens in certain very poor communities—in Sardinia and Greece for instance—where technology has not penetrated and money not corrupted. There people know an austere happiness because certain values have been preserved, truly human values—dignity, fraternity, generosity—which give to life a unique flavor. So long as we continue to create new needs we multiply frustrations. When did the trouble begin? The day when science was preferred to wisdom, utility to beauty. With the Renaissance came rationalism, capitalism and scientism. So it is. This is where we are, what shall we do? Try to reawaken in oneself and around oneself wisdom and a taste for beauty. Only a moral revolution, not a social, political or technical one will bring man back to the lost truth. At least one can do this on his own: give way to joy despite the absurd world and the disorder that surrounds us.[13]

In 1970 the New York *Times* estimated there were

[13] *Les Belles Images*, 1966.

over 2,000 communes in the United States (God knows how they arrived at the figure). It sounds like a lot until one finds how small the groups generally are and how short the life span. Yet the interest they arouse— quite disproportionate to number and achievement—is a good indicator of a general dissatisfaction.

When the Wonder bread has lost its savor and the TV circuses have palled, when school is a bore and the work is not worth doing, what is more beguiling than the prospect of escape to some heaven on earth where every man sits under his vine or his fig tree. It's an old dream and all communards try to make it real, the most convinced settling far from the city following more or less (generally less) the precepts of the nineteenth-century associationists.

A century ago in a period of dissatisfaction not dissimilar to our own, Charles Nordhoff set out to find whether the old dream was working and recorded his findings in *The Communistic Societies of the United States: From Personal Visit and Observation.* As a good reporter he visited over seventy intentional communities spread over a dozen states. He returned a convert, saying he found communal living in all ways a higher, better, and more pleasant life than that of the mechanic and laborer in the cities or the small farmer in the country, since "it provides a greater variety of employment for each individual, and thus increases the dexterity and broadens the faculties of men. It offers a wider range of wholesome enjoyments, and also greater restraint against debasing pleasures. It gives independence, inculcates prudence and frugality. It demands self-sacrifice and restrains selfishness and greed, and thus increases the happiness which comes from the moral side of human nature. Finally, it relieves the individual's life from carking cares, from the necessity of over-severe and exhausting toil, from the dread of misfortune or exposure in old age."

It was a beautiful picture, all sunshine. Horace Greeley painted in the shadow: "Along with many noble

and lofty souls whose impulses are purely philan-
thropic, and are willing to labor and suffer reproach for
any cause that promises to benefit mankind, there
throng scores of the selfish, the headstrong, the pugna-
cious, the unappreciated, the played out, the idle and
the good-for-nothing generally; who finding themselves
utterly out of place and at a discount in the world as it
is, rashly conclude that they are exactly fitted for the
world as it ought to be."

Descriptions of latter-day country communes often
read like comedies of errors not only because they at-
tract the foot-loose and good-for-nothing, but primarily
because many of the members (unlike most of their
nineteenth-century counterparts) are poorly, or not at
all, prepared for the complexities of the simple, rugged
life. Children of high technology have to learn the
vagaries of hand pumps or kerosene lamps, the problems of keeping a wood stove going in wet weather or
the mysteries of the root cellar, nor have they been accustomed to long hours of physical labor and bathing
once a week or even once in a while. And unlike the
kibbutzniks of Israel, they have not been trained in the
kind of understanding required for a life that depends
on mutual aid, sharing, and group interaction. Nevertheless, whether sunshine or shadow prevails, living
outside the system among friendly and helpful people
is a common dream.

Self-help Housing

The lack of simple skills, the atrophy of initiative, and
the dependence on outside aid are some of the results
of urbanization. How far we have gone from the self-
reliance of rural life is seen by comparing what we
today consider self-help and what it means in an underdeveloped country:

Peru. The Indians come   *United States.* There is no
down from the Andes to   way that poor rural fami-

Lima, and as no Indian will deny a kinsman or friend a place under his roof, things get crowded.

The elected leaders organize the newcomers and begin seeking a site, usually an empty piece of land. It is found, mapped, and divided into plots. Meanwhile the prospective tenants gather the basic materials needed for their new homes—poles and mats. They await the signal rolling their *esteras* (woven fiber mats) around sturdy poles, stuffing their household goods into sacks.

The signal given, they move out of alleys and board decrepit trucks. At the city's outskirts, they are joined by others for a night of frantic work. The poles are driven in the soil and the mats become walls and roofs. By dawn what had been a barren parcel of real estate becomes one of Lima's new *pueblos jovenes,* or young communities.

The startled landlord calls the police, who order the huts removed. Angry words, sometimes shots are fired, the police come

lies can become owners of their own homes, except through self-help housing. A program is based on the family's ability to do some of the construction work themselves.

With the assistance of a supervising organization, a group of six to ten families is formed, each family pledges a minimum of 1,000 work hours to the group. They locate land, select house plans, obtain cost estimates, and apply for loan funds needed to buy building materials. While waiting for the loans they study the responsibilities of home ownership, building code requirements, construction techniques, work schedules, record keeping, tool use and care, taxes, fire insurance, landscaping, interior decorating, home maintenance. When the loans are approved, they begin work under a trained supervisor.

Families usually put in thirty hours of work a week, construction time being six to eight months —the total time is twelve to sixteen months.

To make the program

and go, the case goes to court and is soon forgotten.

Shops are opened, bus lines extend their routes, the city is urged to provide water and electricity. Gradually the mats are removed and walls of adobe rise. Billboards from nearby highways become roofs.

This was how El Salvador, Lima's newest *barriada*, was founded last fall. It already has 130,000 inhabitants.

(Synopsized from article by H. J. Maidenberg in the New York *Times*.)

work, there must be a good technical assistance agency to explain everything including how to prepare the loan application, select a site, assist in plan selection, advise on building materials, supervise and train the families in construction skills as well as help with nonhousing problems.

The Farmers Home Administration provides the mortgages; the technical assistance is paid for by the Office of Economic Opportunity.

(Synopsized from *Source Catalog*, Communities/ Housing. Chicago: The Swallow Press.)

"Convivial" (Intermediate) Technology

As an aid to living a tolerable life man had the wit to invent and use tools. After thousands of years the simple skills and useful devices he had developed were quite suddenly changed in character from servant to master. Their use and size expanded inordinately, reducing or eliminating the need for human hands and human brains, exhausting resources and blighting the environment. The centralized management and impersonal planning, mechanical exactitude, and rigid scheduling considered essential to the production mode of the new master takes all enjoyment out of the work process, and though the time spent on the job is shortened by automated procedures, the workday, no matter how short, seems long.

If it is true that productive work is part of our normal psychological need and the work done forms a person's character, we can only conclude that today's work processes are inimical to human beings, for technology in freeing us from the ancient curse of drudgery has brought its opposite—the curse of idleness and her twin demons, boredom and anomie.

Not only is our production mode undesirable but a good deal of what we produce is suspect. Most of the goods made require large amounts of petrochemicals, metals, and other nonreplaceable resources, they are designed for early obsolescence, and most of them, viewed judiciously, are neither necessities nor conveniences, but luxuries. A second conclusion is that it would be an over-all benefit to the planet and those that dwell on it if fewer of these goods were made and the method of making was changed from the automated efficiencies of mass production to a less energy-intensive mode.

The possibility of such changes is no longer in some utopian future. In any rational view, limitations on production, greater selectivity in what is produced, the conservation of resources, a more human scale, and a more humane work style are among the only ways of preventing the massive economic and social breakdowns, prognosticated by such prophets of doom as Oswald Spengler, Ellul, and Heilbroner. As against such doomsayers there are a growing number of people not merely critical of what is but pointing the way to a future that need not end in disaster.

For example, E. F. Schumacher finds that "the technology of *mass production* is inherently violent, ecologically damaging, self-defeating in terms of non-renewable resources and stultifying for the human person," and proposes the term *intermediate technology* to define a technology that is "vastly superior to the primitive technology of bygone ages but at the same time much simpler, cheaper and freer than the supertechnology of the rich," since such a technology "mobilizes the priceless resource possessed by all human beings, their clever brains and skillful hands."[14]

And Ivan Illich suggests a more positive approach to tools saying, "It has become difficult for contemporary man to imagine development and modernization in terms of lower rather than higher energy use. . . . The illusion that a high culture is one that uses the highest possible quantity of energy must be overcome if we are to get tools into focus." Man after all did not use power tools to build the great monuments of the past. But for Illich the word "tool" is a broad one. It includes not only a saw or hammer but whole systems, cars, and factories. In addition he finds that tools that can easily be used by anyone are needed so as to "allow the user to express his meaning in action."[15]

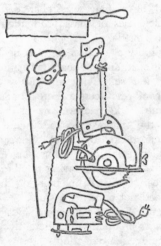

A few variations in a tool.

Paul Goodman, writing on work for unemployed youth in *Utopian Essays and Practical Proposals*, says "We do not invent great programs of work because

[14] *Small Is Beautiful.*
[15] *Tools for Conviviality*, 1973.

not enough *mind* is put to the task. It is not to be expected that the departments of Labor and the Interior,
or even a county administrator of Correction, will dream
up remarkable work projects. A fine architect might,
and might even do it gratis as a public action, but we
do not rely on such men and such motives. Students of
architecture at the university might think up something for youth to build; out of fifty of their inventions
one might be remarkable and feasible. But the university is not on speaking terms with the government.
Or in another genre, a social case worker might have a
vivid sense of some alteration or installation that would
make all the difference to a harried family, and that
youth could do. (This is the line of Carl May's Youth
for Service, e.g. 'The boys built a retaining wall at a
neighborhood center. They scrubbed the floor in the
kitchen, painted the bedroom and bath at the home of
two elderly sisters')."

And Aldous Huxley points the way for the *community*, saying, "Over-population and over-organization
have produced the modern metropolis, in which a fully
human life of multiple personal relationships has become almost impossible. Therefore if you wish to avoid
the spiritual impoverishment of individuals and whole
societies, leave the metropolis and revive the small
country community, or alternately humanize the metropolis by creating within its network of mechanical
organization the urban equivalent of small country
communities, in which individuals can meet and coop-
erate as complete persons, not as the mere embodiment
of specialized functions."[16]

The Family

In social groupings where neither children, money, nor
social position is considered a reason for marriage,
where the family is no longer an economic enterprise
nor a social benefit, and where lovers can be with each
other as long as they like without legal obligation or

[16] *Brave New World Revisited.*

moral blame, people who bind themselves in matrimony must do so out of whim, for there is no need. There are exceptions: to please old-fashioned parents, to satisfy some nostalgia, or even, as in the case of some *kibbutz* youth in Israel, to spite the radicalism of their elders who *didn't* get married.

It is a dramatic time in cultural history when a whole set of customs and traditions related to such a fundamental matter as family ties are in the process of being discarded, since it has long been an article of faith that no society has existed where the family was not a keystone in the social structure; where the family according to many sociologists is not only the keystone but the very arch, since it made society possible by defining social relationships through a traditional method of selecting sex partners.

It is a dramatic change when the social nature of the family is no longer characterized by identification with the father, when a mother-child relationship always considered sociologically incomplete without the father —even when emotionally and economically self-sufficient—is now acceptable. It is a dramatic moment when technology makes it possible for women to compete with men even in physical strength (she can drive a tractor, a gun in her fist is as lethal as in the fist of her brother), when it turns out that women do quite well in politics and as bank presidents, and when, because of the widespread use of contraceptives, she can choose motherhood deliberately. It all adds up to a different world from that of the late 1820s when Mrs. Trollope scolded American society for the systematic exclusion of women from any but inferior activities; the American male, she commented, didn't want his woman to compete in serious affairs; they must learn that women were made for other purposes than "to fabricate sweetmeats and gingerbread, construct shirts, darn stockings and become mothers of possible presidents." In the same vein another feminist, Louisa May Alcott, wrote:

"Aunt Betsey, there's going to be a new Declaration of Independence."

"Bless and save us, what do you mean, child?"

"I mean that being of age, I'm going to take care of myself and not be a burden any longer. . . . I'm old enough to take care of myself; and if I'd been a boy, I should have been told to do so long ago."

After all these years, most women in most places are on the way to emancipation, and by and large have a choice of vocations that may, but need not, include that of wife and mother. Male and female roles while not yet interchangeable are less sharply defined, the yin/yang stereotype blurs. Although being a house-husband is not yet respectable in Middle America, middle-class man is more domesticated than ever be-fore.

There are problems. The old-time psychologist will foresee difficulties when children are unable to recog-nize differences in sex role characterization between parents and so be confused as to their own sex identity. Fewer and fewer children may be blessed (or cursed) with the same (or any) father figure during their for-mative years so the tendency for the mother to become the sole authority figure will grow.[17] If the mother is career-minded, care of the children will be left to hired hands, often of dubious competence.

In 1968 such matters were a cause for anxiety. Of 6,740 women interviewed in a national sampling two thirds agreed that "a preschool child is likely to suffer if his mother works" while four out of five believed "it is much better for everyone involved if the man is the achiever outside the home and the woman takes care of home and family."[18] By 1974 a poll[19] showed that 63 per cent of the men interviewed supported efforts to

[17] A tendency that will increase, for more females are being born than males and the male death rate exceeds the female.

[18] Karen Oppenheim Mason and Larry Bumpass, *Fertility Study*.

[19] By the Roper Organization.

strengthen women's status in society compared to 44 per cent in 1970. More than half the women interviewed said they wanted to combine a career with marriage and raising children, three out of four considered divorce a solution for an unsuccessful marriage, a third saw no reason why single women should not have children if they wanted them. By 1976, with 48 per cent of U.S. women in the work force or looking for jobs, the chairman of the National Committee on Manpower, Professor Eli Ginzberg, found "the flood of women into the work force the most outstanding phenomenon of our century."[20]

The tide runs in favor of sexual equality. A necessary consequence will be the further weakening of our standard household unit—the nuclear family—since typically it depends on a relatively stable relationship between parents and someone whose main occupation is keeping house. As fewer and fewer seem interested in the job and one out of three adults is living without a permanent mate, a variety of substitutes or replacements are being sought.

Without much fanfare groups throughout the country have started coping with the problem. Often they are organized as co-operatives whose members have found the nuclear family inoperative or oppressive and confining, who believe parents should participate equally in child care and career opportunities. Sexual equality is taken for granted and legalized marriage considered unimportant. Typically the co-operators are young, middle-class white professionals but gradually blacks and blue-collar workers are becoming involved.

For these people sexual equality means more than equal opportunity in employment, equal rights in politics, and legitimization of variety in sex relations. It creates the need for a better choice than the nuclear

[20] U.S. women in national work force:
        1960—33%
        1970—38%
        1975—40.7%

family with its problems of instability, its inadequate
and slipshod ways of raising children, its inefficiency as
a social and economic unit, and its isolation from the
community and work process.

We may be sure that when changes in such a basic
cultural pattern as domestic life occur the built environment will soon be modified to accommodate them.

Human Settlements

From earliest times settlements have been located and
arranged to further survival needs and express our gregarious nature. A salubrious site is sought near water
and food, fuel and building material. Shelters are built
to protect against the elements and the outsider as well
as accommodate the people's social arrangements.
Later this simple program is elaborated by the need to
memorialize our myths, the clay pot becomes a ceremonial vessel, the hut is transformed into a temple. The
settlement, town, and city become not only the repository of the culture but also its symbol. Hence no arts
are more closely circumscribed than architecture and
town planning. Politics and economics, custom and
habits, aesthetic predilections, climate, geography,
physical resources, and technology all mold the product; a change in any of them marks the beginning or
ending of a historical period.

Without much awareness we have slipped into a
new period and that is why the old gears no longer
mesh, why things go out of control so readily, why our
cities are in crisis, why our factories are less and less
efficient, why Byzantinism grows, why domestic life is
a shambles and the ultimate invention of the industrial
age—the bomb—threatens all of us.

The postindustrial period has new functions and
calls for new forms. If it is assumed that we survive the
crisis, that technology is controlled, our cities like our
giant corporations decentralized, our factories rede-

signed to fit human ways, social arrangements devised more suited to our psychological needs, and we all learn to live more harmoniously with nature, a safe prediction would be the birth of a new style fit for the new time.

Considering the rate of change, preparation for the new time is overdue, for the increase in planetary degradation is exponential. Our present way will soon be impossible so it is pointless to debate the desirability of *more is better*. The fact is, it is now an impractical slogan. Only a generation ago we thought the danger ahead was the air-conditioned nightmare and the chromium-plated bordello of *Brave New World*. Now if we don't face the facts the likely prospect is that we will be drinking ersatz tea out of cracked teacups, fulfilling the prophecy of *1984* in an overpopulated, undernourished, and polluted world.

Obviously, neurotic preoccupations with man enslaved by the machine, packed sardine-tight in multistoried tiers, can only lead to despair. There are more rational alternatives. What is needed is thoughtful appraisal, a willingness to accept the coming restraints as reform, not deprivation, setting our minds to the hard task of ordering the changes by examining options, charting alternative courses of action, testing them, and then having the good sense and courage to choose rightly.

CHAPTER IV

Control of Technology

The first man of science was he who looked into a thing, not to learn whether it would furnish him with food and shelter, or weapons or tools or ornaments or playwiths, but who sought to know it for the sake of knowing. . . .

—Coleridge

To discover the nature of things is the goal of science. It is a noble task, and neither political expedience, economic considerations, or even ethical principles should be allowed to inhibit the search. The application of scientific knowledge to furnish us "with food and shelter, weapons or tools, ornaments or playwiths" is another matter. Until this century the small scale of such applications limited its potential dangers and so the imposed limits were few—a few safety ordinances in mines, warning lights and bells at railroad crossings. Despite the qualitative change we still tend to deal with technological control in the same way—traffic lights and stop signs have proliferated, there are some noise and smoke abatement regulations, certain food and drug laws, and a few states even have environmental impact laws. Considering how few safeguards there are in relation to the omnipresence of technological elements in our environment—the dams, pipelines, nuclear plants, supersonic planes, or oil tankers—and considering the complexity of their co-ordination, it is surprising and heartening how few black-outs, blowups, and breakdowns we have suffered. What is not so heartening is the way the likelihood of disaster grows as the technological elements multiply.

Increasingly all, or almost all, of us are separated from nature by things of man's contriving, all entangled in life-support systems whose concrete arteries carry blood not generated in our own environment of sun and dirt but through transfusions from distant sources. Sources that will soon dry up not only because they are sapped by the demands of expanding populations, but in no small part because technologies tend to breed technologies. For instance, the air speed of a propeller plane suggests the need for a jet; a supersonic plane, a rocket. As another instance, most of our industries are polluters of air and water; what is more reasonable than to develop a new industry devoted to the making of anti-pollution devices?

We now know that what appears to be the most benign of devices, the most innocent of gadgets, may have adverse by-products or side effects, and so we speak of technological controls, but what sort of technological development needs control depends on whom you listen to and where your interest lies. All too often the truth is hard to get at, or unknown. We live with what we do, as best we can, from day to day; on occasion we view certain things with alarm, but shrink from giving up any luxury, comfort, or convenience. We are told a nuclear plant presents no hazard, few of us believe it, yet in the long run even fewer are willing to face the shortages threatened by the utility company (whom we also don't believe) and so accept what may result in damage to ourselves or our children caused by the failed reactor which (after all) didn't prevent the power shortage.

TWO LAWS DISCRETE

My purpose is not to recommend the dismantling of the mass-producing, technology-oriented society we live in, but rather to have us see it in a reasonable perspective, taking into consideration the benefits it has provided and the penalties it has exacted. Finally, to suggest more satisfactory relationships between people and things than the present ones, for it is surely truer today than in Emerson's time that

> There are two laws discrete
> Not reconciled
> Law for man and law for things;
> The last builds town and fleet,
> But it runs wild
> And doth man unking.

Modern technology and its offspring, automation, have their own rules and if uncontrolled rule out much that is human. When controlled these devices are wonderfully useful and obedient servants but when out of control are devouring, destroying spoilers. When they are used to do badly, work that hands enjoy and do well; when they are given work to do better left undone, then they are monsters. But let's not be anthropomorphic. What I mean is that when machines are designed to suit *thing's law*, when they are remotely controlled by great corporations or conglomerates, then they are enmeshed in the gears of other machines called bureaucracies who transmute people into clockwork mannequins—"servo-mechanical devices with an average weight of 150 pounds and capable of reproducing themselves." Control by such devices of such devices is in our view out of human control, "runs wild / and doth man unking."

SOME GUIDELINES FOR THE SELECTION OF TECHNICAL DEVICES

First, select the device that uses the least nonreplaceable fuel in the running and emits the least amount of pollutants per BTU generated.

Second, choose for durability and repairability. Any consideration of pollution would take into account the useful life of an object (the longer the life, the less on the garbage heap). Repairability is linked with durability, for it is not worth repairing a piece of junk. Repairability should have another facet that deals with transparency or clarity of design, for ideally the repair of most objects should be done by the user; only then is he really master of the device.

A *third* criterion deals with size, number, and kind. Over the aeons nature in its mysterious way has constructed an infinite variety of organisms. Each thrives as long as its size, kind, and proliferation are in equilibrium with its environment. Modern technology has broken this primordial barrier, so we are threatened; once the barrier is breached there is no limit to the mischief that can be created by even minor miscalculations. In weaponry we have gone from stone club to catapult to the bomb, in human settlement from cave to town, city to megalopolis. In air pollution, from the smoke of our ancestral cooking fire to smogs and radioactive dusts. In transport . . . in the growing of food . . .

We have challenged the biological fact. Our giantism has strained our beneficial environment which is perishing. Obviously, then, an imperative in the control of technology is restricting size and extent.

The *fourth* poses a basic question. Do we have the right to withhold a new product that promises to satisfy a real need but that only through long-time testing may be shown not to have unexpected and perhaps disastrous side effects? Thalidomide and DDT are just two well-known examples of (as it turned out) inadequate testing.

At a meeting of the American Cancer Society in 1974 it was reported that "there are perhaps 10,000 new chemicals put into production each year." The result is "we touch, ingest and absorb an ever increasing number of synthetic materials . . . which may have existed on earth but were never part of the immediate human environment." All agree there are dangers; the safeguard lies in careful testing. But what does a pharmaceutical company do with its highly salable new product when the ACS warns: "Since cancer does not show up until 20 or more years after initial exposure to the cancer causing substance, prevention of cancer in the year 2000 is the order of the day in 1974." Should they (will they) hold up distribution for a quarter of a century?

We would not deny the possibility of voluntary exposure by informed or desperate people to untested products; however, prudence would suggest to most of us that if the human race has carried on all these years without the new product, another decade or two should not be an insuperable wait.

A *fifth* and related consideration would deal with that interesting distinction between tools and machines described by Ivan Illich. A tool, according to Illich, is a kind of device controlled by the operator, a specialized extension of the operator's body dependent for correct performance on his skill. A machine, on the other hand, makes the operator its slave, for *it* has the skills: The operator is a tender whose duty may be reduced to watching for the blink of a light which, like the snap of the boss's fingers, could mean "bring me a cigar" or he may have no duty at all like the "fireman" in the diesel locomotive who represents a bit of history. Are such jobs worthy of a man's time and effort? Are they compatible with basic human functions? Surely not! But let's not forget it is we who allow the machine to enslave.

The *final* criterion is more difficult, for it deals with proportion between means and ends, with ethics and aesthetics; in short, with the critique my brother and I called *Neo-functionalism*. In this formulation we accepted the tenet that forms follow function but subjected the function itself to a formal examination. Is the function good, we asked, meaning worthwhile, worthy of a man's time and effort? Is it compatible with other basic human functions? Does it make sense? What are the consequences? The answers to such questions might tell us a great deal even if the object discussed was (maybe especially was) an electric carving knife.

AUTOMATION/CYBERNATION/WORK

Blinded by the customary as well as by fads and follies, we don't see the implications of genuinely revolutionary technical innovations when they first appear. For instance, as late as the 1940s it was said that "fewer than a dozen electronic computers would be able to satisfy the computational requirements of this country." Similarly, those who should have known better considered (some still consider) automatic machinery as just another refinement of eighteenth- and nineteenth-century mechanization.

Mechanization called for a human worker to operate and control the machine;[1] the design had to meet his limitations and abilities. Automation freed the machine from such limitations, for through feedback it can be programmed to control its own operations. From automation of the individual machine to connecting groups of machines into a totally integrated system was a logical development, more radical as a production process than the first assembly line.

Such integrated systems we now call cybernated and it was assumed that around 1980 most jobs that could be cybernated would be. It was assumed that most of the citizenry would be unable to understand the cybernated world in which they lived even though better educated than their forebears, and besides, understanding would hardly be necessary, for the computers would be there to provide answers—if anyone had any questions. In this world there would be an elite—the cyberneticians—who dealt with their peer group—the machines—a time-consuming and interesting occupation. As for the rest of the population (dissidents aside), the government was the employer of last resort, and jobs, especially kept nonautomated, would be invented for the able-bodied and willing-to-work,

[1] Called a "tool" in the Illich usage.

with welfare payments for the balance. "What will they do all their long lives," asked Donald Michael in 1962, "day after day, weekend after weekend, vacation after vacation in an increasingly crowded world. . . ?"[2]

Unexpected weaknesses in the system now provide answers. The first is gluttony: The system is addicted to BTUs in such quantities that we can't afford its appetites. The second is filth: The system is such a polluter that we can't abide its excrement. So without losing the benefits to be gotten from its marvelous machines, we must accommodate them to the realities, since the dream of the National Association of Manufacturers in 1957—"Guided by electronics, powered by atomic energy, geared to the effortless workings of automation, the magic carpet of our free economy heads for distant and undreamed horizons"—was but a dream.

In the same vein and not untypical of his enthusiasms Le Corbusier wrote: "We must choose between the life of the shepherd vegetating among his flocks and participation in a machine civilization." Wealth, he declared, is within the reach of all men, for the world of manufactured products is open to us. The use of the machines will make the wheels turn, standardization will sweep away obstacles, the very universe is reflected in technics, technics being "the conquests of man over a relentless and indifferent nature." (Incidentally this was written in 1944 when relentless, but unfortunately not indifferent, technicians were bombing the hell out of each other.)

The universe is certainly *not* reflected in our gadgetry (what vanity!), and since nature is neither indifferent nor relentless but the "creative and regulative physical power which is conceived of as operating

---

[2] A year later the Vietnam War began to absorb the time of some who were given expensive courses and practical experience in the science of population reduction, others now spend their time in veterans' hospitals, and still others turned out not to have such long lives after all.

in the material world as the immediate cause of all its phenomena," man's attempt to conquer instead of understand and accommodate can only end in pratfalls.

To change the direction of our technology will not mean merely turning the wheel a few degrees, would it were that simple. Over a period of time, there will be many shutdowns and slowdowns, shots will be fired, and there will be large- and small-scale dislocations, vast unemployment, the need for retraining and much rethinking. It is small comfort to know that these are but part of a historical process: Changes in technology have been occurring at quickening intervals since the first shift from agricultural to industrial economies; from the turn of the century but especially since World War II the pace has been headlong, resulting in fabulous increases in output per man-hour, unprecedented additions to the man-made environment, and a great decline in jobs for the unskilled.

Technological unemployment is no new thing. A labor leader recalling the 1850s in London describes "the great trouble that came to the silk weavers when machinery was invented to replace their skills and take their jobs. . . . The narrow streets echoed with the tramp of men walking the streets with no work to do." Over a century later, a United States Secretary of Labor asked, "The issue being joined in our economy today is . . . how can the necessities for continued increases in productivity, based on labor saving techniques, be met without creating . . . widespread unemployment?" His answer was optimistic, but not very convincing. (How could it be when bituminous coal mining production had risen 96 per cent while coal mining jobs were reduced by 262,700 and railroad productivity grew 65 per cent while jobs fell by 540,000?) Fifteen years later we see the problem differently, suggesting, curiously enough, almost opposite goals. *The question is how can the necessity for continued*

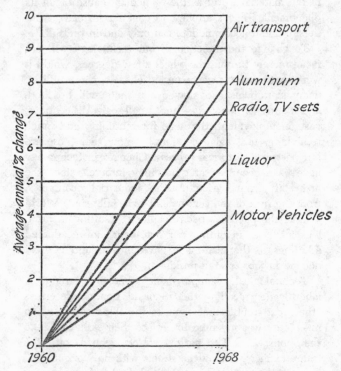

Growth in output per man-hour in certain industries.

*decreases in the use of natural resources, less mass pro-
duction, and more labor-intensive techniques achieve a
reasonable standard of living free from drudgery?*

The aim of the Industrial Revolution was to replace
human with mechanical energy. Such an aim was
hailed by humanitarians, for it was assumed machines
could only do crude work such as quarrying or refined
work such as polishing ball bearings. Having discovered how much work pleasant to man has been
usurped by machines, another kind of aim is
suggested: to replace human energy by mechanical en-

ergy only for the tasks beyond human capacity or simply not worth a human being's time or skill.

WORK

If the function of work is not only to produce goods and provide services but also to be the major activity that develops aptitude, abilities, and character, then how effective is our present technical organization?

To meet the exacting requirements and expanding variety of our technology we are forced to limit our interests to smaller and smaller areas and particularize the things we make to satisfy single functions. Our views and skills are narrowed, the experts learning more about less, the factory employee tending, as Adam Smith observed in 1788, to become "as stupid and ignorant as it is possible for a human being to be." Our production methods compartmentalizing each task make work repetitive and mechanical; the ideal employee in the system being a piece of machinery programmed for the job, devoid of spontaneity and grace, passive and dependable like an ant in its termitary. How quickly, under such conditions, does the long, complex, and cloudy route of evolution curl back on itself to motor action and reaction where reason is no more. It is a great penalty to pay for more knowledge and more goods.

Not so long ago, the labor day had as many as sixteen hours and what with fatigue, inadequate diet, and no hope, those subjected to such regimens were slaves. It was a great victory for the workers when they won shorter hours and better pay, but, as it turned out, these did not emancipate, since it was the jobs themselves that enslaved and stultified. Society, well aware of the degrading quality of the production process, quarantined it from life itself.

The work of twentieth-century architects and plan-

AVERAGE WORK WEEK US		AV. MAN HOUR PRODUCTIVITY*	
1850	69.8 Hours	1860	$0.41
1900	60.2	1900	0.76
1920	49.7	1920	0.93
1940	43.3	1940	1.32
1960	39.4	1960	2.42

*in constant 1950 $

"Never before have so many Americans had so little time to call their own"
1962 (20th century fund)

The anomaly of modern technology.

ners reflects this disdain as well as the modern urge to segregate and specialize. The 1933 Athens Charter of the International Congress of Modern Architects is a neat example recommending "that all future town planning be based on a segregation . . . of social and private life, of working, living and entertainment." Here is specialization, life wrapped in neat and discrete parcels, violating nature's symbiotic ways, abusing our deep need for unity. Paradoxically as the urban ideal once humanistic, becomes technical, the seasonal cycles are simplified so one day is like another and night itself is turned into day. The ultimate goal is to have neither December nor June but scientifically regulated light levels and temperatures adjusted to the planned activities, such as they are. The late twentieth-century office building is the very paradigm: For the typical office worker, it's 9 A.M. zoom up the elevator, soon there's a coffee break, a cafeteria break and shuffle, shuffle in the bland fluorescent shadowless light of the carpeted, draftless, air-conditioned spaces until the swift glide down on the stroke (if there were a bell to toll) of 5. It's all tidy, antiseptic, orderly. No wonder violence on the TV and in comics is popular.

We have not only specialized ways of life, we have homogenized them. We drove people or tempted them to leave the countryside and coagulate into centers where subsistence depends on forms of agriculture which turn out dubious foods all neat in cellophane bags, the farms producing these victuals being just another kind of urban environment—technicians driving or fixing machinery, piloting pesticide spraying planes, or driving huge rigs to distant markets, managers or workers in food processing plants, accountants with their profit-and-loss sheets, employers making deals

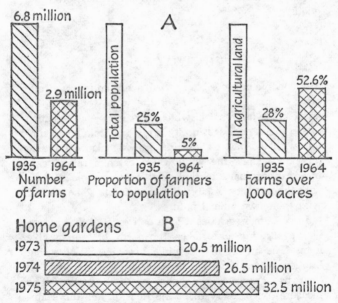

Farming U.S.A.: A. In 1964, 4.5 per cent of all farms produced 42 per cent of all agricultural products. B. A hopeful sign.

with banks and labor unions or contracting for migrant workers, chemists with their additives, salesmen . . . all, almost all, in the grip of conglomerates.

As these enterprises increase in size, greater capitalization is needed. In 1972 it was estimated that it cost $30,000 for machinery and chemicals to support one farm worker's job in the United States. In that same year six of the top food processing plants spent $300 million to advertise their products.

This way of producing food is not for the man with the hoe on his acre or even ten acres so the circle is closed. The small farmer forced off the land swells megalopolis, whose food needs only agribusiness can supply, forcing more farmers off the land, etc. The megalopolis and hinterland increasingly become part of the same automated factory turning out mass-produced goods.

PLAY

Most people are sensible of their needs and periodically must escape the discipline of the work style and the artificial environment in which they live. How touching to see them, enclosed in city grids, maintain some contact with the past by lovingly growing plants, hugging the pots against the windows to catch a ray of sun, how extraordinary to find how many people put up with the nuisance of city dogs to maintain some contact with their own animal natures.

In consumer societies it is to be expected that escape like everything else takes the form of purchasable items. The buying of playthings becomes an increasing fraction of the family budget and the time spent in their use grows as the hours of work decline. The pleasures once reserved for the rich become the example for all to follow; all except the dropouts and the disorganized poor. Powerboats and snowmobiles are bought on the installment plan, second homes, golf clubs, and ski lodges multiply (good roads, only a few hours by car), there are cruise ships, the air lines vie with each other in announcing budget vacation trips to what were once faraway places—a weekend in London, five days on a sun-drenched tropical isle. . . . These are all delights, the question is whether a small planet can long support such pleasures on a mass scale.

PRODUCTS

If we are to develop a mode of production that takes into account the need for meaningful work, the necessity for conserving resources, and the desire for a reasonable level of material comfort, an examination of our tools and accouterments is in order; some must be given up, some given a minor place, some redesigned to fit the new scheme, and others, who knows, may come from some simpler time.

Each kind of product calls for its own production mode. If ball bearings had to be made by hand, we'd use axle grease; to hammer out engine cylinders on a forge would be impractical even for Vulcan and who would turn out cups by Cellini on the assembly line?

In programming the future we must be more particular as to what is produced as well as to how it is produced. A large demand for a product that can be standardized requires the use of our complex machines with their automatic tenders and sensing devices turning out repeats of the same object until the switch is pulled. This mode of production is called *energy intensive*, as contrasted with *labor intensive*, since human intervention is reduced to a minimum. To provide an adequate supply of mass-produced conveniences and eliminate human labor from the boring job of producing them is necessary. What needs examination is what is an adequate supply of what product.

A second way I call *work intensive* rather than *labor intensive,* since it requires a substantial commitment of human creativity, skill, and energy rather than the brute use of muscle the word "labor" implies. In this mode the run of any single object is limited: The object produced, though designed for utility, takes into account the normal desire for variety, the fashionable, and the novel. A suitable environment for such production is not the factory or assembly line but the modest-sized workshops of former times. It is possible that when the atelier is rejuvenated there will be a lively growth of regional styles. But there is no yearning for the old time; the tools used are those selected from modern technology to reduce the hard and boring tasks, making time for the creative ones.

A third sort of production need only be mentioned here, for its relation to technology is peripheral. These are the works created for themselves alone. The brush that Picasso or Rembrandt painted with, the stretched cloth they painted on, and the paint itself were products of a technology. What was painted transcended it and time.

DESIGN OF MASS-PRODUCTION GOODS

If the aim is to reduce the amount and kinds of goods produced by automatic machinery, then in principle no object should be mass-produced, unless it is self-evidently and demonstrably useful and wanted by a large segment of the population (it is to be expected that occasionally we will opt for something of dubious usefulness or downright foolish), or unless the making itself subjects human beings to unhealthy environments or tasks of deadly monotony. The function of automated machines should be to do the inhuman tasks: prepare material for use (extract and convert iron ore to steel, limestone to cement), make tools that aid us in

making things (hammers, plows, engines, computers),
turn out replicas in quantity. . . .

The design of objects for mass production should be
different in kind from other design. The goal is simple
utility, a far different one from that which motivates
the tarted-up packaging of our "industrial designers."
The correct style for mass production was forecast in
the theory (though not practice) of the early Bauhaus
and before that (though for other reasons) in the products of the nineteenth-century Shaker communities. An
economical use of materials is characteristic—when production is in the thousands or millions a gram of extra
weight in each piece in unacceptable. At the same time
durability is important. Since the objects are not made
to satisfy whim or fashion, a long period of usefulness
is wanted. Parts wear out, so easy repair and replace-
ment are essential, a requirement that calls for the
designer to make clear the function as well as how it
functions. Such straightforward design would be a
boon to the layman—he quickly grasps the meaning of
the tool and tends to use rather than misuse it.

Technical change is only valid if it provides more for
less. A jet engine provides more horsepower per pound
so outperforms a cylinder engine, contact lens are in
principle an advance over iron-framed spectacles, plastic dentures an advance over wooden ones, a sheet of
paper over a clay tablet. An exception to both repairability and expressiveness of function is found in minia-
turized elements. The transistors and the printed circuits in a pocket calculator are not self-explanatory nor
are they readily repairable. But then these tiny objects
add little to the middens.

All articles of utility wear out, get broken, and land
on the junk heap, that boon to archaeologists. Part of
the calculation in the selection of materials is whether
they are biodegradable or recyclable, whether if they
are junked, potentially lethal synergistic reactions
occur, as in the case of metallic mercury's trans-
formation to methyl mercury.

FACTORIES IN THE FIELDS OR FARMS?

"Health food" was of course the food for faddists until
the late 1960s. As people have become aware of the
dangers to the land and water in our ways of fertilizing
and spraying, aware of the consequences of indis-
criminate processing of food for better appearance, eas-
ier shipping, and longer shelf life, a change should
occur through market demand for more natural foods.
This change could even happen simply because of increased energy costs, since agribusiness with its sprawl
of fields, processing plants, and distant markets may
not be able to compete with the well-organized work-
intensive small farm except in the growing of seed and
grain crops.

If agriculture replaces agribusiness the variety of
produce offered in the markets will be substantially
less. In exchange, we will, like our forebears, have tas-
tier and more nourishing foods each in their season.
(Later I will discuss what kind of diet we may look
forward to.) The intensive cultivation of small-scale
farm land still found on the outskirts of many European towns and cities suggests the kind of agricultural
system suitable for an economy based on energy saving
and a limited use of technology. An interesting variant
exists in China where along the roads leading to Peking
(and perhaps other cities) trenches are dug. In these
crops are planted, protected in cold weather by transparent plastic covers. At night and when needed a gas
pipe provides supplementary heating. Trucks move
back and forth along the roads transporting the
workers, bringing supplies, and delivering produce. It's
a real dumb, beautiful scheme which gives the people
of this ancient city something they never had before—
fresh vegetables all year round.

Or consider aquaculture. In some countries ponds
are made and stocked with fish which can be brought
to market live eliminating the need for long-distance

The roads lined with greenhouses like this.

hauling and energy-consuming refrigeration, and, not least importantly, guaranteeing the freshness of the fish.

* * *

The need for control of our technology assumes urgency when we recall how tenuous our living space is. Our way of being alive depends on a fragile atmospheric veil separating us from the black hole we spin in. A pitifully thin crust held rigid by the rotation of a molten core is our only foothold in a universe of unimaginable space. How scanty are the few degrees of temperature that represent our survival limit. I said we have challenged the biological fact by allowing technology to threaten our beneficial environment. Since there may not be another such oasis nearer than a hundred or a thousand light-years away, who can doubt that it must be protected?

CHAPTER V

The Need for Utopian Planning

There is in all planning, even if it were ever so earthily rooted in comprehensive studies of facts, an element of belief in reason as an independent force in history and in the freedom of choice by which man can change reality according to his design and so turn the course of future development. In essence planning is an exercise in a non-deterministic conception of history, though it recognizes the limitations put up by existing conditions and forces and their causal interrelations.

—Gunnar Myrdal

The New York City Planning Commission brought out a long-awaited Master Plan for the future development of that city in 1969. In the introduction the planners announced: "We cannot see Utopia. Even if all the money was somehow raised, 10 years from now all sorts of problems will have risen and New Yorkers will be talking about the crisis of the city, what a near hopeless place it is and why doesn't somebody do something."

As it turned out the Plan was found to be no plan at all and quietly shelved. Quite what one would have expected, since the planners had no aim but to reinvent obsolete solutions to obsolete problems and were quick to label *utopian* any proposal that threatened the status quo; "utopian" in their usage matching an observation of Karl Mannheim: "The representatives of a given order will label utopian, conceptions of existence which *from their point of view* can in principle never be realized." It is a suggestive definition explaining why, in general, governmental planning agencies produce mountains of reports explaining why yesterday's decisions were correct (though modification is needed) when in fact they were ineffective or even disastrous. Yesterday's decisions, after all, are part of the "given order," and maintaining it, as Plato pointed out, is the major function of its representatives.

Such a view of planning has a grave objection—it does not take into account the future consequences of present decisions. An even graver objection is that it goes contrary to our innate need to dream of a better future, since in every culture there is a legend of an ideal time, a vision of a golden age, a lost Atlantis, an

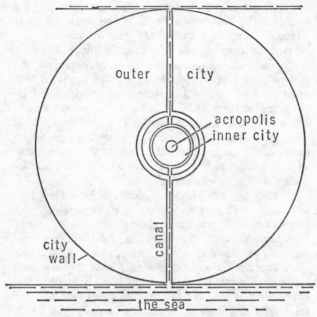

Plan of Atlantis as conceived of by Plato (500 B.C.).

Asgard, a Garden of Eden. The utopian thinkers try to make real these visions—on earth, not in heaven.

It is a noble striving, and every worthwhile plan man has made in some way restates this yea-saying. We survive by it. So it is that the changing facts and statistics of official planning are of far less consequence than the vision of man as a species aiming at perfectibility. Without confidence in such a vision planning for a better society is impossible. The planner who believes he can plan with scope and vision and still be on this side of utopia is deluded, for though he steeps himself in fact and statistic, rejects any but the strictest logic, and accepts no unproven proposition, he nevertheless designs for *utopia*, that is, *no place*, the unknowable—a

fantasy land called the future. What else can he plan
for? Not the past unless he is in the world of *1984*
where history can be rewritten, nor the present, that
slippery moment already past as we think on it.

Because planning can only be a projection of the
planner's view of the future, it is to be expected that
plans may go awry. In our time, events predicted by
"utopians" come to pass with disastrous consequences,
hence distopias such as Huxley's *Brave New World*
with its drug-addicted mannequins moving in environments of glistening plastic and neon tubes or the lobot-
omized people in their numbers marching on as described in Eugene Zamiatin's *We*.

Consequences can be the opposite of intentions. History in no small part is a history of plans gone awry, of
predictions and projections glaringly wrong, of absurd
forecasts and tragic consequences. Yet there is no escape, since a decision *not* to plan is, as I've said, also a
plan. Consciously or subconsciously each step we take,
unless totally accidental, has been given prior consideration; the preplanned co-ordination of muscles to meet
the height of a step or the assumed softness, hardness,
or roughness of the ground is part of an elaborate calculation based on past experience. But what happens
when we have had no prior experience to guide us or if
we make a wrong assumption? What seemed firm foot-
ing is not. The chances of a stumble increase as circumstances vary from the accustomed—a not uncommon
occurrence in our time.

How, then, does the architect or planner cope with
the future needs and ways of man, on what does he
base his proposals? The chances of his being right are
less than ever before, yet he is expected to recommend
expenditures for such heavy and costly things as make
up the physical environment—streets, buildings, towns—
projects that often take years from conception to com-
pletion and when ill conceived, burden people for generations with their ineptitude.

It is not only the extraordinary changes and the

speed with which they have happened but the unexpected by-products and side effects that have made modern planning the most risky of businesses. What levelheaded realist in the nineteenth century would not have dismissed as fiction a forecast of the scientific and technical developments made since that time which we now think commonplace? Indeed they are the very stuff that Jules Verne and H. G. Wells thrived on: elaborate communication systems, culminating in the bouncing of messages off the sides of artificial satellites, the everyday use of calculators that in a minute print out solutions to problems that even ten years ago would have taken years to solve, nuclear power so vast in force as to be incomprehensible, air travel over continents and seas for ordinary folk, landings on the moon and vehicles sent to remote parts of our galaxy. A hundred million rubber-tired machines on our roads is fantastic enough but who could have envisioned the roads themselves with their extraordinary interchanges, ramps, and bridges, each worth a king's ransom and so well engineered as to allow little old ladies to drive seventy miles an hour on the straightaways. To have isolated sixty additional chemical elements, broken the genetic code, developed an elaborate human transplant surgery, made polio and TB rarities among diseases . . . There is no end to the marvels including the pollution that threatens to infect the world and the canker fear in the minds of us all that someone will push what Bucky Fuller has called the "humanity extinguishing button."

In the long run the dreamers such as Verne, Wells, and Bellamy made better forecasts of the late twentieth century than did those practical men who ran things—the Carnegies, Morgans, and Rockefellers. But naturally! Change is rarely in the interest of those in power so they rarely see change occurring and even more rarely the need for it. This is the myopia of rulers, a form of willful distortion which often seems in retrospect to be a kind of madness. Usually it is not madness but an estrangement from reality. Those put in power automatically develop masks to go with their titles and even in the most democratic of countries find themselves in a world different from that in which the rest of us live. They are captives in their security-guarded mansions and bulletproof limousines; they live in an atmosphere of manufactured applause and brass bands, of the grins and handshakes of potentates in similar situations all showing their dentures in the light of flash bulbs. Such becomes their reality while starvation or people blown up are but statistics which may be canceled by the official double talk or altered by the signing of documents none intend to abide by.

History is filled with the recounting of glaring misinterpretations and misunderstandings by power insulated from reality. These impersonators fill the history books— there is a Mussolini mouthing Caesar and a trumped-up Attila with a Charlie Chaplin mustache. On the Russian steppe we've had a latter-day Ivan the Terrible, and most recently in the Capital of our democracy we have seen the spirit of Marie Antoinette in the most unlikely of guises:

> Q. Is it reasonable for the American people to go on assuming, in a hungry world where raw materials are increasingly scarce, that our standard of living each year can go on going up, or do we have to face new responsibilities and even some sacrifices in this country in order to bring about some kind of world order?
> A. Now, here I'm talking off the top of my head. I would think, if we look ahead to the year 2000 and beyond, we have to be prepared to face a world quite different from what we have now. We see it already in energy. I believe that the day of the four-hundred-horsepower engine is over, whether it's this year or five years from now. You're going to see different types of automobiles, and that affects our style of life.

The question was by James Reston of the New York
Times reported in the issue of October 13, 1974; the
answer by U. S. Secretary of State Henry Kissinger.

How interesting to compare the attitude of this
twentieth-century Lord Chancellor with that of another, Sir Thomas More, who with his mask off once
wrote:

> Then consider how few of those that work are em-
> ployed in labors that are of real service; for we
> who measure things by money, give rise to many
> trades that are both vain and superfluous . . . for
> if those who work were employed only in such
> things as the convenience of life require, there
> would be an abundance of them all. . . .[1]

Utopian writing and science fiction are usually
lumped, though not at all alike. Both, it is true, are
in the realm of fantasy, but then so is all fiction. The
mark of the utopian writer is unmistakable—he smells
something rotten, he is convinced it can be changed,
his book shows the way. The test of his influence is
how acutely he views the problem and how suitable
and timely a solution he finds. The utopian element in
any thought will almost invariably generate an adverse
reaction in the conventional mind, for there is in it a
certain something so opposite to current wisdom that
regardless of merit it will be called impractical, unlikely. The truth is that every utopian idea has a he-
retical stink quickly detected by the orthodox who,
unfortunately, are the ultimate decision-makers in
planning of any consequence. Nevertheless, the good
planner must have the habit of utopian thinking along
with the wit to recognize the implications of a utopian
proposal when he makes one. This is not always easy.

For instance: My nephew Woody tells me the
students plan a complaint—even a demonstration—
against another hike in college fees. I point out that
the administration will counter with simple economic

[1] *Utopia.*

facts—there is an inflation, government funding has
shrunk, donors have taken to the woods, etc., how will
such evident truths be answered? It is a difficulty
Woody admits. We discuss the matter agreeing that a
solution must be found which accepts the gray economic picture but nevertheless provides a worthwhile
alternative to the fee hike. Certain facts emerge: (1)
meals on campus cost more than meals in town and are
no better, often worse, (2) rent for dormitory rooms
are not only higher than town rents but town quarters
are more spacious and pleasant, (3) there does seem to
be a lot of unnecessary filling out of forms (not to be
mutilated, folded, or spindled). A course of action is
suggested:

1. Students and sympathetic faculty members from
the university's School of Hotel Management should be
able to ferret out why people in town purveying food
and lodging, managers of small-scale enterprises without degrees in management, who cannot benefit by
economies-of-scale, who pay taxes and make some sort
of profit, nevertheless can provide acceptable food and
clean beds, yet charge less than the university, which is
endowed, tax-exempt, nonprofit, buys in bulk, and supposedly employs people trained in efficient procedures.

2. The Agricultural School is one of the best and
largest in the country, and the campus is set in a large
acreage of fertile land. Wouldn't it be a worthwhile addition to the student's understanding of economy, ecology, and the educational process in general if the Agricultural School organized, and the university adopted,
a program in which all undergraduates worked in barn
and field to raise (say) half the food they ate?

These certainly seem direct and rather simple-
minded suggestions.

What would happen if they were acted on? Consider
just the farming proposition: If such a scheme was accepted, the academic calendar would require change

(summer being the time for farming). A work-study program would be required to allow for the additional activity. Under such a regime who knows what might happen? The new program might tend to broaden instead of specialize the student's skill, knowledge, and interests. Supposing a student began circulating copies of a letter sent Ralph Waldo Emerson in 1840 from the founder of Brook Farm[2] which read in part: "our objects are as you know, to insure a more natural union between intellectual and manual labor than now exists, to combine the thinker and the worker, as far as possible in the same individual. . . . to do away with the necessity of menial services, by opening the benefits of education and the profits of labor to all; and thus to prepare a society of liberal, intelligent and cultivated persons, whose relations can lead to a more simple and wholesome life. . . ." Worse, if students used up their excess energy in tilling wouldn't they be too tired for football? What might happen to phys ed? But the food lodging proposition is worse; if faculty and students examining the comparative costs and quality of room and board found that small-scale enterprises provided more and better for less and if they also noticed that bands of students who fed and housed themselves co-operatively paid even less (with a great plus in the way of communal feeling), might they not conclude something was wrong with the way things were organized? If they did, might there not be a move to dump a good part of the administration, its bureaucracy, and its not-to-be-spindled forms? Might there not be a move to decentralize the administration of the university and place it into the hands of the faculties and student body?

If such consequences resulted from the suggestions of an emeritus professor to a young student, obviously the old codger is a utopian for he advocates ideas "which in principle are unrealizable" from "the viewpoint of the representatives of a given order."

[2] George Ripley.

Yet we live in a strange time; perhaps such suggestions are no longer quite so utopian. The Education Facilities Laboratory's *Generating Revenue from College Facilities* (1974) points out:

> Because of declining enrollments, rising costs of educational services, decreasing income from investments in an adverse market, and a taxpayer revolt at the polls, many colleges and universities are seeking new methods for raising funds, making operational costs go further, and finding partners who can relieve their budgets of the expense of nonacademic services. One solution to financial difficulties is to develop productive uses for underused facilities.

Indicators such as this reinforce the premise basic to this book: *What we won't do voluntarily, necessity will force us to do.*

The problems are complex, difficult, and paradoxical; a world that has gotten progressively less habitable and more crowded calls for larger and more comprehensive plans in order to achieve some sort of balance and a reasonable guarantee of survival. Yet we know that planning has its risks and the larger and more embracing the plan, the greater the risks. It is evident that a small plan with a large error may be rectifiable but a global plan with a small error could be "humanity extinguishing." In our time we have seen dictatorships destroy freedom with their national plans and over and over again have seen that Alexis de Tocqueville was right when he said: "Every central government worships uniformity; uniformity relieves it from inquiry into an infinity of details, which must be attended to if rules have to be adapted to different men, instead of indiscriminately subjecting all men to the same rule." Patently, if a society is to be planned for, its population must conform to the plan, and the more all-embracing and rigid the plan, the more restricted are the lives of those required to obey it. The implications of such an idea are repugnant.

Here, then, is the dilemma:

Physical development cannot be left to chance or small-scale, isolated efforts, for the problems involved in conserving and allotting resources, of protecting the biosphere from pollution, of preventing destruction of life on land and sea, of re-creating and maintaining a symbiotic balance, are global. However, large-scale, comprehensive planning has up to this time often resulted in tyranny, generally proven inefficient, and, in the long run, been unworkable.

How *does* one globally plan and yet preserve human dignity and freedom? The resolution of such a question calls for utopian speculation.

* * *

No one speculates on the future in a time of stability, or on alternative societies when there is no possibility or positive need for change. Nor does one speculate when no new thing has happened to trigger the change.

A new thing had happened to Athens when she lay defeated and exhausted at the end of the Peloponnesian War. Plato's solution for her troubles was embodied in *The Republic*. There was a need for change, though no possibility, when Sir Thomas More, appalled by the misery resulting from the Enclosure Acts, foreign wars, and court extravagance, wrote *Utopia*. The new things triggering change in the Renaissance were the great voyages and the new science so we have such a book as Bacon's *New Atlantis*. The nineteenth- and early twentieth-century utopians were cranked up by those vast changes we call the Industrial Revolution and that age just past whose remembered dates were 1776 and 1795.

We have arrived at another moment in history, a time when the possibility for change is here and the need for change is imperative, for we, a single species, dominate the planet, have the power of life and death over all things, and are in imminent danger of fatally misusing it.

It is an awesome moment when a species of limited capacity and all but unprepared is required to transform itself if its members are to survive. Since biologists such as Julian Huxley have found no evidence indicating that our physical being will change in the foreseeable future, the mutation, for a mutation is required, must take place in our minds; our economics, our politics, our sociology, and our ethical behavior must be recast to suit a culture man has only dreamed of. We must now plan for the actuality of such a culture. The utopians give hints and guidelines as to its nature not given by others: Did not Plato call for equality of the sexes, Thomas More, the need to eliminate poverty in order to eliminate crime, and did not he and the Italian Tommaso Campanella advocate attractive work and short workdays as an essential to human development? Did not almost every utopian condemn war and the exploitation of man by man; were not mutual aid and solidarity stressed as inherent in human nature?

It is true that Plato's Republic was not a republic but a dictatorship, that More's island is described as having fifty-four towns all exactly alike with each street and each house the same, it is true that the most influential of modern utopians, Karl Marx, called for a revolution whose result was a monstrous dictatorship but whose aim was exactly the opposite—"the withering away of the state" making way for "an association in which the free development of each is a condition for free development of all." It is true that utopian ideas are often nonsensical, utopian aims often miss their goals. Just like those of "practical" people.

The Planner's Dilemma

When the means of production and what is produced are being questioned, when religious and social taboos are disappearing, when social groupings are reorganizing in new patterns, when, in short, the structure of society is in transition, the planner is in a quandary. Everything is uncertain, forecasts meaningless, past experience a dubious guide. In such a time prudence dictates thoughtful appraisals, theoretical discussion, and pilot studies rather than planning for commitments to those heavy goods we call the physical environment. Nevertheless, there is building that must be done either because there is a desperate need or because what is, is a damned nuisance and should be changed.

Planning, then, may be categorized under three headings: *measures to alleviate conditions of desperate need; meeting needs which though immediate are not desperate;* and *the long-range commitment.*

First, as many are in desperate need, planning and implementation must often be simultaneous. Solutions must be improvised, the work done quickly. The planner avoids permanent commitments, a finger in the dike is the best simile, and if there is no dike then sandbags may be piled up, rafts built, or the people and their cattle evacuated to higher ground. The planning is interim, the efficiency of immediate utility is the criterion.

Although the physical results of such planning are sheer utility, provisionary, and often wasteful, the spirit in which they are carried out can be of another sort. The work done by the WPA and the CCC in the days of the 1930s depression are examples.

Second, there are needs which though real enough are not matters of survival. For example, there are traffic jams. Shall we double-deck the highway? Here the planner can say no, let us try alternative possibilities before committing ourselves. We could make it expensive for single-occupant cars during rush hours, reduce tolls for car poolers, provide special lanes for buses and run more of them. These are all alternatives; some, or all, who knows, may turn out to be solutions.

There are cases where new structures are wanted but there is no absolute need. The planner's recommendation is based on his judgment—does it fulfill an indisputably human need? Is it of obvious benefit to those who will use it? Does it replace an unaesthetic, unhealthy, or obsolete use? Does it reclaim or protect a natural resource, a historical landmark? Is it ecologically sound? When such questions are answered affirmatively, then the commitment may be made even when its future value may be questioned.

Finally, what are the alternate futures we should plan for? Is it a world filled with half-starved and sickly people choking in their own excrement, or one of happy-faced rural folk dancing on the green, of technocrats pushing buttons and robots busily rolling about serving them food grown on the moon, or life in concrete bunkers and a great mushroom cloud? Of things going along pretty much as they are, only more so or a little less? . . .

These are hard questions and it is not the planner, alone or even surrounded by experts, who is going to resolve the contradictions, dilemmas, and perplexities of our time, nor will the answers come from the bureaucracies whose responses can only be characterized as catatonic. Will the answers come from such as us, a fickle people, prone to embrace fads and follies, quick to manufacture heroes and quick to pillory them? Polls testing our opinion vary like fever charts. Our bureaucracies may be catatonic, but we (dare I say it?) are just a mite manic-depressive, so it's hard to believe us capable of making thoughtful appraisals of our changing circumstances. It's hard to believe we will entertain plans that view the coming changes as beneficial, which suggest ways to reduce the traumas of transition and propose courses of action that may aid in making

the transition orderly. It may be true that our nerv-
ousness, our busyness, our conservatism, and our
shortsightedness are all covers for the malaise described by Giscard d'Estaing: "The world is unhappy. It
is unhappy because it doesn't know where it is going
and because it senses that, if it knew, it would discover
that it was heading for disaster."

If things are all that hopeless, then we should turn
our thoughts to the problems of death, the last judgment, and the resurrection rather than mundane things.
Eschatology, not planning, should be our interest.

* * *

In short, now is exactly the time for utopian speculation. We are in trouble, there is the need for change.
Old things are dying, new things happening.

In such a period we must free ourselves from our old
formulations and start anew with faith in "reason as an
independent force" able to "turn the course of future
development"; we must review our ways to rediscover
what is prejudice and what is fact, what is crucial detail and what is trifle. We must examine the models we
have been emulating, learn to differentiate between the
new and the merely novel. . . .

It's a lot, but what it boils down to is deciding
whether we follow the plans of the hard-nosed, who attempt to extrapolate the future by projecting present
trends, or the utopians, who establish goals, then work
backward from them to the present. It seems to me
that the latter is the more practical approach, since it
charts the future course of day-by-day decisions.

CHAPTER VI

The Double E

To prophesy is a hard task—especially in re-
spect to future events.

—Anon.

In 1946 in the introduction to the final section of *Communitas,* Paul Goodman and I said, "Now let us make a new beginning and collect our conclusions for our own problems in this book: How to make a selection of modern technology? How to find the right relation between ways and means?"

The aim of this book, written over thirty years later, is no different, though times have changed and the author works alone.

Communitas was based on three community models invented to illustrate and analyze alternative means of livelihood and ways of life possible in an American economy whose symbol we took to be an ever-brimming cornucopia. We assumed our vast surplus of means and wealth flowed from inexhaustible resources to be disposed of as we pleased. As we saw it, our problems were not physical but cultural. We did not know what to do with our riches so we spent ourselves and our substance on follies.

It is certainly true that we did and we do spend ourselves on follies, but in retrospect it seems curious that neither Paul nor I saw the threat of our misuse of resources and technology except as "air-conditioned nightmare" nor took into account the world war raging and the planet-shrinking events of the period. Yet by 1940 ocean-crossing planes and hemisphere-spanning communication systems were common, as was the realization that political and economic co-operation among nations was indispensible if there was to be a viable world.

Here, then, all these years later, is a fourth model based on the same aesthetic and ethical standards used in *Communitas* but with premises that reflect additional concerns. Here there are crude physical restraints; scarcity not surplus, not a cornucopia but a small planet with burgeoning populations and diminishing resources. Here I accept the need to control technology since we will soon be unable to cope with some of its by-products (unemployment, pollution) nor afford some of its products (gadgetry, death-dealing machines). Here I assume that certain trends in our culture will become dominant modes—among them a more communal way of life, sexual equality, an altogether simpler standard of living, a decentralization of work and political processes. . . .

As in *Communitas,* this paradigm is embodied in a physical model, for this form seems now (as it did then) the best way for an architect to present a proposal. However, a model of this sort is an abstraction from and a simplification of the real world. It is therefore *not* a model in the sense of an architectural model, as the focus is not on the concrete form but the form-making elements, be they ethical, social, technical, economic, or aesthetic. The purpose of the model is predictive: to sketch a probable future if certain alternatives are selected. I have tried to select alternatives that I assume may find acceptance simply because others (in my estimation) range from the improbable to the disastrous.

Although I will show the plan of a town and even the detail of a house, these are to be taken as illustrations designed to evoke thought, not as proposals for building. As the model is not intended as a blueprint for action but as a basis for discussion, it refers to no site although the climate and geography would be familiar to the dwellers in the temperate zone; there is no particular population although the people are from a high technology background, no doubt American. In locale, then, it is not strictly *utopian* (that is *no place*), but as its premises are optimistic it is *eutopian* (that is a *good place*).

Such a model may be heartening as we are in a time when prophets of doom are in high repute and with good reason, for their knapsacks are full of facts, all with doomsday labels. It *is* a fact that we are in great danger. But then what? Does it mean that we accept the ghastly future predicted by the nay-sayers? *That* to my mind is intolerable; we cannot live with despair. Is it not contrary to our good sense to believe we have no choices or to believe that, having choices, we will not choose those that will enhance rather than destroy us?

ASSUMPTIONS AND PREDICTIONS

I have quoted Gunnar Myrdal as saying that planning is an exercise in a nondeterministic conception of history, therefore based on predictions and assumptions as to the future course of events. Here I assume there are alternatives to the gloomy predictions—reason and faith can triumph—so predict that given a free choice we'll make the right choice since, in the words of U Thant,

> Like it or not, we are all traveling together on a common planet. We have no rational alternative but to work together to make an environment in which we and our children can live full and peaceful lives. . . . Perhaps it is the collective menaces arising from the world's scientific and technological strides and from their mass consequences, which will bind together nations, enhance peaceful co-operation and surmount, in the face of physical danger, the political obstacles to mankind's unity.

But beyond rationality is my confidence that J. B. S. Haldane stated a fact of nature when he wrote, "In so far as it makes for the survival of one's descendants and near relations, altruistic behavior is a kind of Darwinian fitness, and may be expected to spread as a result of natural selection."[1]

The basic assumption of the Fourth Paradigm is that

[1] *The Causes of Evolution*, 1932.

we all seek life, liberty, and the pursuit of happiness
and it is a possible goal.

I also assume those demographers right who forecast
that during the early decades of the twenty-first century the world's population will have doubled and
there may be another doubling before a leveling off in
growth occurs.

A third assumption is that we have reached a pla-
teau in technological change in all branches except the
life sciences.

Finally I predict that by the year 2000 even the
smallest nation will have a stock pile of atomic weapons and assume that with nuclear war imminent, the
nations will meet, vote for life, not for death, and universal disarmament will follow.

THE YEAR 2020

1. Getting rid of armaments has had astonishing effects,
freeing enormous resources for useful purposes. Even
as long ago as 1972 it had been calculated that during
the previous quarter century the arms race between the
Soviet Union and the United States had cost those two
countries $1,500 billion, a sum that (in 1961 dollars)
would have financed fifty years of economic development in the underdeveloped nations, even if a third
was retained for the military security purposes then
considered necessary.[2] By 1973 arms expenditures had
become so outlandish that Kurt Waldheim, the secre-
tary-general of the United Nations, warned, ". . . if
we don't blow ourselves out of existence, we will probably spend ourselves out of existence—this year we will
spend $250 billion on armaments, which is one of the
fundamental causes of the cancerous inflation which is
attacking every economy and threatens the world mon-
etary system with collapse." Perhaps by coincidence in
the same year the Club of Rome called for an annual
investment of $250 billion by the industrialized nations

[2] Prof. Seymour Melman, Columbia University.

to help the poor countries, and added, "Now is the time to draw up a master plan for organic, sustainable growth and world development based on global allocation of all finite resources and a new global economic system." During the year of 1973 millions starved in India and Africa.

With the moral and material burden of armaments removed, people began to see with fresh eyes. It became apparent, for instance, that old Adam Smith had been right—"No society can be flourishing and happy in which the greater part of its members are poor or miserable." Almost overnight world-wide poverty was reduced as the world's wealth of resources and the people's mental and physical energy were directed to peaceful uses. Almost overnight tensions, anxiety, fear, and insecurity bred by military propaganda began to be replaced by feelings of human solidarity and mutual aid—just as Prince Kropotkin had predicted in 1900.

THE DOUBLE E

2. Disarmament had, of course, ended colonialism, and the underdeveloped nations (as they were called) began to receive their fair share. Such sharing would have been an intolerable tax on the planet if the law called *World Conservation of Natural (including Human) Resources* had not been universally accepted. This law, or more accurately this set of principles, was based on ecological and economic studies made in the late twentieth century and incorporated recommendations made by the United Nations as early as 1970 in its *Man and Biosphere,* a program aborted by the national misunderstandings and rivalries of that confused period.

In the historical preamble to *World Conservation of Natural (including Human) Resources* two quotations describe late twentieth-century concerns; one from the United Nations 1974 conference in Bucharest: "It is imperative that all countries, and within them all social sectors should adapt themselves to a more rational utilization of natural resources, without excess, so some are not deprived of what others waste." The other, a warning signed by thirty-two of Great Britain's leading scientists, described the crisis conditions in these terms: "If current trends are allowed to persist, the breakdown of society and the irreversible disruption of the life-support systems on this planet—possibly by the end of this century, certainly within the lifetime of our children—is inevitable."

The premises on which the law is based are simple to the point of banality: "Planetary resources are finite and must be conserved; planetary life depends on maintaining a balance between organism and environment; earth is an oasis of life in space, the human race is probably unique, a species worth preserving. . . ."

King   Master   Not

The logogram now used to represent the law is composed of two letters back to back—the Double E—symbolizing *Economy* (the management of expenses) and *Ecology* (the mutual relations between organism and environment). My Chinese friends pointed out that the ideogram for *king* is like the Double E and that with a slight modification it becomes *master*, while if the two letters were separated and extended it resembled the ideogram for *not*. From which they concluded economy and ecology should be inseparable and not overextended.

PLANNING

3. During the last stages of Western industrial society, the exploitation of land, transportation modes, and engineering design dominated physical planning theory. Although some concern for the psychosocial aspects of physical planning appeared after the civil disturbances of the 1960s, most planners objected to the addition of such nonquantifiable elements to their already heavy load of facts and figures. The computer, still somewhat of a novelty, was hailed as the answer to the overburden and in no time at all turned out elaborate inventories containing billions of "bits" of information all stored on magnetic tape. Out of these, answers were to be generated without too much aid from the human brain. The aberrant results of such a method soon demonstrated that no machine could assimilate, co-ordinate, discard, and rearrange information as a single experience, especially when the information could neither be derived from its elements nor considered as the sum of its elements. In short, there was no substitute for the creative, imaginative mind and the universal outlook. Like all the beautiful devices of the twentieth century, the computer was revaluated and given its proper place on the tool rack.

All twenty-first-century planning for the man-made environment is rooted in the modest principles of the Double E. In spite of the fact that there are many plans that must interlock at major nodes, planning is now much less complex simply because there are no conflicts within or exceptions to the basic premise: *The ecological and economic principles are primary.* Before implementing any planning proposal there are searching appraisals of all its implications, the unlikely as well as the foreseeable, the by-products and side effects as well as the sought-for symbiotic relationships between the natural and the man-contrived. The aim of architects and physical planners is to relate spaces and structures so their arrangement facilitates a convivial rapport between domestic life and work, education and leisure, privacy and community, expressing through their forms an aesthetic vision which makes sense of it all.

In addition to the restraint imposed by the law of the Double E, there is another: the requirement to accommodate the needs of the world-wide organization that came to be called the Basic Economy. It was not philanthropy or simple altruism that led the rich nations to accept this planned division of subsistence goods but fear of the rising power of the Third World (as it was then called), who by the latter part of the twentieth century no longer begged for charity but demanded their share of the world's bounty. In 1975, for instance, a consortium of poor nations claimed as their right "seven per cent of the industrialized nations' gross national product," not in some far future time,

IF THE GROSS NATIONAL PRODUCT HAD BEEN DIVIDED EQUALLY EACH PERSON WOULD HAVE HAD:

AMONG THE RICH

United States	Sweden	France
Population 210,000,000	8,100,000	52,000,000
$6,200.	$5,900.	$4,500.

AMONG THE POOR

Burma	Bangladesh	Afghanistan
Population 29,000,000	74,000,000	16,600,000
$80.	$74.	$90.

Disparity in global wealth according to the World Bank (1973).

but by 1978. Demands such as this were backed in various ways—by withholding raw materials, boycotts, through minor terrorism (kidnaping) and intermediate terrorism (sky jacking). Finally, with their possession of the bomb, even the most obtuse agreed that the old-time handouts no longer worked and concluded that society (which by 1980 meant the world) not only could not flourish "when the greater part of its members are poor or miserable" but would not survive.

THE BASIC ECONOMY

. . . our proposal covers everybody in the society rather than a special group, the unemployed. In this it follows the plan of social insurance, which insures everyone, regardless of prospective need. Everyone is liable to a period of labor, or its equivalent, for the direct production of subsistence goods, and all are entitled to the goods.

And instead of limiting the class of persons, the limitation is set on the class of goods, subsistence goods. This kind is the most universally essential, so it is reasonable to require a universal service; nevertheless, this part of the economy is not allowed to expand its standards, therefore it cannot com-

pete economically or dominate politically.

It is reasonable to speak in this
way of a subsistence minimum
. . . when the minimum can be
produced with a small fraction of
the social labor and there is wide
satisfaction at a higher standard.

—A 1940 proposal called "Planned
Security—Minimum Regulation,"
by Percival and Paul Goodman

4. Global disarmament made international co-operation
possible. The first step was to agree that the right to
participate in the society and earn freedom from want
is the birthright of all. The Basic Economy (now written as a B back to back with an E) was organized to implement this right.

Like the Double E, the principles on which the Basic
Economy is based are few: A fraction of the world's
production is taken out of the economy of all nations in
proportion to their wealth. This fraction consists of the
goods required for a minimum but healthful subsistence for all. There is no variation in quality or quantity
because of higher or lower standards of living as the
goods are *not* for comfort or luxury, but *subsistence*.
These goods cannot be bought or sold; planning, production, and distribution are internationally organized,
locally administered. It is desirable that all able-bodied
people serve a period in the labor force.

Excerpts from a study made in 1984 called "Prelimi-
nary Observations on the Feasibility of a Divided
Economy":
Until the early part of the twentieth century, even in
the most industrialized nations, most of the productive

machinery and labor force was needed to produce subsistence goods. By 1970 probably not more than a
tenth of the gross national product of countries such as
the United States was given to such purposes, perhaps
less, the estimate depending on what is considered subsistence need; in our definition, adequate food, shelter,
and clothing to maintain physical efficiency.

To accurately establish the quantity or provide an
inventory of goods required for minimum and healthful
subsistence is beyond the scope of this study. In a general way it can be said that even as early as 1940
statistics indicated there were materials, techniques,
and a work force available which if less wastefully used
could have provided a reasonable amount of convenience and luxury goods as well as a subsistence ration
for all.

The following comments reinforce this observation.

First, in Great Britain, E. F. Schumacher calculated
the actual amount of time spent in 1970 by the population in what he called the work of "actual producers,"
meaning "not people who tell other people what to do,
or account for the past, or plan for the future or dis-
tribute what other people have produced." Dr. Schumacher found that only one out of six such "actual
producers" was engaged in "actual production," and
these people spent only 3½ per cent of their total time
at such tasks. The other 96½ per cent was "spent in
other ways, including sleeping, eating, watching television, doing jobs that are not directly productive or
killing time more or less humanely."[3]

Second, in 1944 the United States devoted nearly
"one fourth of its total productive power to the manufacture of combat armaments, more than 40% to meeting total war needs and approximately half to supply-
ing total government requirements. Yet the volume of
goods and services supplied to American civilian con-

[3] *Small Is Beautiful.*

sumers was sustained at not far from the highest pre-war levels ever achieved."[4]

"Because our output per capita in the United States is the highest in the world, American civilians would be left much better provided with goods and services than those of any other belligerent even if this country used a substantially larger proportion of its economic resources for war purposes than it does."[5]

During the third year of World War I although 60 per cent or less of our production was allocated to non-war purposes, "the American consumer and his family remained by far the best-fed, best-housed and best-clothed civilians in the world."[6]

Third, back in the middle 1940s, using the estimates underlying such statements, the Goodman brothers calculated what they called the "subsistence fraction, U.S." and concluded that using the mass-production machines and techniques of the times to turn out selected products of high utility but minimum variety, every person would be guaranteed subsistence if they worked one year in four; predictable refinements in technology would soon halve the figure.

In 1970 one of the brothers collected another set of figures that supported this view. He argued that a country producing twice the goods and services of all Europe, including the British Isles, a country with a per capita production 40 per cent higher than Sweden, 60 per cent higher than Germany, 70 per cent higher than France, twice that of Britain, and two and a half times that of the Soviet Union would hardly notice the subtraction of a subsistence minimum from its gross national product.

Fourth, the vast expenditures for military purposes

[4] America's Needs and Resources, 20th Century Fund, 1947.
[5] U. S. Department of Commerce, 1945.
[6] War Production Board, 1944.

typical of the twentieth century could not be counted
only in physical sums, although, as one instance, direct
United States military spending in the 1960s and '70s
amounted to about 10 per cent of the annual gross national product. A greater loss was in the misuse of
human intellect; an expert at that time calculated, "Between one-half to two-thirds of the present engineering
science research and development manpower of the nation is now devoted to military work."[7] Still greater was
the loss to society once described by William James in
an essay titled "A Moral Equivalent for War": "If now
there were instead of military conscription a conscription of the whole youthful population to form for a certain number of years a part of the army enlisted
against nature, injustice would tend to be evened out
and numerous other goods to the commonwealth would
follow!"

And finally, it is, as was said previously, beyond the
scope of this study to detail kinds and amounts of subsistence goods. Nevertheless, a guess as to magnitude
was made by using energy as a yardstick. For instance,
if one took India's average per capita consumption of
37,000 BTUs per day and considered it adequate to
produce a subsistence minimum, then only a twentieth
of the United States productive capacity would be
needed. Making allowances for differences in climate,
less than minimum desirable standards, etc., a conservative estimate would be that less than a tenth of U.S.
production circa 1975 would represent the subsistence
fraction of the United States.

*   *   *

Living conditions among the poor nations were bad
when the above was written, but not comparable to the
1960s when the average per capita income in some
forty of the world's poorest nations (in 1960 dollars)
was roughly $120, less than 35 cents a day, while the

[7] Seymour Melman.

annual per capita income in the United States was nearly $3,000, almost $8 a day, or a difference of 2,000 per cent! Obviously, with a world so divided there was neither peace nor stability.

As the nations began to disarm in the late 1980s it was agreed that the vast stores of skills and resources now free would be used to implement the basic requirement for world peace: *All people must have elementary subsistence as a right.*

The rest was logistics. How can the deprived of all nations be fed, clothed, and housed in the most efficient way? How can all people be insured against want? How can these things be done with minimum damage to global resources, minimum infringement on human freedom? These were not new questions, and efforts had been made to answer them in ways suited to the economies of the twentieth century:

In industrially advanced countries, citizens were guaranteed against want by insurance schemes financed by a tax on the general economy. This method required maintaining the economy at a high rate of production and consumption in order to pay the tax and support an ever-expanding bureaucracy needed to collect the taxes and administer the funds. As a result the democracies were forced to establish controls which increasingly limited individual economic freedom while in socialist countries all were fettered so all could eat.

In the industrially backward countries the poor went hungry unless fed by the charity of their own rich or the undependable and miserly aid of the more affluent countries. The future promise lay in schemes for rapid industrialization of the whole economy to provide development and create employment. Such schemes either never materialized or, if realized, failed to alleviate the plight of the poor. It became obvious that the poor could not be helped as long as a quarter of the world's population controlled 75 per cent of the world's trade and "over 90% of the capital flow from the rich countries to the poor goes through multinational corporations whose aim is to make profit, not to improve local conditions."[8] Not surprisingly a 1976 study reported the "target gross of gross product in the developing regions set by the International Development Strategy for the Second United Nations Development Decade are not sufficient to close the income gap between developing and developed countries," adding, "The principal limits to sustained economic growth and accelerated development are political, social and institutional in character rather than physical."[9]

Conclusions reached from this history:

As the main occupation of the affluent nations was to supply convenience, comfort, and luxury goods and services, the subtraction of the subsistence would make no difference to the socialist states and an acceptable loss to capitalist countries, since the trade-off would be a large decrease in taxes and (if they insisted) unbridled competition or monopoly or price-fixing for all other goods and services.

Aside from threats and politics, the situation among the technically backward countries required swift action as whole populations were in need of subsistence goods for survival. The policy had been: "Give a man a fish, he eats for a day." Now another policy was put forward: "Teach a man to fish and he eats for a lifetime." It was recommended the rich provide the poor with the means to mass-produce subsistence goods and teach them how to use and maintain the machinery. With survival assured, with the energy given by an adequate diet, suitable shelter, and proper medical care, with the learning of modern skills and work habits, the people would soon be able to decide on life styles compatible with both their ways and the new technology.

[8] Dr. M. S. Manhold, formerly president of the European Common Market.
[9] *The Future of the World Economy,* United Nations Department of Economic and Social Affairs.

ORGANIZATION OF THE BASIC ECONOMY

An international committee monitors the Basic Economy organization set up by each nation. Each nation provides the co-operating force through a universal draft. Payment for service is in scrip exchangeable only for subsistence needs.

Production norms will fluctuate as only enough goods are to be produced each year to maintain "an ever normal granary." Subsistence goods being necessities for survival, neither glut nor lack can be tolerated.

Subsistence needs are provided in quantity and kind suitable to occupation and climate. The subsistence fraction is defined as "food, shelter, clothing, and medical care adequate to maintain physical efficiency." However, when there is a need, simple tools and some form of transport are included.

Labor—the amount of time that must be given to secure economic freedom depends on technological development and demand for the products.

Although the function of the Basic Economy is to provide subsistence goods in the most efficient way, the well-being of the producers takes precedence. The schedule of work is designed to avoid long periods of routine and mechanical work with opportunity provided and time allowed for other activities; the co-operators urged to do their service in foreign parts learn new languages, develop new skills and new interests, all with the aim of making the work period a broadening, stimulating, and democratizing experience.

But whether a substitute may be hired to perform the service, what happens to those who refuse to serve, and the like, depends on the policies of each nation.

It is impractical to completely separate the general and basic economies: Medical services, public transportation, power and water supplies, for example, are shared; the Basic Economy service therefore includes work in certain sectors of the general economy.

Providing shelter poses problems. It is easy to stockpile clothes and food and possible to provide services to meet fluctuating demands but impossible to satisfy a large and sudden desire for shelter except by requisitioning space belonging to the general economy. For those that will use them as their only home a Basic Economy shelter is available, and all land planning includes tracts set aside for Basic Economy settlements. It is probable that few (except perhaps the young and the philosophers) in the rich countries would voluntarily seek the austerity of such settlements.

The disbanded military plant, its lands and equipment, are converted to create the initial production centers of the Basic Economy. Thus the ancient prophecy is fulfilled: The swords are beaten into plowshares and the spears into pruning hooks.

STYLE

5. In the industrial age the goal of technology was to reduce the number of man-hours used and increase the amount of goods produced. Automation, computation, and mass production ultimately made it possible not only to free people from all servile and repetitive tasks but from most work, leaving a large number with nothing to do that paid a living wage and was within their competence or interest. In a great city like New York, one of eight was on public welfare in the 1970s, and as the depression deepened a word from an earlier depression, "boondoggle,"[10] again became a synonym for work. Soon, as so many tasks were absurd, all tasks began to seem absurd; there were complaints of sabotage, but it wasn't sabotage, it was frustration.

The postindustrial society has other standards. The

[10] Boondoggle, noun and verb: Being instructed on location, method, time allotted, and given a shovel, you dig an unneeded hole and then fill it up. This is boondoggling or a boondoggle.

worker finds work that suits his idea of a pleasant, sane, or meaningful existence, since his basic economy subsistence guarantee makes it possible to refuse a job that doesn't suit him. This new freedom resulted in shortages of labor during the early years of the divided economy. Fewer comfort and luxury goods were produced and their price rose. A consequence was disastrous declines in sales; in the long run a benefit since no small part of the production was neither useful nor beautiful, resources were conserved, and gradually new consumption habits made it clear that if an enterprise was to prosper it had to accept that "the primary functions of any organization, whether religious, political or industrial, should be to implement the need for man to enjoy a meaningful existence."[11] High wages had to be paid to get unpleasant work done—a recommendation, by the way, of many utopian writers—while all other production began to follow the principle laid down by William Morris: *Design no object which doesn't give pleasure in the making, make no object which doesn't give pleasure in the using.* All design and technology now seeks to meet these requirements.

Broadly speaking, the goods now produced fall into three categories:

First, *the machine style*, symbolized by the ball bearing whose function requires that each be exactly like the next in its series—of equal sphericity, density, polish, etc.—and there be many of them. To make such objects by hand would be, if not impossible, simply not worthwhile. So it is with other machine-style goods, all are shaped for absolute efficiency and minimum use of materials compatible with performance. These goods, completely impersonal, standardized, mass-produced, are the means, never an end. Pure function is sought, and the proof of its finding is in miniaturization, or more poetically, ephemeralization of the object.[12]

[11] Frederick Herzberg.
[12] The development of parts having increasing efficiency as they become smaller and lighter (stone ax to laser beam, spectacles to contact lens).

Machine-style product.

This is the style of pure utility, the style of the Basic Economy, of bridges and dams, of airplanes, computers, saws, hammers, and all other tools.

The theoreticians of this style say, "Fitness to function is the only reason we regard an object as beautiful," and a discussion ensues, say, on forks. *Why mass-produce forks?* True, the shape has been perfected, and like all machine-style objects it uses the minimum amount of the most serviceable material, since an extra gram multiplied by a million is unacceptable to a conserving economy. But that is *not* the question. The question is whether chopsticks, made of a replaceable resource—bamboo—and as simple and elegant a tool as could be devised for the purpose, aren't a purer example of the machine theory.

Second, the symbol for *hand-style goods* could be a sculpture or a painting. The object is personal, the whim of the maker may be a sufficient excuse for its being, and it need not appeal to everyone; it may, in fact, only appeal to the maker. It is made by hand or

Hand-style product (column capital, circa 1220).

with tools which are simple extensions of the hand, and the production is limited by the interest of the maker. An object made in the hand style is what you please and need have no function except to be itself. It may be what was once called a happening. It may be a fine example of the machine style, such as a ball bearing, *provided* the ball bearing is mounted on a pedestal.

The mode of production of the third style is *intermediate*, for it combines many of the tools and techniques of the machine style with much of the personal quality of the hand style. There is no search for maximum efficiency and utility as no large numbers of like objects are to be made, complete accuracy and uniformity are not desiderata. As an example of this mode consider the making of chairs: Chairs for an auditorium seating a thousand should be made by machine, but chairs in one's living room? A man with leisure and a knack for this kind of thing feels it is worthwhile to make a chair

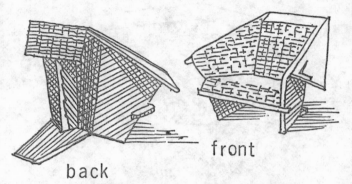

front

back

Intermediate style (Frank Lloyd Wright chair).

as a singular and expressive act, and seeing a chair by
Chippendale, is inspired to create a fine carved chair.
As many people are similarly inspired, there is real
competition with the machine-style product and now
many chairs are hand-made. So with other things:
clothes, housewares, and all personal objects. Here,
then, we have the handicraft movement dreamed of by
Ruskin and Morris, but no longer a dream since it is
based on the freed time given by our advanced technology. "Leisure," Hobbes wrote long ago, "is the
mother of philosophy." We add—and all the arts.

The style tends to be neo-functionalist; form follows
function and the function satisfies ethical criteria.
Major characteristics in this style, as in that of the machine, are clarity of function and easy repairability,
since it is considered undesirable for anyone to use a
device he doesn't understand and inconceivable to
throw it out because a part is broken. In a previous
generation "know-how" was a key word. It is today
preceded by "know-why."

These styles are not mutually exclusive; to the contrary, it is just in their interaction that the form-making
potential is best expressed.

Three good forecasts of current attitudes toward
minimum decency in design were made, one in the
seventeenth century, the second in the early part of the
nineteenth century, and the third in the late 1960s:

Francis Bacon: Houses are built to live in, and not
to look on . . . leave the goodly fabric of houses
for beauty only to the enchanted palaces of poets
who build them with small cost. A building should
only be located among good neighbors and convenient market places, where the air is wholesome,
and the water supply adequate. There should be a
woodland for shade and productive soil for gar-
dening as God Almighty first planted a garden
and indeed it is the purest of human pleasures.
The size, shape and arrangement of the house is
established by convenience, comfort and good
ventilation. Nothing should be done which im-
mensely increases the mass of work, and adds little or nothing to its worth.

Charles Fourier: In every mechanism, whether
material or political, true economy consists in simplifying the play of cogs and wheels and reducing
the number of machines, in diminishing rather
than increasing the expense and the middle men.
This seems a paltry truth, since it is so obvious.

E. F. Schumacher: If the purpose of clothing is a
certain amount of temperature comfort and an attractive appearance, the task is to obtain the purpose with the smallest possible effort, that is with
the smallest annual destruction of cloth and with
the help of designs that involve the smallest input
of toil. The less toil there is the more time and
strength is left for artistic creativity. It would be
highly uneconomic to go in for complicated tailor-
ing . . . when a much more beautiful effect can
be reached by the skillful draping of uncut mate-

rial. It would be the height of folly to make material so it would wear out quickly and the height of
barbarity to make anything shabby, ugly or mean!

Unexpectedly, at least from the standpoint of the
late twentieth century, the spirit of the architecture
seems closer to Chartres than to the Crystal Palace, the
spirit in town planning closer to Sienna than Brasília.

CENTRALIZATION, DECENTRALIZATION

6. As a principle in twenty-first-century organization,
decentralization is the preferred way, as its opposite
tends to go out of scale, is always politically risky,
often technologically unnecessary, and generally economically inefficient. However, in locating and designing routes, whether for trains or planes, water or electrical power, in controlling pollution or preventing
epidemics, allocating or replenishing natural resources
and the like, centralization of authority and comprehensive planning are essential.

To this day it is impossible to discuss large schemes
without remembering the Tennessee Valley Authority,
for it was the exemplar of a great planned regional development, successful as few have been. Here was an
improvement that started with a single natural resource: a flow of water with a head of some five thousand feet, passing through half a dozen states. When
harnessed it provided an area four-fifths the size of
England with hydroelectric power, flood control, a nav-
igation system, soil and forest conservation from which
followed rural electrification, large-scale manufactures,
the development of model farms, educational and
health services.

To develop such a scheme required centralized planning and a central authority. The head of the TVA,
David Lilienthal, in 1944, aware of the dangers in such
an organization, pointed out: "the distinction between

authority and administration is a vital one . . . the problem is to divorce the two." This was done: Administration was decentralized, decisions were based on consent and participation, each at its appropriate level; from the farm family to the neighborhood, through the school district, village, county, state, and region up to the halls of Congress.

The TVA is a heartening example, for it demonstrated that a plan, even when huge in size and scope, need not be a manifest danger. Yet we are right in being suspicious. Other remembrances of the last century are still with us; the grandiose and murderous schemes of Mussolini, Hitler, and Stalin will not be forgotten. *Quis custodiet ipsos custodes?* is still the warning question. Big plans *are* dangerous but when they are needed there are no substitutes, only safeguards. The safeguards are forthright—human welfare is placed before technical efficiency, what benefits the majority has priority; means and ends are inseparable. In the twenty-first century centralized control and comprehensive planning are limited to regional and global networks, the management of the Basic Economy and the rule of the Double E. Here it ends.

The producers of luxury goods and even those of convenience need no regulation beyond that of the Double E and the market place, since their errors in planning may be damned nuisances but never fatal to people whose subsistence has been guaranteed by the work of their hands. To centralize or decentralize, to automate or use hand tools, are matters which can be left to expedience or the good sense, prejudice, or whim of the producers, since the goods produced belong to the economics of affability, not need. Nevertheless, the several styles of production have helped to focus on the vexing question of what should be centralized, dispersed, or decentralized. Surely there would be great difficulty in attempting to centrally plan or produce hand- or intermediate-style goods, and since the production is limited and the potential variety unlimited, no conceivable advantage in it. Machine-style goods, on the other hand, being designed for simple utility, mass-produced, and having a high degree of efficiency as the major criterion, may require concentrating authority, large-scale planning, tight scheduling.

REFORM OF WORK

7. By the middle of the twentieth century the scientific and technical management teams in the industrially advanced countries had developed systems capable of producing all needed goods and services, but efficiency and smooth operation were reduced as long as people manned the machines. People, especially people suitable for jobs needing neither brain nor brawn, were undependable, careless, and expensive, so where it could industry speeded the use of automated processes. Unemployment grew as did the taxes needed to support or restrain the "technologically" unemployed. In 1970 a New York City poster asking "What will you do when a computer takes your job?" expressed the trouble of the times. Ultimately two facts became clear: Fully automated processes were theoretically possible but not as practical as people plus machines, since automated machines could make goods but not buy them, a bad thing for the economy; and they deprived people of a major psychological need—useful work, a bad thing for the society. It also seemed a fact that designing work processes suitable to human beings, as some Swedish factories had done, was in the end more efficient than the by-products of the old-time assembly line—absenteeism, malingering, and sabotage. The *coup de grâce* given the old way of organizing work happened after the Basic Economy was introduced—with a guaranteed subsistence too few took the kinds of jobs offered.

During the last decades of the twentieth century three general principles emerged as basic to postindustrial production:

First, a program of work designed on psychological and social as well as technological considerations. The program provides for diversified employment designed to aid in the development of sane and healthy people, as well as to produce goods.

Second, consultation with all experienced workers in the design of the products, the machines that make them, and the plants in which they are housed.

And third, participation by all workers in management. (The most important question is still unresolved: *Who shall decide on what is to be made?* Workers, management, the market, or some social, ethical, or political principle?)

A major change in production techniques is seen in the increase in small-sized shops making intermediate-style goods as well as parts for machine-style goods. Considering how long ago petroleum and electricity eliminated the need for concentrating machines around the steam-powered single-driving shaft, it is surprising that the economies of small-scale decentralized procedures took so long to assume their place as major productive means. This dispersal, plus the reforms in the work process based on worker participation and more flexible scheduling, has again made it possible to relate the means of livelihood to the way of life. Home and workshop, often combined in the same building or neighborhood, are now a lively force in educating the young, forming communal ties, fostering creative work, and developing pride of place.

ECONOMY OF SERVICES

8. In the early part of the 1970s a person in the technologically advanced West consumed fifteen times more energy and polluted his environment twenty-five times more heavily than his counterpart in the third world. A result in no small part of the fabrication and use of

harebrained elaborations which had become the major product of the perverse technology, as its exchange and consumption had become the major activity of society in the last stages of the machine age. The rule of the Double E and the workings of the Basic Economy ended these extravagances.

A whole branch of twenty-first-century technology is devoted to rediscovering or inventing simple ways to

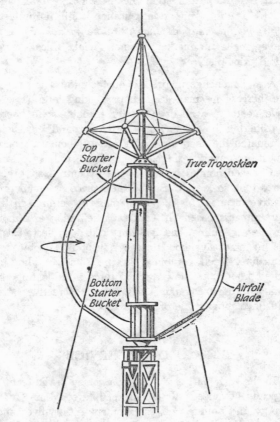

Vertical axis wind turbine (circa 1970).

use natural forces in a nonpolluting way—capturing solar heat or wind force, using the rise and fall of tides, the evaporation of water, the harnessing of volcanoes, as well as the more mundane conversion of waste materials. Many of the devices, discarded by the Industrial Revolution, are back in common use (for instance, the windmill and water wheel) and many methods considered uneconomic when it was believed resources were inexhaustible are now of major importance in the economy. Two related and homely examples show the bent and method of this technology.

In most countries agricultural waste accounts for over half the solid waste. It is readily convertible into electrical power and fertilizer by controlled decomposition, and should be used not only because of its latent power but to prevent it from becoming a pollutant.

Where should conversion plants be located? Should they be small or large?

First of all, it is not efficient to use these wastes in large-size plants as local supply will be inadequate; disposal of large amounts of waste liquids and sludge poses resource problems if not transported to agricultural land; generation of electricity results in waste heat for which no convenient local use can be found.

Therefore, local plants for local use are recommended. The plants should be of minimum practical

"Why plant dead posts in the ground and wait for them to rot? Why not plant live trees instead and let them bear fruits and nuts?" (Philadelphia Agricultural Society, 1819).

size and be located at intervals near farm sites, mini-
mizing transport and transmission costs. In such an arrangement, sludge and liquids, being excellent fertilizers, are immediately available to the farms; waste
heat from the plant is used for heating of farm buildings and hothouses, warming chicken houses and
artificial fish ponds for year-long production; windmills,
water wheels, and solar collectors can be used as small-
scale supplementary power sources; as twenty-first-century planning intimately relates town and country,
town garbage and other wastes can be conveniently
converted in these same plants; the electricity generated is used locally.

A second example is in the use of water, which, if
we can trust Sir Arthur Evans, has been used for
flushing away wastes since the time of King Minos at
Knossos. A striking example of late twentieth-century
inefficiency was the continuation of this method. In the

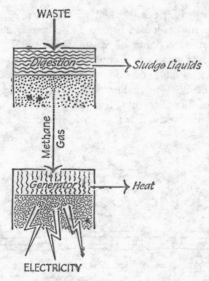

Converting waste to use.

United States the daily water consumption per person averaged 140 gallons, *one gallon* of which was used for cooking and drinking. In New York City the purest of water was brought from the mountains hundreds of miles away and flushed away after being purposely polluted at the average rate of perhaps a gill of urine or a half pound of excrement to eight gallons of water. This vast amount of newly poisoned liquid then had to be carried through miles of sewer pipe to plants designed to make it harmless, or sometimes just dumped raw into rivers and bays.

Oriental people have used what is euphemistically called night soil as fertilizer for centuries, and over the years (one remembers Buckminster Fuller's Dymaxion house of the 1930s) a variety of toilets have been invented which treat the wastes, sterilizing them but keeping the useful phosphates and nitrates for fertilizer. The toilets designed by the new technology are similar.

The aim of any mechanical system is to achieve 100 per cent utilization; anything less creates a twofold loss: Resources are wasted and what is wasted becomes a pollutant, pollution being often nothing other than a result of bad technique.

LIVING ARRANGEMENTS

9. Compartmentalization, specialization, and mechanical scheduling were characteristic of the twentieth-century living: Work was quarantined from other affairs, domestic life had its compartment, as did play; the young were kept separate from the old, family from family, sex from sex, means from ends. Theory and practice rarely mixed. Though there was much talk of democracy, segregation of people by color and/or income was common. Maps by planners looked like kindergarten coloring exercises: *commerce* in one color here, *manufacture* there in another. In the residential districts were zones for separate houses on one-acre

plots, while in others there might be attached dwellings twelve to the acre, or apartments housing two hundred or even four hundred families on a similar acre.

Architects, early in the last century, had reinvented the "open plan" to overcome the excessive compartmenting of space in homes of the previous era. It did little to change living habits of people who had, or aspired to, a separate bath and toilet for each family member, second homes, country cars and city cars. Another characteristic of this fragmented period was the extraordinary shifting about of people: the poor trekking from city slum to suburban factory, the better off from suburbs to downtown office, the quick business trips of a thousand miles in a day, the children bused to school from here to there, a weekend dash to the "country" and return. Everybody jerking along as if in the chase sequence of those early movies, all seemingly bewitched in a disjointed time.

It seems paradoxical that with all the obvious brittleness, fragmentation, and specialization a philosopher of the period could find that "the aspiration of our time for wholeness, empathy and depth of awareness is a natural adjunct of electric technology. . . . The mark of our time is a revulsion against imposed patterns."[13] If this was what people aspired to and *that* was how they lived, psychiatry, not sociology, was needed to examine conduct that appeared to be demented, and indeed, it was a period when psychiatrists did very well.

* * *

Despite appearances, change was in the air. Led by the young without an ideology, without organization, a shift toward other living arrangements became apparent during the early 1960s. Haircuts became unisexual, as did clothes. Dungarees worn by the youth of both sexes to deny sex and class distinction soon became a uniform, serviceable and cheap, worn everywhere, the

[13] Marshall McLuhan.

more faded and patched the better. The young people slept on floors although there were beds, and if they hung up their clothes at all, hung them on nails although there were closets. The brassiere went the way of the corset, the razor went out and the beard came in. For the young, it was a rough and ratty period, the action sometimes excessive but generally toward simpler and more direct living arrangements, which as time passed became the accepted style for all ages. Symbolic were the public toilets: In the South the signs marked "colored" and "white" were torn down, yet (although bodily functions were no longer considered shameful and nakedness immoral) it was not until the 1980s that signs reading "men" and "women" were painted out.

Camaraderie between the sexes and the discarding of prudery achieved an openness especially marked in the upbringing of children. It took until the last decade of the century for education to become voluntary, although compulsory laws for attendance at church had not been a requirement in most civilized countries for at least a hundred years. (Teaching morality, the courts ruled, is at least as important as arithmetic, so if the state didn't require the one why should it quibble about the other?) Once attendance was not compulsory, many schools became "popular academies in which there is neither pupil nor master, where the people come freely to get free instruction if they need it, and in which they, rich in their own expertise, will teach many things to the professors who in their turn shall bring them the knowledge they lack."[14]

By 2000 such "popular academies" had become an integral part of all community activity; libraries, restaurants, shops, were all considered environments for learning, as were the ateliers and work places within the town, the factories and farms on the outskirts or in the countryside. It was not as chaotic as it sounds, for

[14] M. Bakunin, *God and State.*

then, as now, electronic linkages and the memory banks of computers provided the basis for an orderly curriculum.

Nowadays, schools for more advanced study are always convenient to or part of the Basic Economy production centers, though Harvard, of course, remains on the Charles, Cambridge on the Cam, and the Sorbonne in Paris.

Domestic arrangements: The typical institution around which daily activity was organized, the twentieth-century nuclear family, is pretty much a thing of the past, since it was wasteful of resources, vulnerable in time of trouble, and the least friendly form of domestic life conceivable. Households now vary in size and organization. The loner and single-generation blood kin family are found, but the majority of people have opted for family groupings composed of those related by affinity and interest more often than by blood.

Architects used to be bemused by the plans of châteaux and manor houses which seemed to be lacking in all privacy, and in fact, privacy in the twentieth-century sense hardly existed; the rooms were used as passages and were almost interchangeable, the same space often used for eating, sleeping, work, and entertainment.

The twenty-first-century house plan is in many ways closer to these old houses than those of the last century. A more communal style of living is reflected in the large public rooms and general spaciousness, since living and working accommodations are often needed for households numbering twenty or more people. Some are even larger, such as those organized by the followers of Charles Fourier, who have formed households where a hundred or more families live and work together, sure that "upon seeing the advantages, the conveniences and the enormous profits of this union, all will promptly imitate it." This housing designed to accommodate the changing social groupings is gradually replacing these twentieth-century storage units called apartment houses, as well as the detached cottages of suburbia.

The emerging street pattern is also reminiscent of an older time: The town plan is compact as if contained within walls (beyond is the countryside). The streets are narrow by the old motorcar standard, and although there are no uniform replacements and few legal restrictions, the individual houses, as in the streetscapes of medieval towns, relate to each other in a strikingly easy way. This, of course, is not chance but the result of an evolving architectural aesthetic based on a close analysis of function, a straightforward use of appropriate materials, and a respect for the Geddesian triad of "Place, Work, and Folk."

TRANSPORTATION

> I like a man who is proud of the
> place where he lives. I like a place
> proud of the people who live there.
> —Abraham Lincoln

10. Among the generations of man there were centuries of pyramid building, centuries of cathedral building, and a century of automobile building. It is understandable that people would spend their treasure to celebrate kings or gods, but for a people to spend their treasure in celebrating mobility is hardly likely. In retrospect it seems unbelievable that both the young and the mature of the twentieth century were seized by this madness which killed more people, wasted more resources, was more polluting, and led to greater migrations of people than the combined wars of that bellicose century. During the height of the automania, a zoologist observed that in animal herds excessive mobility was a sure sign of distress and asked whether this might not be true of his fellow human beings. Perhaps it was distress, perhaps . . . but what historian can list

Pedespeed (1870).

all the causes that led twentieth-century man to race
from highway to byway, tunnel to bridge? Suffice to
say that he seemed to be constantly going from where
he didn't want to be to where he didn't want to stay.

The folly of automobility is now over. As the stric-
tures of Double E priced unnecessary transportation
out of daily life, people discovered the deplorable conditions in which they lived and began to improve them.
Now the place where one is tends to be the place
where one wants to be; as a consequence almost three
quarters of the rubber-tired vehicles have disappeared.
The saving in petroleum alone can be gauged by remembering that in 1973 the United States dedicated
30 per cent of its total energy consumption to what
was called "internal combustion mobility." More important was the effect on health. Eliminating the pollution caused by these vehicles, and the generally slower
pace (once people got accustomed to it), are credited
with a marked reduction in the incidence of respiratory
and stress diseases. As one would expect, there are few
traffic accidents.

The twenty-first century has the problem of dismantling over half of the most elaborate, extensive, and costly structures ever built by man, the infrastructure on which the automobile depended: garages and service stations, roads and highways, tunnels, bridges, and viaducts. Those routes that remain in use have had their magnificent engineering finally tested—they are reserved for high-speed traffic only, buses and trucks often move at a hundred or more miles an hour on the straightaways. The material from the demolished structures is, of course, not junked, for just as in Renaissance Rome palaces were built of stones and lead taken from the Colosseum, steel and concrete from tunnel and viaduct are being recycled for use in building new towns. A rather curious feature in the modern landscape is a by-product of these road demolitions. Stretching for hundreds of miles are the smoothly contoured and leveled rights of way of discarded highway systems converted into extensive lineal farms for large-scale mechanized agriculture. Many a six-lane highway is now a thin concrete ribbon on which farm machines chug.

Although there is a great deal less movement of people and goods than was common during the latter part of the twentieth century, traffic is substantial. Bus, truck, rail, and waterway systems have been reorganized and operate as integrated and flexible networks. Rubber-tired vehicles, whether for passenger or freight, have, like other tools, obeyed the functionalist dicta of the machine style; superfluities have been stripped away, durability and repairability built into the simplified designs. The motors based on the efficient pollution-free models of the 1980s use a variety of fuels from mixtures of hydrogen and oxygen to the now scarce petroleum derivatives.

The main means of transportation in nineteenth-century America, the inland waterways, have had a renaissance. These rivers and canals, 25,000 miles long, passing through forty-one states, were by 1970 carrying less than 16 per cent of the freight despite the fact that hauling by boat and barge used less than a third the energy per ton of cargo than required by trains, and a hundred times less than planes. Nowadays the economies of water transport are sought, as are the pleasures of travel by boat.

A major shift has occurred in overland air transport. Most standard fixed-wing planes of the twentieth century have been rejected in spite of their superb design, since the noise pollution along the rising and descending flight paths was unacceptable, as was the inordinate amount of land required for airport runways. The obvious solution was to improve the helicopter and the vertical take-off and landing (VTOL) planes. The landing pads now in use, being small in size and designed to confine take-off noise, are located close to the areas they serve, while the huge and distant airports are being phased out, except those in desert areas or along the coast servicing the fixed-wing planes still used for overseas and polar flights.

For short daily trips, skates, bicycles, and a variety of tricycles are common, along with the small slow-speed buses which crisscross the towns, and though railroad trackage is much used for long-haul transportation, high-speed buses and trucks run between towns and serve less densely settled areas.

There are many who, thinking back or reading about the convenience of the private automobile, dream of

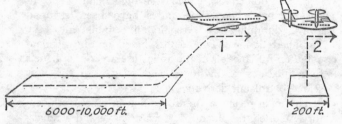

(1) Conventional plane. (2) Vertical take-off and landing plane (VTOL).

the good old days and would, if they could, get themselves a car, and sometimes do. Private cars, however, are damned expensive to buy and to run, the tax is high, the speed limit is low, and there is adverse propaganda (*cars are wasteful, they pollute, the Surgeon General's office warns they are dangerous to health . . .*).

There are still automaniacs but incidence of the disease is now minor except among racing fans.

A TOWN AND ITS ENVIRONS

11. The intention of twentieth-century town planning was to provide more convenient living arrangements for people, but instead it was warped out of all sense to accommodate the bulkiest item in every household—the family car (or even two), which accompanied every occasion: home to work, home to shop, home to school, home to home, and back again. The omnipresent element in every streetscape was the car. The banging of car doors, the starting or shutting off of car motors, was the prelude and postlude to all outdoor activity.

Every part of the physical plan reflected this preoccupation—the shopping strip, the cloverleaf, and many-laned highway had replaced the market square, crossroads, and lanes of old towns. A new space-time scale had developed. Dimensions on the order of seventy miles per hour became a requirement achieved by tunneling under rivers, blowing up hills or bulldozing them into easy grades; huge swaths of land were asphalt-armored. As speed increased, distance became of small consequence, new developments leapfrogged over old (*old* often meaning twenty years) creating the ecologically disastrous and aesthetically distressing landscapes of the period. This land use was called "sprawl," and the suitably descriptive word coined to describe the resulting combination of suburb and slum was "slurb."

The automobile alone did not make planning for people impossible. It was but one example of the missing limiting dimension—the human scale—historically the measure of all things made by us, for us. This primordial yardstick was replaced by the measuring rod of a technology whose limits, being well beyond average understanding, led to many a crackpot twentieth-century invention, some monstrous and some just funny. In physical planning the loss of a comprehensible and usable scale led the imaginative to create those weird concoctions known as Future City, while the conservative sought to preserve some semblance of a previous size and order by legalisms such as rules preserving old towns and buildings, deed and zoning restrictions designed to prevent the new from seeming so new. These laws seemed and were, in fact, arbitrary and regressive. Why, it was asked, should air-conditioned buildings not cover their entire plots, why limit building heights when elevators could reach cloud nine, why windows when the lights were on anyway, why not cities of 10 or even 100 million spread from coast to coast, why not pave agricultural land, since food could be grown hydroponically on the moon or created synthetically in the most unlikely ways . . . ? Fortunately we now need not debate such matters since they are no longer relevant.

Establishing the right size, the reasonable land use, density, or location is now not based on tradition, whim, or speculation but on the economic and ecologic considerations embodied in the Double E and the common-sense attitudes of people who are users rather than consumers, settlers, not nomads. Slowly the cacophony of the town scene has been orchestrated; the disparate elements—form and structure, color and texture, variety and repetition, solid and void—have been resolved by the magic of people building in harmony with their environment and according to their own measure.

LAND USE

12. Twentieth-century economics held that insofar as each unit of land is different from another and the differences have economic significance, unequal demand is created so land costs will differ. Such considerations led to intense use of land having the highest cost often regardless of the consequences. The restraints imposed by the Double E now prevent such abuses. As an instance, undesirably high densities are made unpractical, since in present practice the conservation laws restrict the use of elevators and moving stairways to buildings of special purpose, thus the height of buildings is restricted to the stair-climbing ability of the inhabitants. It is not zoning laws that restrict a building's location of ground coverage but the requirement that it be made comfortable by maximum dependence on the ancient means—sun and shade, exposure to breeze, protection against the gale.

Like the elevator, mechanical ventilation and air conditioning are reserved for special situations—operating rooms, laboratories, concert halls, tunnels, and submarines. A building technology dependent on gadgetry belongs to the past since it was wasteful, catered to the architects' laziness, and threatened to fill the world with identically shaped boxes or, worse, buildings shaped by ego.

The Double E, of course, suggested better uses for the most precious resource of all—our time. The debilitating twentieth-century commute from home to work and back again is over, except for the few who work in the automated nuisance industries or mines located away from the towns. With most travel by foot, bike, or short-haul bus, common sense dictates a close relationship between work and living places, and since all is designed for the convenience of people moving under their own steam, recreation space and the countryside are near. The planner, instead of basing his

layouts on the circulation of bulky vehicles and their
storage, bases himself on the movement of people passing through pleasant places. That romantic Viennese
Camille Sitte is in style, and John Ruskin is quoted:
"The first school of beauty must be the streets of your
city. . . ."

As in all good plans, convenience and delight merge.
Nature's variety and man's skill are seen at the eye
level and pace of the pedestrian, not through the wind-
shield at sixty miles an hour as in automania days. A
sudden rise, a river's edge, the prevailing breeze, the
arc of the sun, all enter into the calculations of the
urban designer establishing street directions, landmarks, and boundaries, the juxtaposition of built and
open spaces, the siting of buildings. . . .

A Renaissance street. Stage set by Sebastiano Serlio (sixteenth century).

METAMORPHOSIS OF METROPOLIS

13. Huge cities had become progressively less habitable and lost the larger part of their population. Unsafe to live in, uneconomic to manage, they had become, through the inept decisions of central governments, the last resort of the poorest and least urbanized people.

Each day buildings were abandoned, cannibalized, and burned out, ultimately leaving surreal cityscapes—broken walls and bottles, starving cats, and the wild ailanthus growing from the cracked pavements. It became obvious that even if there were money for rebuilding (which there wasn't), rebuilding would be a fruitless enterprise.

In New York a planning official,[15] looking at the desolation in his once great city, had a sudden flash of inspiration which showed its shore lines, meadows, and hills returned to the beauty they once had had. "Let's," he said, "turn the South Bronx green, replace every vacant lot and every abandoned building with a tree farm or an agricultural farm. . . . In the farm areas, crops could be grown for local consumption or shipped for profit to Hunts Point Market. Employment for the areas would be developed while improving the quality of the community itself. Area welfare residents might participate while agricultural cooperatives could provide employment for local youngsters after school."

Slowly and then one after the other, as the idea took hold, the old towns re-emerged: Claremont, Melrose, Morrisania in the Bronx, Williamsburg, Greenpoint, all the way out to Flatbush in Brooklyn. In Manhattan the original lanes and roads of the Indians and the patroons began to show themselves under the broken asphalt; the old grid laid out in 1807 and completed in the early twentieth century fades into the original topology.

As the physical pattern changed, so did the pattern of government. The municipal agencies, overstaffed,

[15] Martin Gallent, Vice-chairman, New York City Planning Commission, 1974.

overpaid, and underproductive, which had monopo-
lized all city services and brought the city to bank-
ruptcy were disbanded, and in their place were developed neighborhood-government units which had the
authority to purchase services from other units, from
private concerns, or from their own personnel.[16] The
world-famous fantasy known as Manhattan Skyline no
longer symbolizes a citadel of business but a museum
city, a tourist attraction like Venice or Paris Centre.

South of Fifty-ninth Street the architectural historians have, like good foresters, selected the best in the
forest of skyscrapers for preservation. The others have
been dismantled, since for any practical purpose the
energy costs entailed in using them were excessive. As
examples: The Chrysler and Empire State buildings are
preserved as a kind of joking commentary on an era,
and Cass Gilbert's Woolworth tower has been completely restored as has McKim's Municipal Building.
There is still a continuing debate among the members
of the Landmarks Commission on the fate of the twin
towers of the World Trade Center. Should they be
razed? Those opposed say they are the ultimate architectural monument to the waste and arrogance of
machine age America, so obviously of historical importance. The aestheticians claim the towers are over-
bearing, their location on the island's edge gives the
skyline a lopsided look, they dwarf the Statue of
Liberty. Tear them down, they say, as do some conser-
vationists who believe the salvaged aluminum and steel
can be put to better use.

NEW TOWN THEORY

14. The Industrial Revolution created and developed
the metropolis, its aftermath destroyed it. During this
latter period, then called the "crisis of our cities," innu-
merable theories were propounded and plans drawn

[16] Very like the recommendation of Prof. E. S. Savas, once
First Deputy City Administrator of New York.

ranging from the plodding efforts of bureaucratic Grad-
grinds to the fantasies of genius, all showing ways of
altering the old to fit the changing conditions or prov-
ing the sole solution is to start afresh with startling
ideas, bright from the forge of Hephaistos.

Looking back it is a surprise to find that it was not a
Le Corbusier, a Kenzo Tange, nor even a Frank Lloyd
Wright who forecast the principles of postindustrial
town planning, but a Victorian, John Ruskin writing in
Sesame and Lilies in the lush prose for which he and
his period were known:

> Through sanitary and remedial action in the
> houses that we have; and then the building of
> more, strongly, beautifully, and in groups of lim-
> ited extent, kept in proportion to their streams and
> walled around, so that there be no festering and
> wretched suburb anywhere, but clean and busy
> streets within and open country without, with a
> belt of beautiful garden and orchard around the
> walls, so that from any part of the city perfectly
> fresh air and grass and sight of far horizon might
> be reachable in a few minutes walk. This is the
> final aim.

Was the aim a pre-Raphaelite vision of a medieval
town, Ebenezer Howard's Garden City, or the Goodman brothers' New Commune moved into a new century? Surely none of these, yet in every period there
are works that forecast what is to come. But when the
future becomes the present we find there has been
some subtle change; we now see what was in the light
of what is. It has changed and we too have changed.

PLANNING FOR DAILY NEEDS

15. The layout of a town may be a slow process, the result of simple accretion—there is a path, a hut is built
on it and then another, a new path meanders from the

old one and then another. . . . To plan a town *de novo* is another matter. The slow development, the unrecorded decisions, the multiplicity of plans so small as to seem no plans at all, the trial and error, are replaced by the planners—stage designers whose settings are in the real world designed for actors who are not acting but living out their only lives. Set and action are based on scenarios, but whether or not they are followed depends on unforeseeable circumstances and a tendency toward improvisation by the participants. There are exceptions, such as penal colonies and military installations; these may be organized with some certainty that the unfortunate inhabitants will follow the script. Luckily, not many of us are cast in such roles, or live in such places.

I have explained why rational beings plan, why they must isolate from the endless possibilities, bypaths, and meanders a course to follow. We set boundaries, we make commitments, we limit our freedom. Our simplest acts (to take a step, for instance) imply motive, implementation, and consequences; in short, some sort of plan, and the larger and more comprehensive the plan, the more it restricts us, dictates our ways of thinking and doing.

Surely the greatest danger to those planned for is the tendency of planners to imagine them as ciphers who will respond (as in the Platonic dialogue) exactly as the planners' argument requires. Planners who do more than manipulate statistics, planners who seek to "turn the course of future development," are often accused of playing God, especially by those so brainwashed by convention as to believe any other way of life, any change from what is, to be tyrannical, anarchical, or just nonsensical.

Inventors of ideal schemes are especially prone to this kind of criticism, and not without reason. Yet in a time when the emerging future is quite unlike the passing present, when repetition of our present built environment is unthinkable, it would seem prudent to have *something* in mind, some logic, some hypothesis that will inspire confidence in the direction that planning should take.

Here I have discounted the prophecies of humankind destroyed or robotized and, to the contrary, assumed better choices will be made; by the year 2020 the environment will be protected by something like the Double E, freedom from want guaranteed by something like the Basic Economy. For such a time I sketch an architectural setting designed to foster a way of life freed from the remnants of late Victorian prudery and twentieth-century industrialism. To this end open and built spaces are provided to accommodate diverse activities, including:

Child Care: Excepting for the mother's nursing of the infant, it is quite customary for both parents, assisted by siblings, friends, older people, and (occasionally) professionals to share the responsibility.

Education: (a) Children and adolescents learn in the mini-schools and from the life around them. Households, workshops, and farms are all considered learning environments. (b) Youths as early as age sixteen may start their Basic Economy service, often considered a crucial experience, a rite of passage. (c) Specialized education, whether artistic, technical, scientific, or academic: The work is carried on where and as the subject requires—in universities, hospitals, factories, workshops, farms, in theaters, night clubs, on the streets, at sea, in the wilderness. . . .

Production of Goods: (a) Hand- and intermediate-style goods are produced in home workshops. (b) Mass-produced goods are made in factories located within the town or on its outskirts. (c) Mines, quarries, timberlands, fishing grounds, dictate the location of extraction activities.

Production of Food: (a) The kitchen gardens, orchards, and related facilities are located at the towns' borders. (b) The larger farms and grazing lands are in the green belts surrounding the towns.

Basic Economy Centers: Located where most convenient for efficient production, these centers combine
production activities as well as schools, living quarters,
and other amenities.

Domestic Life: Houses in the variety and sizes required for the many different kinds of households, all
located within the town except those forming part of
the large farms and remote industries.

To this list add the hospitals and public service
buildings, the spaces needed by people selling and repairing things or needed by professionals—lawyers and
accountants, architects and painters, piano players and
dancers. Also included are the museums and television
studios, printing plants, concert halls, swimming pools,
tennis courts, chess clubs. . . . And let us not forget
space for the philosophers, dropouts, and dreamers, living in their Basic Economy shelters and wearing their
Basic Economy clothes.

I assume all these things and happenings in an ambiance that fosters improvisation and invention, easygo-
ing, without nine-to-five schedules (except for those
that want them!).

A POPULATED AREA

16. In this paradigm our first diagram called "The
Zones" shows the development of a town and its environs. It consists of a compactly built up center, a ring
of gardens, another of larger farms, and, beyond, open
country.

The built-up part of the town, four squares miles in
area, houses the activities of 128,000 people at an average density of 50 to the acre. So disposed as to be less
than a mile away from anyone in the town are the
sport fields and courts, swimming places and picnic
grounds. An acre of garden space is allotted to every
10 inhabitants. These allotments are a mile in width
surrounding the town and bordered by a ring road.

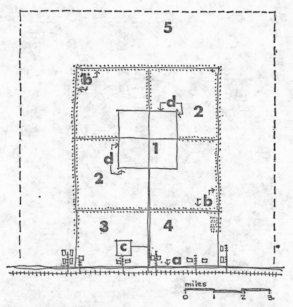

The zones: (1) town, (2) kitchen gardens, (3) large-sized farms, (4) Basic Economy food production center, (5) grazing, open country, (a) highway and railroad, (b) along ring road: farms, power plants, food processing, Basic Economy camps, (c) airport, (d) outdoor sports areas at corners of town.

Along the road are centers (to be described shortly) that service farms and gardens; factories; the borders of large farms; and the Basic Economy settlements.

Some five miles from the town center is the main highway and railroad, reached by the ring road and a road leading directly into town. Between town and highway are large, mechanized farms and a Basic Economy food production center. Dispersed along the main transportation routes are the large-sized factories, refineries, and the like, as well as the VTOLport. Around this entire complex of uses is the green belt, as nearly untouched nature as man can abide.

Although one third of the planet's land area is habitable, 70 per cent of the world population crowds into areas comprising only 7 per cent of this habitable area. Even this minimal land use allows 43 acres per person.

The area covered by this plan is 100 square miles. The average population density is 1,300 people to the square mile, substantially less than the late twentieth-century urban average. Nevertheless, this use of land is not extravagant, as a small calculation shows.

In 1970 the urban areas of the United States had an average density of 2,500 people to the square mile. The average population density of the entire country was 56 to the square mile.

In contrast, assume only 10 per cent of our land was developed in a fashion similar to the "populated area" just described with 90 per cent of the population living in such areas. What could our population number?

The answer is—over half a billion.

TOWN

17. Diagramatically the town is divided into four districts so disposed as to bring the goal of most daily trips within easy walking distance or short bike or bus rides. It is but a five-minute walk to the end of the built-up area from any district center while the ring road is only two miles away. Except for nuisance factories and the like, segregation of function is avoided: work places and living places are often the same, eliminating commutation and making most activity part of the intimate, domestic, community scene.

Each of the districts is also divided into four neighborhoods.

The political structure of the town is simple: The neighborhoods elect representatives to the district councils, and the district councils appoint the town's officers, who in turn select a chairman.

Out of this diagram emerges a plan sketched to suggest an ambiance of informality, unpretentiousness, and friendly scale where one would hope to find, unexpectedly, some little masterpiece of civic art.

There are a variety of squares and plazas. Here in the neighborhoods are found small shops and perhaps some special activity that attracts visitors from other parts; in the districts, seats of local administration, clinics, cafés. There is a market center of conviviality. Here one may barter a chair one has made for a painting, here is a fellow getting his prize for the best cauliflower. Here are bikes for sale and saxophones, and the local restaurant famous for its omelets, or is it the fish brought in live from the neighboring pond? The Town Center is the site of the major shops, the City Hall, perhaps a museum, a television studio and

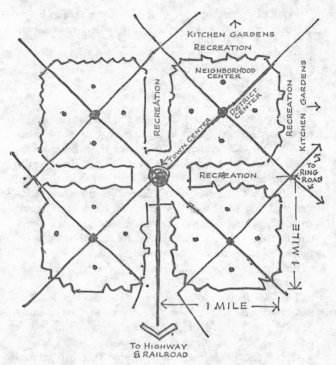

Diagram for a town with 128,000 people per square mile. Density: 50 persons to the acre.

concert hall, a factory producing some object for which the town is famous. . . .

In general the street pattern is based on a regular module, though varied to take advantage of the topographical conditions as well as provide a variety of streetscapes. The houses front on two streets, one for play and pedestrians, the other for the limited vehicular traffic.

There are four major athletic areas, each with its swimming pools, ponds, playfields, and courts, each convenient to the district it serves.

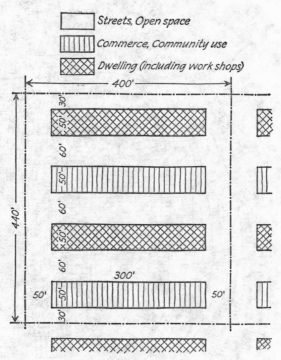

Establishing density in the town. Dwellings: average height 3½ stories.

Leading out from the built area are roads that, as they meander toward the ring road, serve the kitchen gardens. Along some of these roads and paths enterprising gardeners, following Chinese farming practice in the 1970s, have built lineal greenhouses. Others are more direct, connecting city streets to the ring road, since trucking through the town is prohibited. Lining the ring road are small farms and related light industries.

Beyond the ring road are large farms, and the open country.

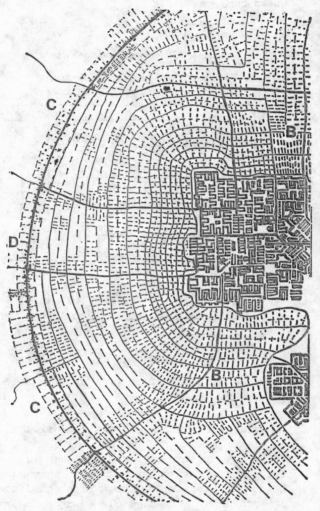

A town plan based on the diagram. The principles are:
"(1) to have most functions within walking or bicycling
distance, and (2) to have nothing zoned in isolation ex-

cept nuisance industries." (A) Recreation areas, (B) kitchen gardens, (C) the ring road, (D) farms.

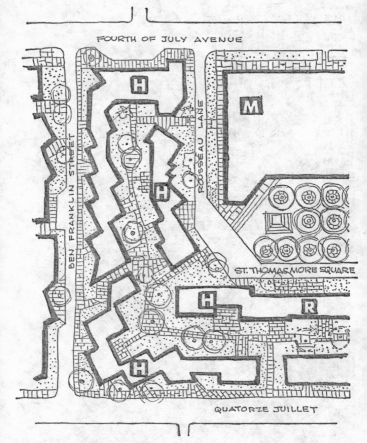

Street pattern: (M) Museum of Discarded Technology, (H) households, (R) restaurant.

A street . . . As in preindustrial towns the blocks are short and the street width tends to vary, though few are as broad as those in twentieth-century cities. However, as in medieval towns the intersections often

Street scene.

widen into plazas which are "not avenues of motor or pedestrian traffic but are places where people remain. Places of work and home are close by, but in the city square is what is still more interesting—the other people."[17]

. . . and the houses on it. A street will usually be lined with three- or four-storied buildings, more often than not containing home and workshop. These houses vary in size but none are as large as those in last century's cities, nor as small as those in the old suburbs. The "grain" of the street (as urban designers used to call it) is closer to Paris before rather than after Haussmann.

[17] *Communitas.*

A variety of households. Main floor: (A) kitchen-commons
(B) workroom.

Not untypical are the house plans illustrated. *The
paired house* on the left is shared by some thirty
adults and children in two households. One produces a
variety of small parts for an electronics firm while the
other designs and makes rather modish women's
clothes. The street floor of the house is divided between the workshop and the farm-style kitchen-living
rooms, a busy and sometimes noisy place whose activities often spill out onto the paved terraces. Above is a

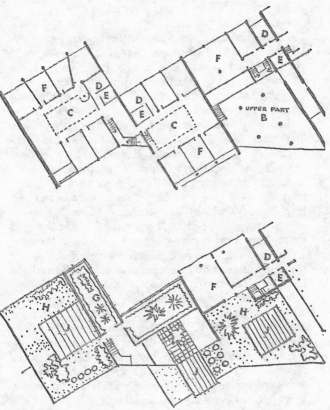

Upper floors: (B) workroom, (C) living room, (D) bath, (E) toilet, (F) private room, (G) greenhouse, (H) terrace, (J) solar collectors.

double-storied quiet living-library space surrounded by the household's private rooms. The toilet and bath are communal (see Chapter XI). The roof is a garden on which is often set greenhouses or sheltered areas for sun bathing.

The house on the right is shared by a sculptor and painter, a graphics artist and printer, each with their apprentices and households.

GREEN BELT

18. Prior to the twentieth century most productive United States crop land was located at the outskirts of our cities, and even as late as 1950 half such land was still to be found in and around the metropolitan areas. By 1975 farm land near cities became a rarity as government programs favoring highway programs and detached, single-family houses had sent the city sprawling into the old suburbs and the suburbs far into the countryside. On a pleasant weekend the result was endless miles of cars, bumper to bumper as people sought a little fresh air, a little quiet, the smell of growing things. Fifty miles out they found the streams they had helped to pollute, by which they picnicked. Returning in the evening, they stopped at "farm stands" along the road to buy the "local produce," grown more often than not a thousand miles away, agribusiness having driven out the small farmers and developers having bulldozed the farms into housing or industrial sites.

In any sane view the twentieth-century despoliation of the landscape was perverse, as was the kind of planning that fostered it. To the conserving society of the twenty-first century such patterns of development appear not merely perverse but almost criminal, since they had no merit except quick money for a few at unacceptable economic and ecologic costs for the many. It was not as if no alternative scheme existed, just the opposite. As far back as the sixteenth century Elizabeth I had banned new building within three miles of London's limits, and since her time the *green belt*, as it got to be called, has been a recurrent theme in town planning.

In the 1960s there were such curiosities as a President's Task Force on Beauty designed to salvage bits and pieces of the countryside and designed to battle what an English professor[18] had described as the "excruciating ugliness associated directly or indirectly with the motor vehicle. . . ." Such efforts were not new. As

[18] Colin Buchanan.

an instance among many, Benton Mackaye[19] in the 1920s had called for a stop to the invasion of the countryside, proposing the "Indigenous America and Confining the Metropolitan America," by creating what he called *intertown*: "This does not mean it would be urban environment, on the contrary, it would be a rural environment. *By no means* would it be a suburban environment."

As a way of containing the explosive growth of twentieth-century cities, the green belt had little success; it was abandoned in Tokyo, and Chandigar—Le Corbusier's planned city—followed the same route. The green belt in the planned city of Brasília, like the outskirts of all large cities in the less developed countries, became the site of shanty towns during the great migrations of the late twentieth century, and whatever open areas surrounded cities like Boston, New York, and Chicago disappeared into suburbs and shopping centers with the countryside a mirage on the distant horizon. Whether the green belt was too remote to be useful as a "lung" for the great city remained a moot question among the city planners until the question lost its point as the great population clots thinned out in the 1990s.

Whether an old place is reconstructed or a new one projected, the green belt is now essential, since every town grows at least some of its food, open space for sport and recreation must be near at hand, and the Double E safeguards the fields and forests. All agree with old Ebenezer Howard—"nothing gained by crowding." All agree with old John Ruskin—"a sight of far horizons within a few minutes walk."

In the Green Belt

The Kitchen Garden. In the last decades of the twentieth century it became increasingly difficult for people to buy fresh, unprocessed food. Back in 1975, for instance, the farmers of New Jersey (then called the Gar-

[19] Designer of the Appalachian Trail.

The kitchen gardens.

den State), long the major suppliers of vegetables to a
vast population (including the 16 million inhabitants of
the New York City area), found it more profitable to
give up this huge market and switch to grain and soybean crops. Garden-fresh produce rose in cost, suggesting to many that either they eat the often tasteless, and
always artificially ripened and preserved products
grown in distant places, or they grow their own. The
experiences of old-time advocates of the simple life
such as the Borsodis and the Nearings took on unexpected significance. Had not Ralph Borsodi proven "a
completely vegetarian family could live entirely out of
a kitchen garden and orchard occupying not more than
one acre of land . . . large enough to supply fresh vegetables during the growing season and for canning and
dehydrating during the winter. . . ."[20] Those that
could started gardens, and soon back yards, empty lots,
and the lawns in front of suburban houses began producing lettuce and tomatoes, and peas and cucumbers
clambered up the sides of tenement walls. By the
1980s the house garden was a customary sight and hothouses in the form of plastic domes were, if not common, not unexpected.

Although the intensively cultivated gardens of the
twenty-first century with their greenhouses and fish
ponds, berry patches and orchards of dwarf fruit trees,
produce a good portion of each town's food, cultivating
them is no backbreaking drudgery since the heavy
work is lightened by the communally owned tractors
and tools needed for field work, the scrubbers and
pressure cookers used in the kitchens.

Despite propaganda and the high cost of meat, not
many people are vegetarians, so few look to grow all
the food needed for sustenance. Land planners, therefore, set aside about half the acreage recommended by
Borsodi almost a century ago; in a temperate climate
with good soil the allocation is about an acre for every
ten persons.

[20] *Flight from the City*, 1933.

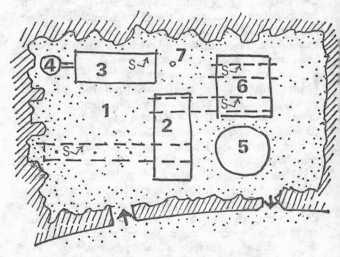

A service station on the ring road: (1) parking area, (2) agricultural implement storage, (3) kitchen for canning, dehydrating, storage, (4) smokehouse, (5) composting tanks, (6) power generator house, (7) windmill, (S) solar collectors.

Along the ring road. This secondary highway is the town's trucking route. Along it are factories which because of land area needed or shipping requirements are better located outside of the built-up sections; moderate-size farms producing a variety of foods, fish, fowl, hogs, and dairy products; and the multipurpose service stations. (These structures important to the local economy combine a number of useful elements: a power plant which converts organic wastes from town, garden, and farm to fertilizer and electricity; a garage and maintenance shop for farm machinery; deep-freeze lockers and a kitchen equipped for dehydrating and smoking; a greenhouse and root cellar. Sometimes a mill is included to grind the local corn or imported wheat. The stations are powered by waste heat from

View of a service station.

the generating plant, by windmills and solar collectors.)
Finally, there are landscaped areas set aside for parks
and as sites for the Basic Economy settlements.

Along the through routes. Convenient to the railroad
and main highway are located the extensive, mechanized farms growing grain and pulse crops, the buildings of heavy industry, a production center for Basic
Economy goods, the VTOL airport. . . .

Countryside. About four miles away is the ring road
of the next town. Between are meadows and woodland,
streams and ponds.

A farm along the ring road—silos, windmill, solar collectors.

ORGANIZATION OF A BASIC ECONOMY
PRODUCTION CENTER

The aim of the centers is to produce the required
quotas of subsistence goods and maintain high quality while expending the minimum of material, energy,
and time. This mechanical efficiency would be intolerable if the physical and psychological welfare of the
co-operators was not protected by the rule of the Double E, and even then it might be unacceptable if the
goals of the Basic Economy were not so simple and
direct—*to provide the means by which all could produce a guaranteed subsistence earned through their
own work.*

The goal is simple but the planning is not, for al-

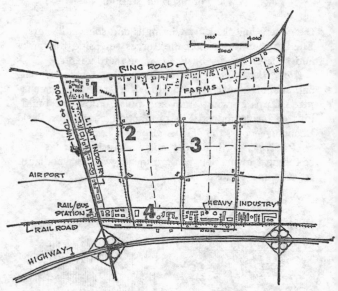

A Basic Economy production center: (1) agrobiology college
and housing, (2) service centers, (3) the farm, (4) processing,
storage, and shipping.

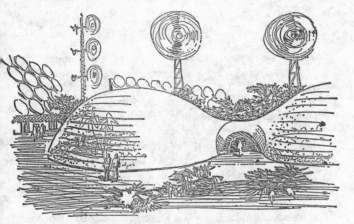

The college greenhouses.

though standardization and uniformity is stressed and
the goods limited to objects of basic utility, many
different kinds of materials and skills enter into the
making. Ore and oil must be extracted, crops grown,
machines fabricated, cloth woven, food processed. . . .
Each production center is designed for its use. Some
are large, some small, some are in cities, some at quarries or mines, sometimes a center located in an isolated
area may be the nucleus of a new town.

In this model the production center takes the form of
a mechanized farm. The area is about three thousand
acres in which are located housing and other amenities
for a work force of six hundred as well as the greenhouses, shops, processing and packaging plants needed
for this type of farm. In addition there are the buildings required for a small college of agrobiology.

The farming methods combine the efficiency of
twentieth-century agronomy with the old (and re-
newed) virtues—composting, resting and replenishing
the soil, converting waste and residue to useful products, avoiding pesticides.

THE REGION

Let us again return to the TVA for a bit of comparative history. Franklin D. Roosevelt, in 1933, advocating the creation of the Tennessee Valley Authority, said, "Many hard lessons have taught us the human waste that results from lack of planning. Here and there a few wise cities have looked ahead and planned. But our nation has 'just grown.' It is time to extend planning to a wider field, in this instance comprehending in one great project many states directly concerned with the basin of one of our greatest rivers. This, in a true sense, is a return to the spirit and vision of the pioneer. If we are successful here we can march on, step by step, in a like development of other great natural territorial units within our borders."

In spite of nationwide hostility, the TVA became a reality, not because it was a masterful way to preserve and direct natural resources for human needs, but because the Great Depression (as it was called) had jolted people out of their complacency, frightened them into accepting new ideas.

It took the world-wide crisis conditions and depressions of the 1970s and '80s to awaken the comfortably established to the need for change; nonetheless, there was widespread opposition to the introduction of the Double E and the Basic Economy. In the United States the measures were called un-American, an interference with the sacred constitutional rights of citizens to mess up things as they saw fit. Besides, such schemes were impractical, utopian, socialistic—they would never work. All very like the attacks on the TVA, whose constitutionality was challenged in the courts on forty different occasions. The Double E and the Basic Economy were similarly challenged and like the TVA, ultimately upheld by the Supreme Court.

Nor did other nations accept the world-wide regulation of resources and the creation of the subsistence

economy because of their reasonableness and humanity. As in the United States, acceptance was based on
dread of impending social and economic chaos. (It was
also the· time when the clock of the atomic scientists
stood at one minute before doomsday and planetary
pollution had reached disaster proportions.)

The Regional Plan

In these early decades of the twenty-first century, mutually dependent regions co-operate to maintain demo-
graphic, economic, and ecologic balances since no
place has the combination of arable land and water-

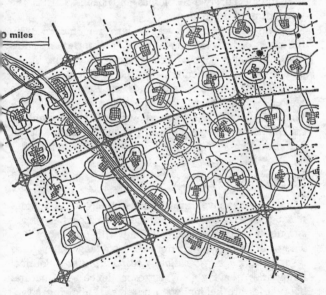

0 miles

. densely populated part of a region. Three thousand square
ɪiles with thirty townships. Average density is 1,400 persons
ɪr square mile. Highways are approximately twenty miles
part.

ways, quarries and mines, oil field and forest, needed to produce the variety of goods required in modern society. Although local products are preferred for patriotic as well as practical reasons, an active export-import exchange is an important element in the economy. As the hypothetical region we are describing is in the temperate zone, more apples are eaten than pineapples, more grapes than grapefruit, more strawberries and asparagus in the spring, prunes and potatoes in the winter, the obvious way of reducing the wasteful intermediary services of former times. But it is not merely a practical matter: An awareness of climate and season is fostered, a pride in a place and its distinctive foods and industries, its ways of doing things, and its special style in clothes and slang. This is the patriotism of the region.

World-wide, what saves modern regionalism from the curse of provincialism is good transportation routes and electronic communication as well as the interpenetration of local cultures by the products and international work experience of the Basic Economy. In the United States regionalism is fostering a kind of geophysical populism which allows for great political differences and a good deal of economic and cultural variation.

The Present Recalls the Past

Since nations have thrown down their arms, nationalism seems to have lost its meaning. Local flags are sprouting everywhere, all different with one exception: They all bear in no matter what language the words *co-operation, participation, responsibility*. Political boundaries having no correspondence to natural boundaries are beginning to be erased, allowing large-scale planning without artificial restraints and controls from distant capitals. As of this writing (2020) some national governments have already been replaced by independent regional federations bound together by similar traditions, language, and interests. Some ask whether we are on the way to the old city-states but without walls, animosities, or class distinctions. It is possible, it could happen.

However, for me the most hopeful note is a saying recently inscribed on a new town hall. It is not from the mouth of a god or guru but from that of a modest nineteenth-century English electrician, Michael Faraday, who once said, "All this is a dream. Still examine it by a few experiments. Nothing is too wonderful if it is consistent with the laws of nature, and in cases such as these, experiment is the best test of such consistency."

PART TWO

Introduction

My primary purpose in writing this book was to relate the discussion on ecology with the future direction of physical planning and architecture.

Starting with the premise that the world was rapidly being made uninhabitable by our overuse and misuse of nature's bounty, I asked whether we were on an irreversible route. If we were, then no planning was needed, eschatology was our dish; out we'd go with a whimper or a bang.

Such an end is, at least for me, unthinkable, so I asked whether high-technology societies could be reorganized to establish a more satisfactory relationship between people and environment; whether such a change could be made without sacrifices in creature comforts or in social ways that we would find unsatisfactory or unacceptable.

To answer such a question led me first to examine quantitative aspects—population forecasts, rates of energy consumption, amounts of pollution, etc.—to establish the dimensions of the problem. Then going back to history I examined such simple things as how people ate, bathed, and moved about, asking whether the old ways were functionally satisfactory, less wasteful, and at least as pleasant as their modern counterparts. If they were, could we learn from them and so develop a new style more suited to our "oasis in space"?

The essays that follow are based on such examinations. I trust they will provide a factual background for many of the recommendations made in this book.

CHAPTER VII

People and Food

"A population tends to increase to its starvation limit."

—Thomas Robert Malthus

Thomas Huxley once estimated that if all the progeny of a single aphid survived, "in 10 generations the weight of them would be more than 500 million of stout men." This sums up the population problem.

In 1798 Thomas Robert Malthus wrote an essay in which he pointed out that all species of flora and fauna, including man, increase faster than the means of sustenance. Fortunately, nature has its checks and balances which maintain an equilibrium, so the chances of being overwhelmed by aphids would be slim since "Necessity that imperious all-pervading law of nature restrains them within the prescribed bounds. The race of plants and the race of animals shrink under this great restrictive law; and men cannot by any efforts of reason escape from it."

Malthus discussed two kinds of restraints on overpopulation by man. Positive checks (*catastrophic*): "are extremely various and I include every cause, whether arising from vice or misery, which in any degree contributes to shorten the natural duration of life. Under this head, therefore, may be enumerated all unwholesome occupations, severe labor and exposure to the seasons, extreme poverty, bad nursing of children, great towns, excesses of all kinds, the whole train of common diseases and epidemics, wars, plagues and famines."

Preventive checks (*purposeful*): "So far as it is voluntary it is peculiar to man and arises from that distinctive superiority in his reasoning faculties which enables him to calculate distant consequences." Malthus describes the troubles of poor people with large families and believes the father must "doubt whether he should follow the bent of his inclinations" when he sees he can't support his offspring.

Derided by the working-class movement as a capitalistic genocidal plot, attacked by the church for advocating birth control, and disregarded by most, the Malthusian pessimism had no place in the nineteenth and early twentieth centuries. The Industrial Revolution would eliminate poverty, for there was no limit to the increase in production, everybody would be well off, the poor raised from their misery without sacrificing the comfort of the rich. It did seem in that time of fantastic technological growth coupled with the expansive exploitations of new lands and colonial people, the world—meaning the Western world—was capable of providing all its people with all things.

It was not an unwarranted optimism. One by one the "positive checks" listed by Malthus have been drastically reduced thanks to improved sanitation and medicine, labor-saving machinery, better working conditions, and mass education in hygiene. Fewer children die at birth, more people live longer. However, the "preventive checks" among the poor in general, but especially among the poor in the technology-deficient countries, have not worked, or hardly. "The rich," as the old song had it, "get richer and the poor get children."

The demographers forecast world population will double in twenty-five to thirty-five years and most of the increase will be where the people are poorest. World population in 1971 was 3.71 billion, a 74-million increase over 1970, and at this rate it will double by 2006. In 1976, 72 per cent of the world's inhabitants lived in the technology-deficient nations, more than half in southern and eastern Asia. We may expect that in the year 2000 there will be 3.4 billion people in those countries. Many will be living in crowded conditions.

A comparison between a land-rich and a land-poor country reveals what crowding can mean. The average population density per square mile in the United

States is 56 people. People are not evenly distributed, most living in what the Census Bureau calls "urbanized areas"—cities and suburbs in which are home, offices, shops, and factories but *where no crops are grown or cattle grazed*. These urbanized areas have an average population density of 2,500 people to the square mile.

Bangladesh has an over-all density of 1,300 people to the square mile. Of the 75 million people, only 8 per cent live in cities and towns. The population growth is 3 per cent a year but it is believed this will decrease slightly in the foreseeable future. Taking this decrease into account, in twenty-three years the average population density of Bangladesh will be 2,600 per square mile or more than the density of our urbanized areas. *Where then will food be grown?* In 1973 Bangladesh had to import not only 2 million tons of food but all minerals, chemicals, coal, and most of the cotton it needed. Will old Malthus be right with his catastrophes? Are starvation, misery, pestilence, and probably war the only way to brake the growth? Or can we hope for a better solution?

* * *

In 1972 the United Nations Statistical Year Book reported that the gap between the have and have-not nations was rapidly widening. In broad terms, from 1960 to 1970 in the developed countries the total per capita output, industrial and agricultural, increased by 43 per cent while the increase in the technically deficient countries was only 27 per cent. The caloric food intake per person per day in the United States, Britain, or France was over 3,200 while the intake per person in countries like Indonesia, Somalia, or Bolivia was under 1,800. Each individual in the United States used the equivalent of 11.1 metric tons of coal in 1970 compared with a world per capita average of 1.9 metric tons.

It appears that population figures by themselves don't reflect environmental impact, so let's look at the relationship between people and what they consume. The Menton Statement (1971), a message signed by 2,200 scientists from twenty-three countries, pointed out, "It has been estimated that a child born in the United States today will consume, during his lifetime, at least 20 times as much as one born in India and contribute about 50 times as much pollution to the environment. In terms of environmental impact, therefore, the most industrialized countries are also the most densely populated." Professor Jean Mayer, of Harvard, voiced a similar attitude earlier (1969): ". . . there is a strong case to be made for a stringent population policy on exactly the reverse of the basis Malthus expounded. Malthus was concerned with the steadily more widespread poverty that indefinite population growth would inevitably create. I am concerned about the area of the globe where people are rapidly becoming richer. For rich people occupy much more space, consume much more of each natural resource, disturb the ecology more and create more land, air, water, chemical and radioactive pollution so it can be argued that it is even more urgent to control the numbers of the rich than it is to control the numbers of the poor."

Thus we have a Malthusian and a non-Malthusian viewpoint, both leading to unhappy conclusions.

My aim is not to tell the Indonesians or Brazilians to be more prudential; I'll leave that to some native guru who may convince them that "a neglect of an effective birth control policy is a never failing source of poverty," as Plato warned in his *Politics*.

As the rate of population increase in North America, with a population of 220 million, is only 1.3 per cent a year and Europe's (minus the Soviet Union) 462 million people increase but 0.8 per cent yearly, the industrialized countries have already achieved a high degree of fertility control. This is especially true of the United States, which ranks twenty-fifth among the nations in life expectancy, with a birth rate among the lowest. However, an unpleasant fact for American parents to accept is that we give birth to perfectly fine little children who in no time at all are turned into voracious mouths by the mores of a consumer society.

* * *

Claims made by such a group as the Committee on Population and the American Future in 1972 that slower population growth will cause total as well as per capita income to rise faster completely misses the economic and ecological argument. The point is not to reduce population to zero growth in order to expand the gross national product but quite the other way around; the gross national product should be decreased while providing all with a more satisfying life in a "cleaner, greener land." We can only hope that part of such a life would be spent in helping the less lucky.

As we expect the doubling of the world's population around the year 2000 with a second doubling thirty-five years later, most food scientists seem to agree on the improbability of feeding these multitudes especially with present techniques and allocations of resources. The demographers may be right when they say many people will be born; the question is whether the grim Malthusian check will kill them off.

In 1729 Jonathan Swift made a "modest proposal" for ending the famine in Ireland. May I remind you that the full title was *A Modest Proposal for Preventing the Children of Poor People from Being a Burden to Their Parents or Their Country (by fattening them and eating them)*. Is it time that it be dusted off and presented as necessary or even desirable? Probably, for "among the 2½ billion people living in the world's less developed countries, 60% are estimated to be malnourished . . . 20% are believed to be starving at this moment. . . ."[1] Who would have thought a by-product of soap and clean water would be famine, or a by-product of the instruc-

[1] Dr. John H. Knowles, President, Rockefeller Foundation, March 1974.

tion given in Genesis—"Be fruitful and multiply, and replenish the earth and subdue it"—would be misery?

*   *   *

It is not to be expected that we go hungry to feed half the world but it is reasonable to expect more rational utilization and sharing of our resources in times of world-wide scarcity. We have a present duty to feed the starving. We also have a duty to look to our own future, for soon we may not be so well off since it is capital, not income, we are spending.

In spite of our vast land reserves, we have been using up our agricultural soil instead of using it. We churn more and more fertilizers into it and spray more and more pesticides on it to harvest diminishing amounts of produce. Agribusiness has replaced agriculture, introducing methods whose consequences were unplanned for and unexpected for both people and products. A meaningful way of life was destroyed for millions, forcing them off the land into the cities, where, in most cases, a less than satisfactory lot awaited. Meanwhile, the quality of food deteriorated, as crops were grown, harvested, and marketed to maximize profits, not satisfy nutritional needs or taste buds.

In exchange, we have had huge increases in production on smaller acreages with less human labor, thanks to machinery, fertilizers, and pesticides. Let us not forget that if we had continued using 1900 U.S. methods of cultivation which took 1½ acres to feed an average American, we would have needed to add 400,000 acres a year to our farm areas or the equivalent of another Iowa every decade just to keep up with population growth. It is not a paradox that the industrialized nations are adequately fed though only a small percentage of their work force is on the farm, while two thirds of the world where famine is an ever-present possibility have most of their people in agriculture. Let us not blame a technology that provided us with many benefits, but let us not celebrate it either. It has gone astray, become an increasingly wasteful and dangerous way to produce food; we can no longer afford it. When 5 million tractors in the United States use 8 billion gallons of fuel and we find this is the energy equivalent of the food produced, we must re-examine our ways.

There comes a time when sheer quantity makes a qualitative difference, when the law of diminishing returns sets in. It may be true that "one ton of nitrogen is the equivalent of 14 acres of good farmland" (Jean Mayer) but if I double the fertilizer on 14 acres, do I make it 28 and if I redouble it . . . ? Obviously there are limits.

*   *   *

If our aim is to conserve irreplaceable energy, improve our health, and help feed the hungry, there are at least six things we are doing wrong:

1. *We are expending more fuel than we should on producing, processing, shipping, and selling food.*

In 1970 the energy contained in the food the average American ate was less than one sixth of the energy required to produce and deliver the food. A startlingly small percentage of this energy was used in the actual production of the food as shown in these 1963 estimates (using millions of calories as the measure):

Agriculture	1.2
Food processing	2.7
Transportation	0.2
Wholesale/retail trade	1.3
Home	2.5
Total expenditure per year	7.9 million calories per person

When one considers that for the almost 8 million calories of expenditure the average result in food value is a little over a million calories, it seems an unduly costly way of getting food on the table.

2. *We fertilize excessively, use pesticides indis-criminately, polluting field and stream and sometimes poisoning flora and fauna (including people).*

In 1949 an average of about 11,000 tons of fertilizer nitrogen was used per USDA unit of crop production; by 1968 the use was increased to 57,000 tons for the same crop yield! "Obviously a great deal of the nitro-gen fertilizer did not enter the crop but ended else-where in the ecosystem" (Barry Commoner). Pesticides are no different. The amount of pesticides used per unit of agricultural production increased 168 per cent between 1950 and 1967 because the pesticides killed off the natural insect predators of the target pest and the pests themselves became more resistant.

3. *We damage our most basic food ingredi-ent—water—and destroy that which lives in it.*

According to the World Health Organization, barely 500 million people enjoy the luxury of water from a tap. More than nine tenths of the people in the tech-nically deficient countries don't have enough water, and what they have is often not fit to drink. Lakes, rivers, and other fresh waters have been used as sewers. As populations and industry grew, so grew the pollution.

The oceans and seas show here and there that even their vastness will not long support the overfishing of advanced technology or the degradation of oil spills, garbage dumping, and industrial wastes. The Mediter-ranean is now called a dying sea, Lake Erie is dead.

4. *The processing of food is often detrimental to food values and therefore to health.*

The $161-billion food and beverage industry of the United States is either doing us a service by preparing us for the science fiction time of the all-synthetic diet or, as many claim, perverting our tastes and perhaps slowly poisoning us by selling processed foods rich in refined sugar, modified carbohydrates, artificial colors and flavors and the like, but poor in the natural goodnesses of foods fresh and untampered with. The food we eat must have something missing, for in 1970 a federal survey covering ten states revealed "a significant proportion of the population malnourished, or was at a high risk of developing nutritional problems." As the evidence piles up, government bans grow, forbidding cyclamates, MSG in baby food, DES in cattle feed, etc. But bureaucracy works slowly especially when it deals with big business or beloved products like bacon for breakfast, a dish called by Dr. Michael Jacobson "probably the most dangerous food in the supermarket" since it is preserved with cancer-causing sodium nitrite.

5. *In a world short of food for people, we devote too much acreage to growing food for animals.*

Half the harvested land in the United States is planted with crops used for animal feed. As cattle consume about twenty-one pounds of vegetable protein to produce one pound of meat protein, they are quite inefficient as food factories. Reducing our livestock population by one-half would free about 100 million tons of grains for human consumption, according to former Assistant Secretary of Agriculture Don Paarlberg. This amount would meet the caloric deficit of the nonsocialist countries four times over (Frances Lappe).

6. *The average American eats too much and too many of the wrong things.*

We eat badly, 40 per cent are overweight consuming on the average 126 pounds of sugar a year and supporting in the process a $3-billion candy industry. The average American eats 21 to 25 per cent fewer vegetables, fruits, and dairy products than he ate twenty-five years ago and 50 to 80 per cent more sugary snacks and soft drinks. We eat less grain, twice as much beef and veal, 2½ times more poultry than we did forty years ago. It is not a balanced diet and we're not healthier by eating it. A nutritional survey made by the Department of Agriculture (1955–56) bears this out since it found that as the nation got richer, it spent more on health care, its food industry produced more new foods, and many American diets became nutritionally worse.

* * *

With our huge arable land resources, our technology, and our native abilities, we can feed ourselves more healthfully, substantially aid the undernourished in the world yet consume less energy and pollute less in the process. The solution is to be found in shifting the emphasis on what we grow and how we grow it, in reducing the intermediary handling presently required to get food from producer to consumer, and in modifying our diet.

Twenty or even ten years ago, this would have seemed an unrealizable program to recommend to the American people. Today, thanks to the "health food and organic food freaks," the excesses of the food conglomerates, and the growing realization that it is one world and a small one, it now seems possible.

CHAPTER VIII

Cooking and Eating

It may be safely averred that good cookery is the best and truest economy, turning to full account every wholesome article of food, and converting into palatable meals what the ignorant either render uneatable or throw away in disdain.

—Eliza Acton, *Modern Cookery* (1856)

Aside from snacks, coffee breaks, and cocktail parties each one of us eats about eleven hundred meals a year and it is estimated we spend some one thousand hours at it. The amount of time taken in preparation, cooking, and cleaning up per person per meal is obviously a variable depending on the diet and the amount of rationalization or mechanization.

The kitchen used to be called the workshop of the house and like all workshops went from hand to machine ways. America led the way, for here (not counting the ante bellum South) we've always had a chronic shortage of household help and a female population constitutionally averse to drudgery. As early as 1841 Catherine Beecher wrote a *Treatise on Domestic Economy* in which along with feminist propaganda she discussed in detail ways of making every household task—from choosing seed for the garden to cooking and cleaning— more efficient. Ms. Beecher found the typical kitchen a place where "cooking materials and utensils, sink and eating room are at such distances apart that half the time and strength is employed in walking back and forth to collect and return the articles used." It was also Ms. Beecher's opinion that "the true housewife makes bread the sovereign of her kitchen," which meant the wood stove was going full blast winter and summer. What then was more sensible than her recommendation to place the stove in an alcove separated from the kitchen by glazed sliding doors, or more convenient than her proposal for built-in sink, drainboard, and continuous work surfaces with storage spaces below and above?

Out of such beginnings came, though no credit has

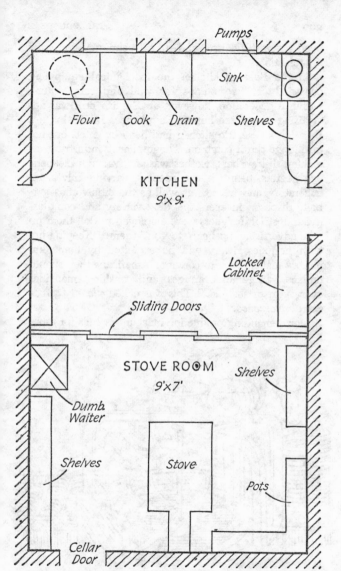

Plan of the Beecher practical kitchen. *Is the dumbwaiter used to send meals to a dining room above or to bring supplies from the cellar?*

been given, Taylorism and other techniques for work organization.

In the Beecher kitchen the mechanical equipment consisted of "two pumps for well and rain water"; within a generation, however, an English firm was advertising over three hundred appliances fueled by gas. By 1893 an electric kitchen had been invented but not until 1930 did it catch on. The appliance industry grew making dishwashers, clothes washers, vacuum cleaners, egg beaters, blenders, can openers, carving knives, refrigerators, and freezers as well as the omnivorous garbage disposer, in ever-expanding variety and complexity. Industrial designers were employed to doll them up and advertising agencies to tout them: "Keeping-up-with-the-Jones rivalry will be exploited by home appliance makers . . . to convince Americans they should replace refrigerators, ranges and washing machines every year or so. . . ."[1] This was called *planned product obsolescence.*

Our demanding production mechanism calls for more

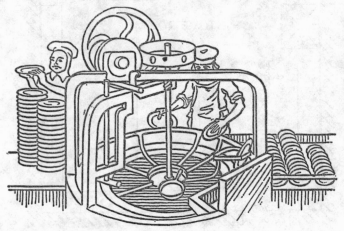

M. Eugène Daugin's machine for washing dishes (Paris, 1885).

[1] *Forbes,* 1956.

than replacing the obsolete, even when obsolescence is speeded by the Jones rivalry. New needs must be generated, new products made to supply them. Our never-failing know-how comes up with a sought-for innovation—convenience foods. Food with no fuss, no mess, practically predigested and sold in their own throwaway cooking bags or baking pans hardly required a private arsenal of appliances to process and put on the table; the kitchen, neat as in a television commercial, can become an example of conspicuous consumption like the Victorian parlor, or disappear. So can the dining room.

Although rich and poor eat their TV dinners in front of their TV sets, American interest in hearing and reading about cookery is extraordinary. Recipes are compared as eagerly as hospital experiences. The sale of cookbooks is enormous. Television programs devoted to sauces and sautés rank high. Most newspapers have food columns, slick magazines on food sell on the newsstands. How extraordinary, then, to find how banal home cooking generally is and how uniformly terrible is the food in public eating places except at a select few. No wonder the kids drown it in catsup and wash it down with Coke. No wonder the grown-ups who drink each need a hundred pounds of grain a year converted into beer and bourbon to numb their palates.

To eat poor food through poverty is excusable, but we have no such excuse: The average American has available to him a ton of grain a year (five times as much as the average person in a developing country) of which he consumes only 150 pounds directly, the balance having been converted to meat, milk, eggs, beer, and bourbon.[2]

It takes no gift of observation to notice that Americans lead the world in their inclination toward foods suited to the toothless: hamburgers, hot dogs, mashed potatoes, chili, noodles, soft breads, overcooked vegetables plus an inordinate addiction to sweets and car-

[2] 1968: Dr. Lester Brown, Overseas Development Council.

bonated drinks. The result of such choices is not unknown, for as far back as 1837 Sylvester Graham was
telling his fellow Americans, "If man were to subsist
wholly on alimentary substances in their natural state,
or without any artificial preparation by cooking, then
he would be obliged to use his teeth frequently in mas-
ticating food and by so doing not only preserve his
teeth from decay, but at the same time and by the
same means, would he thoroughly mix his food with
the fluid of his mouth." The same kind of message with
a lot more scientific backup is given today by Dr. Jean
Mayer: "Nutrition must play a major role in preventive
medicine which in turn is our major hope to lengthen
and improve the life of our citizens while reducing the
cost of our health system. Our medical expenses have
risen from $12 billion in 1950 to $106 billion this year
[1972] with essentially no improvement in the life
expectancy of our adult citizens."

It's an anomaly. We use more and more fertilizer,
pesticides, and machines to plant, nourish, protect, and
harvest our crops and we use more and more power
and machines to store, refrigerate, package, and ship
them. We use more and more newspaper and television
time to advertise and more space to display and sell
food products and use more and more gadgets and devices to prepare them for eating. We consume more
meat, vegetable, and dairy products at each meal than
any other nation. Nevertheless, we often eat not only
tasteless food but food that isn't good for us. It is to be
hoped that old Anthelme Brillat-Savarin was wrong
when he said, *"La destinée des nations dépend de la
manière dont elles se nourrissent."*[3]

DINING

Some years ago when my brother wrote *Utopian Essays and Practical Proposals*, we collaborated on a

[3] "The destiny of nations depends on the way they feed
themselves."

chapter in it called "Seating Arrangements" in which we observed:

> Eating is eating, yet how we sit down to eat springs from whole systems of moral attitudes and social structures. . . .
>
> (1) In some primitive societies there is communal preparation of food, but each one withdraws with his portion to some safe nook and eats privately. The economy is communal but eating is clearly regarded either as a strictly biological function, best practiced with no table manners or concern for others, so that one may gorge or regurgitate spontaneously, and strictly in secret or more likely, as a dangerous function ridden with taboos, much as we in the west regard sexual intercourse and (apparently) excretion. To some ob-

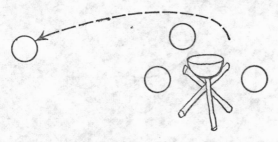

> servers, too, the privacy has seemed to indicate a lively suspiciousness, as if each one feared that the others were going to snatch the food out of his mouth or as if while engaging in this biological indulgence, he were vulnerable to attack and had better sit with his back to a tree.
>
> (2) Civilized people have always regarded eating as a social activity [and have devised several] common plans. . . . Depending on the class structure, those who prepare the food either sit down at the common table or are excluded. The act of eating and drinking together is made to serve as a

relaxing and pleasurable background for being together, for family feeling, enlivened conversation,
to allay distrust for business deals, etc. To be sure,
to socialize the biological activity means also to in-
ternalize the eating taboos, and there is developed
a system of disgust and, as a safeguard against it,
table manners. (Some persons, therefore, who
don't wake up and put on their good behavior easily, prefer to have their first cup of coffee in solitude, the way animals eat.) The round dining

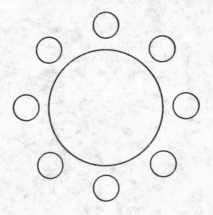

table of the bourgeois home tends to a tight sense
of family and is cement for the Oedipus complex,
it is one of the chief schools of inhibition and
there may be little conversation. The normal meal
of the long table, where the host and hostess sit
far apart at either end takes us back to the table
of the king and his nobles whose presence at the
king's biological function (his *coucher* or *lever* or
dining) is of charismatic advantage. A remarkable
American variant of recent times is the convention
banquet where the mass may eat in small sociable

groups, whereas the important people sit at a kingly table on a dais, from which ceremonial speeches will eventually pour forth.

(3) It has also remained for the Americans to arrive at the least plausible of eating plans, seated at a public counter and looking neither to right

nor left, like pigs at a trough. The plan is essential to the needs and mores of our organized society. We eat in company to avoid loneliness and on an assembly line for efficiency of production, distribution and consumption. Yet we eat in solitude to avoid surveillance and the anxiety of talking to strangers. Shared solitude is an excellent condition for flights of fantasy that cannot come to overt expression.

To these observations, we can now add a fourth example, the TV eating arrangement, which harks back to the first example and has the shared solitude of the

previous example though the setting may be slum or the very lap of luxury. Here the flights of fantasy are externalized and ready-made, seen through the transparent veil of the boob tube.

It's a relief to turn from this scene to an Arcadian description of John Humphrey Noyes of another world in another time: "At the back of the house there was a long shed with a rough table down the center, and planks, for seats on each side, on which 30 or 40 people sat. I was kindly received by them, and invited to dinner; and a good dinner it was, consisting of coarse brown bread piled up in broken lumps, dishes of large potatoes unpeeled and some potato-soup, and a supply of melons for the second course.

"I sat beside a Dr. Hard, who noticed that I took a little salt on my potatoes, and he remarked to me that if I abstained from it, I would have my taste nicely improved. . . . There was no animal food of any kind except milk, which one or two of them used. The women waited upon the tables but the variety of dishes being so small, each person attended to himself so that waiting was rendered almost unnecessary. All displayed a rude politeness."

CONVENIENCE FOODS

Since 220 billion meals a year are eaten in the United States, it was to be expected that the enterprising would develop an industry that converted the mass-produced raw materials into mass-produced meals, for, whether the production chain is mine/assembly line/auto dealer's showroom, field/assembly line/public feeding place, the problems of making, processing, and selling differ only in nomenclature, not in methodology. Since the hearth is the primordial heart of the home and people are conservative, one would have assumed a strong resistance to ready-cooked meals. A moment's thought dissipates such an idea for several reasons. Ready-mades are not looked at as novelties but simply extensions of the old preserving techniques of drying, pickling, and canning.[4] As households diminish in size and women work outside the home, cooking for few or hurriedly is simply not worthwhile. Unlike the French, most Americans seem to have no natural appreciation of food (hence their interest in reading about it as a cultural activity). For a people with underdeveloped taste buds, convenience food *tastes* better. And as a corollary, few Americans have a talent for cooking. Convenience foods *do* taste better than Mom's.

Therefore, as Americans are prone to believe what advertisers tell them, especially when it caters to their indolence, it takes no flight of fancy to forecast that all things being equal, most people would accept a convenience food diet if the price was right.

But as fuel increases in cost, the price will become less and less right, since such a way of preparing food often requires up to fifteen units of primary energy to deliver each unit of food energy to the consumer, with the fourteen units being eaten up on the factory, farm, in processing, packaging, freezing, and shipping at minus ten degrees Fahrenheit.

[4] This is, of course, not true; the change is qualitative for there is a real difference between aiding the cook by giving a choice of out-of-season products and eliminating the cook.

There are other objections to the ready-cooked-meal industry. First, the human work involved, excepting for the few high-skilled technicians, is reduced to the stupidest drudgery, since "convenience food systems need fewer preparation and food employees with less or no previous training."[5]

Second, the products and their preparation needing additives to preserve or change color, to create or enhance flavor and odor, to prevent spoilage, are often bad for the health; the tarted-up looks pervert good taste.

Third, the mode of production requires large capital investment resulting in centralized control, bureaucratic management, and conglomerates. It eliminates regional differences, for the products must be uniform and the volume huge to have a profitable operation.

And finally, the food turned into merchandise must cater to a mass taste, and as no such taste exists, it must be manufactured through national advertising. The result at its best is the airline meal—foods of various monotony served from Seattle to Key West.

Food considered as merchandise suggests that "in many cases the brand name of a desired product and the size of the package may be all that is required to describe the merchandise." The merchandise of the future, we are told, will be sold in "at least three quality lines . . . because processors will discover that one line of foods cannot possibly meet all needs. They probably will be called Gourmet, Institutional and Standard,"[6] leaving to Victorian England that monument to *haute cuisine*—Alexis Soyer's *Gastronomic Regenerator* with its 2,000 recipes, one fancier than the next.

How far away in time and space all of this is from what was considered "only natural" as late as 1929: "It is only natural that in the U.S.A., cookery should be more cosmopolitan in character than in any other land, since the population is made up of more racial strains

[5] *Hotel & Motel Management*, March 1970.
[6] Ibid.

than any other. It is also natural that in so large an
area, with so many different climates, there should be a
great dissimilarity in different regions both in food materials and in methods of preparing them."[7]

But the ultimate objection to precooked and pack-
aged food is simply that *it deprives us of one of the
most fundamental, human, pleasant, and homely of all
the arts—cooking.*

Precooked food became common during the Industrial Revolution, as did food adulteration. Who was to
do the cooking when all worked in the factory? Where
was the cooking to be done when neither bake oven
nor fuel was available in such fast-growing industrial
towns as Manchester, England, where in 1804 not a
single public baker was to be found. Eleven years later
only half the population prepared its own bread. And
was it not normal for the public baker to increase his
profit by finding ways to speed up and cheapen the old
baking ways? Soon yeast replaced leaven as a starter,
alum was added to improve color and texture, bean
and potato flour found their way into the wheat, plaster
of Paris, even ground-up stone was added to the
dough. And so with all the foods. It is touching to read
excerpts from a warning given in 1843 to the Rochdale
Pioneers: "When you have a little store and have
reached the point of getting pure provisions, you may
find your purchasers may not like them, nor know them
when they taste them."

The olfactory sense is blunted and perverted by mis-
directed agronomy and the concoctions put together by
"food technologists." The natural flavors become unrec-
ognizable, the future of good eating is in jeopardy, not
only for the poor, as in Victorian England, but for all
people. This is no pleasant prospect, for I share with
most a fondness for a decent meal. I agree with Brillat-
Savarin that what you eat you are and am even willing
to go along with Charles Fourier "by imagining a
union established between the gastronomers and those

[7] Encyclopaedia Britannica, 1929 edition.

blessed in the culinary arts, where one can envision a
social order devoted to pleasure and especially gour-
mandism, . . . a voluptuous and learned group of the
highest utility meriting it the title of Palladium of Wisdom since it is associated with the most useful of sciences, the guaranteed hygiene of health." However, I
must leave to Monsieur Fourier the balance of his
imagining: "each person will be assured 5 good meals
a day, not including the interludes which will consist of
4 light snacks of about 5 minutes each."

The wives' old task of preparing three meals a day,
day in, day out, is drudgery because of the repetition,
not the work. How much more so if done alone, as happens in most homes today, and what a waste of effort if
the meal is for the typical small family. Convenience
foods represent the technical solution to such a condition. Considered as a social phenomenon, the decline of
the home-cooked meal paces the decline of family life.

ECOLOGICAL EATING

What the cook cooks depends on his choice among the
comestibles available. Up until 1800 what was available was the fresh things, each in its season, and the
dried, smoked, and pickled things. Simple choices out
of which great cuisines grew. Nicolas Appert's invention of canning, hailed by gourmets as reversing the
seasons—"that clever artist to whom we owe the pleasure of eating little green peas in February, goose ber-
ries and apricots in March"—has turned out to be a
mixed blessing, resulting in luxuries becoming commonplace, the rare, exotic, and the unexpected made
banal. Appert's canned foods, bouillon cubes, and preserved milk were luxuries—O that they had remained
so!

There are economic, ecological, and moral reasons
why we must change our diet in the next years. We

will not be able to afford the costs of feeding so much of our grain crops to animals who, as protein makers, are vastly inefficient, in ratios of 21 to 1 for cattle down to 5.5 to 1 for poultry. Our heavy use of agricultural land is depleting the soil and what necessitates this intense use is that half the harvest each year is fed to livestock. We are beginning to understand the relationship between good diet, unadulterated food, and health. And finally, we may (should?) start choking with guilt on our present diet as we come to realize that each wasteful meal could fill many hungry mouths and still leave more than enough for our own.

What this diet may be is suggested by the recipes given in some recent books.[8] However, my preference is the traditional foods which people living in poor and often crowded countries have thrived on. An example is Italy, where in ancient times the Romans spoke of a proper meal as one that went *ab ovo usque ad mala*, or, as we'd say, from soup to nuts. Today the average Italian eats either a heavy soup, macaroni, or rice as a first course rather than the antipasto, for these are filling and take the edge off hunger. The meat course, if there is a meat course, can then be a small one. Meat is a dish for the rich, served by over half the families in Italy only on Sundays, if then, and, animals being scarce, the Italians, like the Chinese, eat the entire beast. Liver and lights are part of the diet; *Coratella*, for instance, which includes lamb's liver, lungs, and heart, is considered a delicacy, as is the roasted lamb head, *capozzella*. It's an old custom. Deer kidneys, sow's udders, and a basin of wild boar testicles appeared on the menu in a fifth-century Roman banquet. Typically the cuts served are those we consider inferior, often ground for boiling or stewing, and though Italians rarely taste roast beef, steaks, or chops, they have developed sausage making into a fine art and do extraordinary things with sparrows and other little birds.

[8] Frances Moore Lappe, *Diet for a Small Planet*, 1971, and Ellen Buchman Ewald, *Recipes for a Small Planet*, 1973.

As no point in Italy is more than one hundred miles from the coast, fish is comparatively plentiful; nevertheless, the frugal Italian uses seafood Americans discard—squid, conch, skate, octopus, eels, sea urchins. Vegetables are basic. They expand the main dish, are often eaten raw or are boiled and served cool with oil and vinegar.

Pastries are reserved for festive occasions. Fruit and cheese are the dessert, generally eaten together. The cheeses! Gorgonzola and Bel Paese, Parmesan, and Reggiano of the north, Straacchino in Milan, Pecorino in Rome; in the south the fresh cheeses, ricotta, provola, mozzarella as well as provolone, are all names to be savored.

Liquors made with grain are foreign to Italy, whiskey being strictly for the types who ape American movies. For the traditional Italian, wine is a food, not an intoxicant; grappa, that distilled punch in the nose, is for the forlorn.

Who knows whether the legend of a Chinese maiden teaching her Italian sailor lover the art of noodle making is true or whether Marco Polo, returning to Venice, brought along with silk and gunpowder, spaghetti from the court of the great Khan of Tatary?

To me there are curious and elusive similarities between the Italian and Chinese cuisines, though in actual taste, appearance, and way of serving they are as far apart as the China Sea is from the Mediterranean. The Chinese share the Italian fondness for pasta and rice, and both diets include more vegetable and grain products than meat, fish, or fowl. A major difference is the Chinese use of pulse, especially soybean, as a major source of protein; indeed, the inventiveness of the Chinese cookery could rest on the myriad forms, liquid and solid, and the myriad uses given this simple and plentiful legume. Bean sprouts, bean milk, bean curd in several stages, bean skin, and the varied soy sauces are

used in probably half the dishes of this remarkably
varied way of preparing food.

It is hard to say whether the Chinese developed
their culinary ways and explored the realm of food
(from pigs' ears to ducks' tongues, sharks' fins and
jellyfish skins, to tree fungus and swallow's nest) for
economy, nutrition, or sheer epicurean curiosity, for all
three are there.

There are literally endless ways of preparing the
food; let us here mention just two: stir-frying and
steaming.

The ingredients of a stir-fried dish will generally be
1 part of meat, fish, or fowl to 2 or 3 parts vegetables,
or simply vegetables, sliced, shredded, or diced and
quickly cooked in a little oil over high heat. It is a
cooking method having a fourfold advantage: Little
fuel is used, only small amounts of meat are required,
nutritive value is preserved, the taste is enhanced by
combining flavors and through quick cooking.

Steaming in the traditional way has similar advantages though cooking time is generally longer. The
utensil used is usually a set of bamboo trays which fit
one over the other (called a steaming cage). Depending on the number of dishes wanted, these trays are
piled one on top of another up to about seven. They
are placed in a wok partially filled with water and
placed over the flame which need not be large, for
once the water comes to a boil, it is the steam and not
the fire that does the cooking. Anything that walks on
land or swims in the sea, anything that grows (except
fresh leafy vegetables, which are considered too delicate), eggs, and breads (called dumplings and made
with or without fillings) can be used in steamed dishes.
Black-bean-steamed sea bass and rice-powder-steamed
meat are classic dishes in the style. Even some soups
are considered better steamed than simmered, being
found purer in taste and more limpid in texture.

THE CONVIVIAL KITCHEN

The advantage gained by a group of neighbors pooling their knowledge in selecting menus, co-operatively marketing and sharing in cooking and cleaning—both the pleasant work and the chores—seems obvious. More problematical is eating together, for most of us have lost the habit of easy socialization. Such ventures now occur as isolated examples; if they became common, economies would surely be made in buying, fuel use, and household management, and (who knows?) habits of mutual aid and forbearance might result. In built space, the reduction in costs would be striking. Suppose five families were an acceptable household size (the number would depend on location, custom, choice), then, instead of five partially used kitchens/ dining spaces there would be one, generous in size, equipped with the best of appliances. It could be a separate structure as in many medieval houses, or more likely be part of a floor in an apartment house or built into a row of houses.

Having a technology sophisticated beyond our needs, we use it to the extent allowed by our ecological and economic means and acceptable to our social ends. Within these boundaries let me speculate on a space and its fitments designed for the making and consuming of convivial meals. What springs to mind is the happy scenes painted by seventeenth-century Dutchmen who loved the polish of copper pots and flames in great hearths. It's a warm and cozy image but our new learned thrifty self asks about all that heat going up the chimney and those fat-assed girls and fat-jowled men. Maybe this is not a picture of the good life but rather a wishful projection by the deprived, like Fourier's five meals plus snacks.

There is a reasonable frugality leading not to deprivation but to elegance, an example being the traditional Japanese house, with its variety of design principles made familiar to the West by the functionalists:

exposed construction using minimum materials, undecorated surfaces, sliding screen walls creating multiuse spaces or an open place, a paucity of furniture (the matted floor is a seat, the bedroll is tucked away when not in use). Less well known is the functional elegance of the cooking and warming devices, all simple in design and all aimed at the conservation of fuel. Let me give a few examples from a lovely book written in 1885 by an American zoologist, Edward Morse, *Japanese Homes and Their Surroundings*.

Stoves: "In a typical arrangement there are two recesses open in front and on the top for quick cooking, and heat is borrowed from these for a pot space at the back. The small size of the wood used for fuel will strike any Westerner."

Braziers: "It is a convenient and economical device for cooking small messes or boiling water, charcoal being used for the purpose." The charcoal vender makes a fuel by using bits of charcoal, "mixing them with some kind of seaweed and then forming the mass into round balls the size of a large orange. These are dried in the sun and seem to burn very well."

Fireplaces are "in the center of the kitchen—A kettle is suspended over the fire by a chain and other kettles are huddled around to be heated. Overhead a rack hangs from which fish or meat are suspended, and thus the smoke which ascends from the fire is utilized in curing them. Sometimes a large cushion of straw is suspended above the smoke and little fish skewered with pointed sticks are thrust into this bundle of straw like pins in a pin cushion." The fire is laid in sand and often a copper box, having round holes at the top for the *sake* bottles, is filled with water and set in the heated sand.

It is slightly embarrassing to compare our use of the *hibachi* (heaped high with charcoal to broil our franks and burgers on a summer day) with its use in old Japan where it was "an inseparable accompaniment of

every home from the most exalted to the humblest."
The hibachi is a sort of portable fireplace around which
the family gathers to drink tea, gossip, or warm up.
"When the hibachi is properly arranged, it is customary to heap the ashes in a pyramidal pile about the coal
and mark a series of radiating lines upon it. A single
stick of coal buried vertically in the ash will burn for
several hours." Dr. Morse adds, "Whenever you call on
a friend, winter or summer, his very first act of hospi-
tality is to place the hibachi before you. Even in shops
the hibachi is present or is brought in and placed on
the mats when the visitor enters."

Like all kitchens of the past, the Japanese kitchen
had no way of keeping things cool except by hanging
them in a well or in a cold cellar. But then there wasn't
much need. The meat was fresh-killed or smoked, the
fish brought live from the market, butter and milk were
not in the diet. We may therefore presume that when
our diet changes, our mammoth fridges and freezers
will become relics and in their place will be small refrigerators (for milk, butter, plus a few frozen delica-
cies) used mostly during the warm months. For the
balance of the year, we'll have a well-ventilated larder
built in or attached to the exterior wall of the kitchen.
In most climates the problem then will be not how to
keep things cool but how to prevent freezing in winter-
time (an electric coil or a midget space heater will do
it).

Aside from twentieth-century extravagances, the
form of kitchen appliances has followed their function;
a Chinese wok is the right shape for stir-frying, a
French omelet pan for making omelets. We may therefore presume our equipment will change in form and
kind as our diet changes. Tomorrow's recipes and the
need for fuel conservation will surely not want the siza-
ble broilers and roasters now in vogue but may call for
low-heat reservoirs (connected perhaps to the solar-
heated hot water system) for the slow cooking of

beans, soup stocks, and stews. For quickly made dishes, we may learn from the classic Chinese stove whose ceramic top holds heat and has in it an opening shaped so the curved bottom of the wok sets into it, exposing a maximum surface to the flames.

Oh, and dishwashing! In medieval times one ate on slabs of bread and then ate the plate, while all the West, until Renaissance manners caught up with them, ate with their fingers. Except for the rich, these customs continued until the Industrial Revolution brought in, along with cheap cotton goods, the plethora of plates and eating hardware common to Victorian tables and bequeathed to us. Dishwashing is drudgery—wasteful of time, soap, and hot water. The engineer's answer was the home dishwasher and then the paper and plastic throwaways, neither, like convenience food, acceptable to a conservation-minded society. The obvious answer to the dishwashing problem is not to invent gadgets but to reduce the number of dishes. Shall we use our fingers for forks and a slab of bread for a plate or adopt a more civilized solution? Perhaps a pair of chopsticks, a spoon, and a bowl, all a Chinese uses for most home-style meals, would do.

In the morning paper one day I read "General Mills, Inc. is currently test marketing two meat analogues called 'Country Cuts'—frozen, ready-to-eat cubes with the flavor and texture of chicken or ham."[9] Bemused by this piece of news and mulling over what I had just written, I picked up my copy of *Walden*. Thoreau wrote, "There is some of the same fitness in a man's building his own house that there is in a bird building his own nest. Who knows but if men constructed their dwellings with their own hands and provided food for themselves and families simply and honestly enough, the poetic faculty would be universally developed, as birds universally sing when they are so engaged?"

[9] New York *Times*, October 12, 1974.

CHAPTER IX

The Use of Energy

An occasional convulsive tremor or the smoke drifting from some Vesuvius or Mauna Loa reminds us that under the earth's thin mantle is a molten mass. If we could tap such a source, we'd have a *perpetuum mobile,* since enough energy would be released by cooling it just one degree Fahrenheit to run all existing power plants for the next 20 million years. Luckily, this prospect is far away, for if we had such power it would not be long before our greed, vanity, and ineptness would bring the world we know from the biblical sixth day to the day before the first.

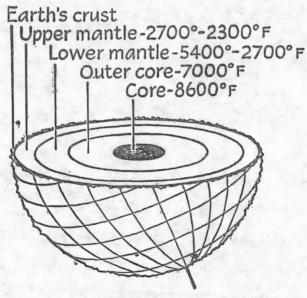

Earth's crust
Upper mantle-2700°-2300°F
Lower mantle-5400°-2700°F
Outer core-7000°F
Core-8600°F

The heat inside.

When we think of past societies, we judge their culture by their poets, painters, and philosophers; their power, by their kings and warriors. Since the nineteenth century in the Western world a new standard has been set, simple and measurable, better suited to the understanding of conspicuously consumptive societies: *A country's greatness is measured by the amount of energy it uses.* No one will question that this belief is shared by East and West in our time.

*   *   *

There have been various estimates made of annual energy use in the United States, and the consensus is that it represents about one third of the world's yearly production—a lot for a nation containing only 6 per cent of the world's population. We are also told that by the year 2000, the world's population will have doubled, our own increase will be not more than a third but our demand for energy will increase exponentially, reaching, according to a forecast of the Department of Interior, 191,566 trillion British thermal units. A number such as 191,566 trillion is of course meaningless without some sort of scale to measure the order of magnitude. A look at our past use of energy may help: U.S. energy consumption in 1900 was 5,000 billion BTUs. By 1951 it had grown to 25,000 billion and jumped to 70,000 billion in 1971. The National Petroleum Institute (as might be expected) projected consumption at 120,000 billion in 1985. These figures are still astronomical, so let's try another order of magnitude, the average daily use of energy by individuals in a few countries: In 1970 the average Japanese consumed 200,000 BTUs, the Englishman 430,000, the American 850,000. In less-developed Brazil during the same year, the average daily BTU consumption was 184,000, while if we take India as representing the third world, we discover the average Indian got along on 37,000 units!

We all have been taught that a British thermal unit

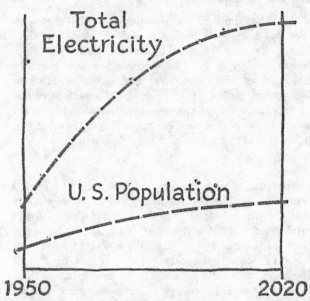

A "plausible" projection: *"The flatness of the population growth as contrasted with the steep arc of energy growth makes it clear that it is the per capita increase in consumption which is primarily responsible for the ascent of energy growth"* (Dr. Ralph E. Lapp, 1972).

represents the quantity of heat required to raise the temperature of one pound of water by one degree Fahrenheit. But concretely what *does* 37,000 BTUs mean? This example may help. In 1972 the Gulf Oil Corporation posed a problem: *How much energy is used by an average American commuter in an average American 4,000-pound car traveling at average speeds on an average highway?* Taking everything into account from extraction of raw material to the finished product for all elements—car, tires, road, oil, gas, and the like, the answer was 24,000 BTUs per mile of travel. In other words in ten miles of travel, an American driver used about the same amount of energy as the Indian had for all his weekly needs. Unbelievable!

In 1974 Pope Paul VI said, "A full human life, one endowed with freedom and dignity will be assured to all men and all people when the earth's resources have been shared more equitably. . . ." Does this suggest that the average Indian should have not only the amount of food he needs (his average diet is at least 500 calories below the accepted minimum and 1,500 below the United States intake) but a more equal share in the world's production of energy? Yet if India and other nonindustrialized countries representing 2,000 million people got, not the equal of our American daily energy income, but the 200,000 BTUs of a Japanese, would not the world soon be sucked dry of petroleum, mined clean of coal, and probably so polluted as to be uninhabitable?

Let us return to more ponderable considerations.

* * *

Of all the oil believed to be ultimately discoverable in the United States, about half had been found by the end of 1970. Most remaining oil is in the "frontier areas" (Alaska North Slope, Atlantic Offshore, Gulf of Mexico deep waters). We have lots of coal—3 trillion tons—but only some 150 billion are economically minable with present prices and technology.

Professor William D. Nordhaus, a Yale economist, expects the United States to almost exhaust domestic petroleum resources by 1980 and also expects that as these run out prices will rise making the cost of mining coal feasible. He forecasts that from 1980 to 2000 we will increasingly depend on imports, and about 2120, coal and oil will be exhausted and the breeder reactor of the nuclear age will take over.

All forecasts by the proponents of the ever-expanding economy end with the panacea of nuclear power. They claim there is no hazard; nuclear power is safe—as Gulf Oil Company put it—"despite some fears still remaining among members of the public because of its origin as a destructive weapon." Nonetheless, such "members of the public" as the MIT-based Union of Concerned Scientists finds nuclear plants in the present state of the technology a menace and it has been pointed out that by 1980 the power reactors of the world "will produce annually as a by-product, more than 40,000 pounds of plutonium that extracted from spent fuel rods could provide enough weapons-grade fissionable material for more than 2,000 Hiroshima-size bombs."[1] In addition, everybody agrees radioactive waste is a cause for concern especially as some of it remains lethal for thousands of years and there seems no way to get rid of it. Burying the waste at sea is unsafe and, what was thought a solution, burial deep in the salt mines of Kansas or Siberia has been found "unsuitable." Perhaps there is no way to safely dispose of these wastes since they are from Pandora's box.[2] As to the box itself—what does one do with an abandoned nuclear reactor?

It takes no great imagination to visualize a desert world of the future, with here and there great hulks emitting their invisible deadly breath, monuments to . . . it's hard to say—temerity, shortsightedness, greed? Perhaps it is true that the most important technological question of our time is to what degree the electric power industry should switch to nuclear power plants.

Aside from survival there is the question of economics, for not every expert believes nuclear power can be a source of cheap and unlimited energy. A spokesman for the Energy Research and Development Administration found that "if projected growth rates for nuclear power hold true in the next decade or so, uranium production must expand faster than the output of

[1] New York *Times*, May 14, 1975.
[2] "No technically or economically feasible methods have yet been proven for ultimate disposal of radio-active waste—a grim legacy from the nuclear program to future generations." Petition signed by 2,300 U.S. scientists on the thirtieth anniversary of the bombing of Hiroshima.

virtually every raw material, including oil, has thus far in the 20th century,"[3] a message repeated by the Stockholm International Peace Research Institute: "Unless activities are stepped up soon and huge new reserves mineable at relatively low cost are found, there may well be a uranium crisis in the mid 1980's."

It would seem the 1971 forecast of S. R. Eyre is not without foundation: "It is by no means certain the power from fusion reaction will ever be available and indeed the whole future of fission energy is now in dire jeopardy: consumption of the relatively rare uranium 235 in non-breeder reactors could result in complete exhaustion in a mere fraction of a century, resulting in a situation where nuclear power would be *more* expensive than power from fossil fuels and water."

As we enter the last quarter of the century, we find that in addition to the 221 nuclear power plants operational or on order in the United States there are 274 operating or planned in twenty-six other countries. Taking into account what we know and what we can guess, it is a frightening commentary on the suicidal bent of our time. One wonders—are we exploring the moon and Mars as a preview of the future of our planet earth?

The legend has it that Prometheus stole fire from heaven in a reed and gave it to man. Zeus in revenge created Pandora, who later opened the box from which every human ill escaped. This fable may now relate to a time whose mid-point was the fateful day of 2 December 1942, at 15.25 when one by one the cadmium control rods were pulled from the atomic pile and a nuclear reaction became self-sustaining. Einstein may be the Prometheus in this story, or is it Fermi? Pandora? Pandora is us.

* * *

The state of our technical arts is adequate but what leaves much to be desired and needs revaluation and

3 John A. Paterson, Chief of Evaluation, ERDA, 1975.

change is the choice of things that should be made, the way they are made, their distribution and use.

In this context, we ask what other sources of energy are available. The sun and wind, the tide, the fall of water, hot springs and volcanoes, the forests, sum it up. Of all these beautiful and mostly self-replenishing sources, it is only the waterfall, man-made or natural, that now provides any significant amount of energy. As to the others, the most optimistic prediction is that in twenty-five years harnessed geothermal power in the United States will equal our hydroelectric output (about 2.3 per cent of electricity presently produced). We harness the tides a little, collect energy from sun and wind hardly at all.

What of wood? Hardly a hundred years ago it was

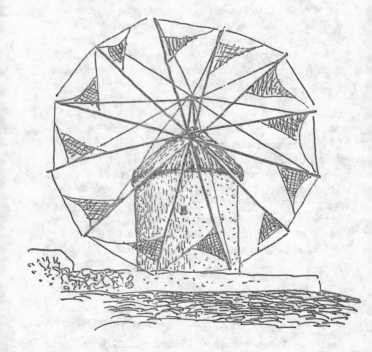

used for 80 per cent of all fuel needs, and even today, incredible as it sounds to us in this land of high technology, an estimated 1.3 billion people use wood as their sole resource for cooking and heating. Because a third of humankind depends on wood, the forests of Asia and Africa are being depleted.

Disaster is compounded since dried animal manures are increasingly used to replace scarce firewood so depriving the soil of its natural fertilizers. In India, for instance, 300 million tons of manure a year are turned into dried cakes for burning. (This is equivalent to a third of India's chemical fertilizer consumption.)

*   *   *

We must now look back and ask whether it was necessary for the people of New York State to increase their use of electrical power by 10 per cent in the years 1965–75 while the population increase was only 0.6 per cent. Did our New Yorkers living in Westchester County really need a 50 per cent increase in the number of cars they use when their population only increased 10 per cent? Was it really necessary to practically junk our railroads between 1940 and 1967, thus forcing among other things an increase in air passenger miles from less than 27 million to 334 million which in turn required an increase in gasoline consumption from 22 million to 512 million gallons? We might also ask whether it is reasonable or desirable for man to slowly suffocate himself by proliferating devices which exhaust lethal quantities of carbon monoxide into the air he breathes.

On the basis of present trends one optimist has figured that for the United States to become self-sufficient in energy by 1985, we would require 435 new nuclear plants, 8 shale oil plants, 18 oil-from-coal plants, 30 gas-from-coal plants, and 10 geothermal plants, while another has pointed out that while today our nuclear plants furnish but a fraction of our electrical power, the aim should be for them to furnish over half by 2000. Are these goals reasonable or desirable for us and if so, then why not for the rest of the world? Chauncey Starr, of the University of California, estimated the present per capita energy consumption in the United States as five times the average for the world (including the United States). Assuming the world population increases by 100 per cent in the next thirty years and that population achieved the 1973 standard of living of the United States, the world-wide annual consumption of energy would be ten times the present amount.

Is this a reasonable, desirable, or possible goal for a small planet?

* * *

AUTOMOBILITY

> The car is fast becoming a threat to health, safety and comfort in city areas.
>
> —Leonard Woodcock,
> President, United Auto Workers
> (1972)

The Ford Foundation's *Exploring Energy Choices* (1974) provides three interesting scenarios, based on three alternatives for the future.

First, if *present trends continue:* this would require a "very aggressive" development of all possible energy resources, including those involving some danger (great expansion of nuclear power, considerable pollution) and those that would change the character of the lightly populated parts of the country (rural, ocean front, unindustrialized).

Second, if we *develop energy-saving technology* as a technical aim but do not attempt any significant reduction in the American standard of living, we will need expanding sources of energy—for example, coal and shale oil in the Rocky Mountain region.

Finally, if we accept *zero energy growth* that "would emphasize durability, not disposability as goals," we will be able to "substitute for the idea, 'more is better,' the ethic that 'enough is best.'"

This last proposition is the only one we believe desirable, but the report leaves unanswered "what is enough" as well as "enough of what." These are easy questions for the poverty-stricken masses to answer—enough food for us and our cattle, enough water for our parched fields—but for those like us far from the problems of survival, there are no clear-cut answers. To us, the day before yesterday's luxuries are yesterday's conveniences and today's necessities. The automobile is the obvious example.

From a luxury for the few, the automobile became a necessity for the many. Its mass use changed our ways of planning human settlements, becoming in many ways the decision-maker in design. Its convenience makes us lazy, its ubiquity destroys our townscapes, and its roads and parking lots use a disproportionate amount of land. To manufacture, maintain, and sell, the car employs a good-sized chunk of our skilled and unskilled work force; the gasoline required to fuel and the oil to lubricate it take a large part of the petroleum we use. By-products are air pollution and junk piles. It is the very image and symbol of the wasteful ways we cherish.

The automobile makers have been blamed for producing big cars when it was obvious that compacts were adequate for most functional needs. What the critics failed to see is that the car buyer sought, in addition to transport, ego reinforcement, the satisfaction of being the guide and master of a sleek bulk whose very name—be it Mustang, Comet, Thunderbird—evokes the free spirit.

The average man's love affair with his motorcar is no secret. Those on the assembly lines and in the bureaucracies denied power and initiative in their daily chores express their individuality, decision-making ability, and courage on the road by speeding, cutting in, braking within inches of disaster; at the curb in front of their houses, tinkering with their engines or polishing the coachwork, the pride of ownership is in their eyes. Bolstering the illusion of personal control and freedom is a real need in an economic structure that tends to offer more and more people less and less meaningful occupations—occupations that don't test the mettle but do wear down the spirit.

Who will deny that "folks in the United States," as General Motors announced in 1948, "are inclined to like flash and dash. Because of that, the popular American cars are big, fast, high powered, advanced in styling and asparkle with chrome." With such a demand, utility was never a criterion so it's not surprising that the average mileage per gallon of American cars fell from 15.3 mpg in 1940 to 13.7 mpg in 1969.

As resources diminish we are learning we could never afford the general use of cars weighing an average of 4,300 pounds nor the amount of gasoline required to move them. Nor could we afford urban transportation and land use planning requiring the majority of the working population to spend inordinate amounts of time and energy in daily long-distance shuttles from home to work. We are slowly learning that it is quite wasteful for 86 per cent of the Los Angeles–Long Beach metropolitan area work force to commute by automobile especially when 97 per cent of the cars have one rider. Across the continent the situation is but slightly different: 80 per cent of the commuters from New York's Suffolk and Rockland counties drive cars to work, and, in the New York region as a whole, 640,000 cars transport workers to their jobs each day and at least four fifths carry only the driver (U.S. Census, 1970).

In 1925 the United States had 17 million autos to serve a population of 116 million people. By 1970 we had 100 million cars with a population of 204 million. The projection for the year 2000 is (was?) 320 million autos to be used by 280 million of us. (By contrast, in Denmark, there is one car per four people, while in Indonesia there are three per thousand!)

As all this horsepower has to be fed, it's not surprising that since 1947 our annual consumption of petroleum products rose from 1.9 billion barrels to 5.6 billion, and not surprising that at this rate of increase the consensus is that *world* petroleum resources will be exhausted in thirty to forty years.

Coincidentally another resource that may be depleted is breathable air, since nationwide, 40 per cent of the air pollution is due to emissions from motor vehicles, and in the cities the estimate is 80 per cent. In New York City where only 27 per cent commute by car, the Department of Air Resources estimated in 1970 that cars, buses, and trucks poured out 77 per cent by weight of all the city's air pollution and found the Empire City's pollution typically three times higher than the danger point established by federal standards. Like other marvelous technical feats of the twentieth century, the automobile by its sheer multiplication has become a destructive force.

Comparatively speaking, all our other uses of energy pale into insignificance when we consider what it takes just getting ourselves and our goods from place to place. Our autos and trucks consume 40 per cent of all the petroleum used in this country and that is one eighth of all used in the world. Clearly, for the job that needs doing, it is too much.

The answer is not to ban the car, but, as with other tools and machines, to control its quantity and speed, size, complexity, and use as well as reduce the poisons it emits. For instance, a 2,000-pound car uses half the materials of a 4,000-pound car; a cruising speed of 50 mph should be acceptable to a species who up to seventy-five years ago only traveled faster when they fell off cliffs.

Also we must speak again and again of the need for transparency and repairability in tools. The car is no different. Let us strip away the gadgets and chrome and return to fundamentals of good, simple, and safe performance with attention to efficient choices resulting in lower pollution emissions. Perhaps a bit of redesign is needed? A return to the steam engine? Perhaps more of Rudolf Diesel's or Felix Wankel's engines instead of the one we favor. Not least is durability; a new model each year is so clearly folly it needs no comment. Our automobile designers have catered long enough to our vanities and adolescent dreams, the time has come for more mature design.

Finally, it is unreasonable to assume that we can possess one car for every two inhabitants and maintain a habitable world. Suppose the People's Republic of China with 750 million people decided on a policy to "overtake and surpass us" in car ownership? Or India with 570 million? We agree such possibilities are highly unlikely. What is much more than likely is that we'll run out of gas, so we might just as well adjust our planning now.

To conserve resources, to reduce accidents on our highways, to stop degrading the environment, can all be brought about by controlling the use of the car. This control directly affects the scope of our physical activities and how they mesh with those of our neighbors as plans based on such considerations strive for configurations that eliminate intermediary services that waste time, materials, and energy with no resulting benefit.

Over the years we have built not only a great number of factories to produce cars but all the supporting services in their multitudes; what will we do with this redundancy of parking lots, garages, and filling stations? I can imagine underground garages converted to root or wine cellars, or even presidential libraries; service stations to cafés or community workshops. But what *does* one do with redundant over- and underpasses, cloverleafs, and six-lane highways? Sort of big for kiddy slides and roller skating, but maybe good for bicycling and for sleigh riding in the winter?

Traffic crossover on Northern Boulevard, New York City (1940). "*Supplies a good example of parkway intersection, landscaped surroundings and parking areas as one unit*" (International Congress of Modern Architects, 1942).

COMMUTATION

It sounded like something wished for, rather than actual, when the Census Bureau announced that one of its findings in 1970 was "for every ten Americans who go to work by public transit, there are seven who walk." "In the suburbs," they added, "there are eight." Alas, it was that we didn't rightly read: The joke was the word *public*, for though 5.7 million Americans *did* walk to work, 60 million *drove* in their own cars. Even in the cities—excepting New York—public transit is a minor part in the nation's daily commute. In Los Angeles, 86 per cent of the workers go to work in their own cars, in Chicago 67 per cent, in Washington 74 per cent. Only in New York City do we find the other way round—59 per cent do use public transit.

The automobile created the demand for the good road, the good road created a demand for more cars, which called for more good roads—ad infinitum. "The nation's highways have been able to disperse our factories, our stores, our people; in short, to create a revolution in living habits. Our cities have spread into the suburbs, dependent on the automobile for their existence." So read the *President's Advisory Committee on a National Highway Program in 1955*. Lewis Mumford, far from seeing this as a benefit, commented, "When the American people through their Congress voted . . . for a $26 billion highway program, the most charitable thing to assume about this action is that they hadn't the faintest notion of what they were doing."

Back then when General Eisenhower was President, one of the reasons he gave for advocating the 42,500-mile highway system was, "In case of an atomic attack on our cities, the road network will permit quick evacuation of target areas." As the commuter finds his car in the daily traffic jam, moving (if at all) at ten miles an hour, it seems Lewis Mumford, in addition to being right in condemning the peacetime effect of the road system, would be proved right in an atomic war (that is, if anyone survived to tell of it).

One of the results of our highway building is that the largest city in America now surrounds New York City. These suburbs contained 8.9 million people in 1970, over a million more than the city itself, and

spread over 2,100 square miles, some 600 miles more
than Los Angeles and its suburbs combined. Spread
City, as it has been called, has such a low density
(some seven people to the acre) that it cannot support
public transportation since the simplest system requires
five to ten families (twenty-five to forty people) per
acre to be economical.

Increasingly suburban areas have divorced themselves from the towns that spawned them. Even in a
center like New York City, half the employment is now
in the periphery and most suburbanites neither work,
play, nor shop in the city. The sponsors of the National
Highway Program claimed in 1955 that "the automobile . . . had brought the city and the country closer
together, it has made us one country, and a united people." Exactly the opposite is true. In New York City
(and it is no exception) 2 million whites fled the city in
the last twenty years, while in the suburbs the 95 per
cent white population strive to keep it that way.

Autoland

Suburbanites are, as the 1955 report said, completely
dependent on the private automobile: to get to work, to
school, to visit, to buy a newspaper. All these trips
require not only wheels but someone to guide them,
hence the two-car family with Mom chauffeuring the
children. Later, of course, when the children become
"of driving age" three cars are needed, each requiring
space at home, on the road, and at the parking lot.
Each car (if the family is frugal) represents sixty horses
who, we are told, stand immobile for twenty-two hours
each day.

One would think that with a suburban population
density of about two families to the acre, lots of people
would have kitchen gardens. There are no statistics but
anyone's eyes tell him nothing is raised except "foundation planting" and lawns in Spread City. There are

no chickens, cows, or pigs raised, just lots of cats and dogs.[4]

The speculative builder, balance sheet in hand, says that to produce the suburban house type (single family, detached) at least cost, land should be as little marred by nature's eccentricities as possible. Trees and hills are bulldozed and rocky outcrop blasted flat to reduce road and sewer costs and permit convenient duplication. If a little nature rape results in a lower sales cost, will the consumer quibble? If more profit, will the developer complain? Planning with nature, on the other hand, takes wit and sensibility, qualities that when applied, use up time and money, both, as we know, always in short supply. In the old days streets were laid out in rectangles with all plots alike, simplifying survey work and land speculation; now the roads are curvilinear ("picturesque"). Forty years after Radburn the cul-de-sac street pattern is popular but Clarence Stein's best contribution, the dual circulation system (the road side of the houses is for service while at the rear are found pedestrian paths in a park), doesn't appeal to developers or home buyers.

Architects and planners well aware of the disastrous ecological impact of suburban sprawl have proposed (a) "cluster" zoning (groups of houses bunched together leaving the surrounding land in its more or less natural state) or (b) Le Corbusier's *unité d'habitation* (isolated multistory apartment towers in the greenery). Neither of these propositions suits the locals, for they fear—and who can prove them wrong—once the cluster or the tower is built, no one can guarantee the open space will be kept open, especially if property values increase.

While such schemes would preserve some natural

[4] "The President of the Association of Fish Canners in Morocco once told me that a cheap canned fish developed for the middle eastern market, primarily Egypt, brought a better price in the United States as cat food. One third of the canned fish sold in the United States is in effect pet food" (Georg Borgstrom).

features, neither alleviates the transportation problem of Spread City. That can only be solved by the streets of a metropolis or the close-knit plans of those small towns which we think so great when in the hills of Tuscany or on the plains of Normandy. (Yet as we speed away, we remember how difficult it was to get a good shot of the cathedral without finding all those cars in the view finder.)

It does seem that something more drastic than planned communities such as Reston in Virginia and Cumbernauld in Scotland is required. A program comes to mind: "bringing into cultivation waste lands, improving the soil, abolishing the difference between town and country by a more equitable distribution of population over the country and by combining agriculture with manufacturing industries." But I guess it won't do being dated 1850, being written by Marx and Engels, and being from *The Communist Manifesto*.

Mobility

Have we reverted to a more primitive society? From a people settled in city or farm to a nomadic life? It would appear so, for in our time, some of the greatest mass migrations in history have occurred. In foreign lands for the same old reasons—war and famine. Here the story is different. Our poor, on the whole, have been seduced into mass migrations by the misguided policies of well-meaning big-city bureaucrats, while many in the middle class are moved around as if they were pawns on a chessboard by the corporate structures in which they function. Among all of us there is the ever-present desire to conspicuously consume, so trips to Puerto Rico or Paris are not exceptional; romanticized by airlines and hotels, tourism probably calls for dispensing more gasoline per customer than any other part of the economy except the daily commute.

It is a fine thing to travel, to see strange places and

new faces. I would believe an energy-conserving society will afford this luxury for those who want it. The traveler may drop out of the sky in London or Prague just like today except that he will then spend a month wandering the byways on foot or by bike. Perhaps stopping to sketch along the way. Sketch! It takes more time and skill than snapping away with the camera but what's the rush? Besides, what with the shortages of materials, both camera and film may become outlandishly expensive.

The root definition of commutation is "to change one thing for another." But there is no point in going from the frying pan into the fire or jet to Damascus to drink Coca-Cola at the Hilton Hotel.

*   *   *

How the use of many modern devices tends to isolate people! The driver, solitary in his car, the radio blaring, windows closed, his eyes fixed on the concrete ribbon unrolling at seventy miles an hour, is the very image of man in the artificial world he has made.

CHAPTER X

Pollution

Everything comes from everything, and everything is made from everything, and everything can be turned into everything; because that which exists in the elements is composed of those elements.

—Leonardo da Vinci

We're prone to boast, fabricating false images of our abilities, exaggerating our achievements; we begin to believe a computer is a brain because we call it one and we have a glib way of referring to "spaceship earth." These are poor metaphors, for our printed circuits and tapes are mere hardware and those contraptions we hurl into the upper air are flimsy things made of string and oddments; their technology when compared to nature, as rudimentary as the chipping of stone arrowheads.

A century ago scientists were promising the conquest of nature. Nowadays we pretend to know better, yet we still seem intent on changing the horn of plenty into Pandora's box, changing that part of nature which has been beneficial to us into malevolence. The land, sea, and air we pollute poison only us, for to nature the airlessness of space is as much part of her as that mile or so of earth's atmosphere in which we move as do goldfish in a bowl.

In our time we have gone far in transforming the oasis on which we live—forests into deserts, lakes into morasses—as if our aim were to return the planet to an earlier stage: rocks and lifeless space bathed in hydrogen and methane gases, ammonia and watery vapors.

The ways of modern man have been destructive to his habitat. In a state of nature the animals graze, manure the land while they live, and when they die their bones enrich the soil on which they grew. Now we cage the animals in concrete feed lots, and the massed droppings pollute the nearby fields and streams. We salt over wintry roads to melt the snow, the brine runs off, the water in nearby wells is no longer fit to drink, the brackish ground water kills trees miles away. As if by intention we have managed to multiply simple processes so that substances, useful to man through the ages, are turned into poisons.

The most obvious example of our polluting capacity is the mounting trash heap that threatens to engulf major parts of the industrialized world. In all lands as affluence grows, so grows the garbage heaps. For instance, in 1967 the major dumping area in Tokyo Bay was full, and with wry Oriental humor the city named it Dream Island. Now the only dump left overflows and the garbage must go elsewhere. The question is where? Ryokichi Minobe, the governor of Tokyo (with wry Oriental humor?), said, "When it comes to physical environment, Tokyo is a far from ideal place to live in. In fact, I must admit Tokyo is decidedly unsuitable for living. Indeed, this is the most frustrating part of Tokyo's life."

In the 1970s the situation in New York City is no different, for here is generated 30,000 tons of refuse daily[1] and like Tokyo and its own suburbs we are running out of land to dump on. New York sewers pour 400 million gallons of raw sewage into its metropolitan waterways, and another 629 million gallons of "inadequately treated" sewage ends up in the Hudson River and its harbor. Such conditions led the Federal Water Pollution Control Advisory Board to recommend a moratorium on all new buildings until adequate sewage treatment plants are built.

This city provides a classic case of solutions attempted by treating defects instead of eliminating causes as the following proposition demonstrates. *The more sewage plants that are built, the less contamination by raw sewage.* However, the more sewage plants, the more sludge. (Sewage sludge is what is left after sewage water is cleaned in a treatment plant.) In New York City the sludge is dumped into the sea, a reprehensible practice soon (it is hoped) to be banned under the Federal Pure Water laws. An alternative is to

[1] More than Tokyo, Paris, and London combined!

burn the sludge, an intolerable proposal for a metropolitan area where the air is already far from meeting
safe health standards. Another alternative is to dump
the sludge on land. This would require fifty-five square
miles a year to handle the output from existing sewer
treatment plants; adding the sludge of those under construction would raise the area needed to 165 square
miles per year. Since there is no land available for such
purposes, there is nothing to do but continue dumping
into the New York Bight as we have been for the last
forty years. *Problem:* Twelve miles off Sandy Hook is
a "dead sea" which each year expands and now
threatens Long Island bathing beaches.

Or consider Long Island, that eastern suburb and
major recreation area of New York City. We read of its
water supplies contaminated by the outflow from individual cesspools discharging 400 million gallons of untreated waste each day into the underground reservoir
which constitutes the island's only source of drinking
water. So there is a cry for sewers. Opponents of
sewers see another picture. If sewers are built, then
there will be a dry Long Island, its vast water supplies
being pumped out to sea through the sewage treatment
plants, its creeks and wetlands drying up, its waterfowl
and sea life disappearing. In 1972, examining the problems facing the New York region, William Ruckelhaus,
then head of the federal Environmental Protection
Agency, said it: "This situation indicates how the handling of one environmental problem often leads to another."

In 1973 the National League of Cities and U. S.
Conference of Mayors reported it costs our cities $6
billion annually to dispose of trash and within five
years they will run out of places to dump the junk totaling 250 million tons yearly. It seems a lot of money
and a lot of junk but what was to be expected when
between 1940 and 1960 our garbage pile increased by
130 per cent while our population increase was only 33
per cent.

A product in one place is beneficial, in another a poison; sludge is an example. In 1967 the annual production of chemically produced fertilizer was 15.5 million tons, apparently not nearly enough to provide for both rich and poor nations. Sludge happens to be a perfectly splendid fertilizer. Why, one wonders, is it a problem instead of a resource?

A second example is that in early 1975 a presidential advisory committee recommended a "resumption of an all-returnable beverage container system" as it "could almost immediately save an energy equivalent of nearly 5 million gallons of gasoline per day . . . equal to the estimated energy yield by 1978 from a crash program to produce oil from shale rock—a project which will involve the expenditure of billions of dollars in capital investment, unprecedented environmental disturbance and the daily creation of a pile of waste rock six times larger than the Lincoln Memorial."

Those bottles, cans, and cars that fill our dumps and junk yards cost our cities $6 billion a year to destroy although it has been estimated some 16 to 24 per cent of this junk is recoverable, the metals alone worth $5 billion if recycled.

Still another example is paper. Georg Borgstrom wrote: "It had been estimated that if the paper waste of the United States was collected and transformed by chemical methods into sugar, this would take care of one-third of the caloric needs of the U.S. population." It's a likely estimate, since in packaging alone, the forecast was a 63 per cent increase between 1958 and 1976, most of it paper, 90 per cent landing on the scrap heap.

None of these examples is meant to suggest that I think it economical to cut down four hundred acres of trees to turn out an edition of the New York *Times* and then sweeten our breakfast coffee with recycled newsprint, or economical to junk a refrigerator for its metal. Aside from other considerations, although recycling slows the exhaustion process, each conversion is a downgrading; "there is no free recycling, just as there is no wasteless industry" (Professor Georgescu-Roggen).

In 1970 the Federal Clean Air Act was passed. It called for reductions in emissions from automobiles by as much as 90 per cent by 1976. Just two years later the Tri-state Transportation Commission representing New York, New Jersey, and Connecticut estimated that by 1985 there would be a 50 per cent increase in travel by automobile and a 60 per cent increase in trucking. Since our engineers have found no economical way of reducing pollution from gasoline engines by any substantial percentage, either the law must be changed or there must be fewer engines used. As all agree, enforcement of the law will benefit public health, and as goods must be delivered and people make their journeys, it is obvious that shipping freight by rail and people by train or bus is the solution simply because less fuel is burned per ton of goods or pound of passenger delivered.

The difference in fuel consumption between rail and road is not minor. By automobile (1969) it takes 1,775 gallons of fuel to move five hundred persons at two per car 100 miles. To move the same number the same distance by rail required 250 gallons. A trailer-truck consumes about 960 gallons on a Chicago–San Francisco round trip. The same load on a piggyback train would require 230 gallons. As almost a quarter (24.8 per cent in 1974) of our total energy use goes into powering transportation, there are compelling reasons for change. But desirable as it may be, a switch from road to rail, from private conveyance to public, is not simple, since most people now live in scattered patterns dependent on the automobile. It will take time and effort to redress the pattern so that once again towns are scaled to walking distances and dense enough to warrant public transportation.

According to Barry Commoner, total production—as measured by gross national product—increased by 126 per cent from 1946 to 1971 while most pollution levels have risen at least several times that amount due not to increases in the manufacture of basic food, shelter, and clothing (which have just about kept up with population growth) but to all the conveniences, comfort and luxury items we have produced, from synthetic detergents to snowmobiles. The result has been the enormous surge in fuel demand which characterized this period (as well as providing the figures used to forecast future needs) resulting in the present crisis. It *is* startling to find that in less than a decade—1963 to 1972—United States consumption of petroleum products went from under 11 million barrels a day to over 16 million.

The problem is always one of selection. Since there is no wasteless industry, what shall we give up if we want to reduce pollution? If we want more and more things, we'll need more power to make them as well as run them. Nuclear power will be the recommended option even though "at the present time there is no harmless peaceful use of atomic radiation except as a meticulously controlled tool for atomic research"[2] and there is apparently no safe way of getting rid of radioactive wastes.

In 1974 the Atomic Energy Commission described the need for shutting down ten nuclear plants because there was insufficient space to store their nuclear wastes. Presently these plants have large pools of water next to each reactor to accommodate the discharge of a fuel load in the event of an emergency. The shortage of storage space led to placing so much waste in these pools they no longer serve the purpose for which they were designed. An alternative suggestion was to allow the use of the pools for storage if special "shrouds" were made as shields. However, this was rejected since it "would open up a new risk of sabotage because removing the shrouds would turn the basins into uncontrolled and uncontained nuclear reactors." Another

[2] National Academy of Science, 1972.

approach would be to ship the spent fuel to places outside the United States. The hitch is that small amounts
of reprocessed fuel could be made into nuclear bombs
as the task of safeguarding the material from theft
presented "almost unsurmountable obstacles."

Although there is no way of getting rid of radioactive waste and no economical way of avoiding the pollution resulting from the present manufacture of nuclear power, plants are being built everywhere.

When environmentalists scream, the public relations
message is changed from "No danger at all" to "Well,
maybe some, but not to have the plant is worse." Typical in this line is a report on the proposed Indian Point
nuclear plant #3 on the Hudson River not far from
New York City where it is agreed "Significant danger
to fish and other aquatic life could be expected even if
the plant was run at half capacity" *but* permission to
build should be granted because "probable environmental impact" had to be balanced against possible
"emergency reductions" in metropolitan area electrical
supplies.

Is this the only choice? In a place like New York
would it not be wiser to reduce power requirements by
cutting down on floodlighting, electric displays, unnec-
essarily high lighting standards, construction of sealed-
tight buildings needing all-year artificial climates, structures whose heights may have no relation to desirable
human usage but do require high-speed elevators, and
so on? Are these too much to give up in order to have
some surety of a healthy environment, possibly even
one in which we can survive?

Environmental pollution is pervasive. The International Labor Organization reports that the hearing of
forest workers is being impaired as a result of noise
generated by power saws, pneumatic hammers, tractors, and other machines. But other damage is less
measurable. What is the result of the purposeless noise
pollution caused by big-city sounds—screaming ambu-

lances and fire engines, the groans and grunts of badly made truck and bus brakes, the roar of subways. . . . And what of the purposeful pollution—the rowdy music coming from transistor radios, the sugary noises seeping out of walls, the television commercials? We may not know what effect visual pollution has on our physical being, but surely the architecture of used-car lots and development houses lifts not the spirit nor can we believe anyone is benefited by the sight of spilled garbage, beer cans by the highway, or auto graveyards.

Then, of course, there is the variety of stinks special to our modern technology, all warning signals to which we pay little heed.

Pollution is not merely a by-product of bad technology, it is a side effect of living itself. Our problem is that we pollute with substances and in ways that do not amalgamate with symbiotic processes favorable to us, so we are poisoned. *We*, not nature, for all is grist in nature's mill whether it be cancers and leprosies, the swirling vapors of Venus or purling brooks and the trill of birds.

CHAPTER XI

Hygeia and Cloacina

To demonstrate the fervor of Christianity in medieval France, Henry Adams in *Mont-Saint-Michel and Chartres* tells us the faithful built eighty cathedrals and five hundred churches of cathedral size between 1170 and 1270, "which would have cost according to an estimate made in 1840, more than 5,000 millions to replace. Five thousand million francs is a thousand million dollars and this covers only the great churches of a single century." When one considers that being part of such an endeavor was believed to be a guarantee of blissful eternal life, it seems a small effort when compared to our worship of the Goddess Hygeia a millennium later who promises much less.

Surely rarely in history has there been a cult with so many willing adherents who so lavishly gave of their time and substance to build to their goddess household shrines, shrines of gleaming porcelain, ceramic, and polished metal. Never have there been so many tracts and pamphlets distributed, such well-paid priests in person and on television screens exhorting the faithful to possess themselves of unguents, fluids, and pastes, perfumed, bubbling, wet and dry in infinite variety to be used in increasingly elaborate ceremonials; for the ritual bathing of the parts, eyes, legs, underarms, crotch, etc., each requiring its own blessed treatment whose purpose is to make us animals smell like flowers, grow hair or remove it, and (though there is no money-back guarantee) magically halt the aging process.

The ritual, like eating in certain savage tribes, is carried out in secret, a custom that may have developed because in Hygeia's shrine is included a fitting dedicated to another—the unmentionable Cloacina, goddess of the Roman sewer. This fitment is as concealed as means allow, and the noise created when sending the offering (well mixed with the purest water) to the subterranean dwelling of the goddess is considered singularly embarrassing. Which does not prevent public announcements extolling the virtues of benefices in the form of douches, tablets, and liquids all designed to speed the offering through the intestine and then to Cloacina's storehouse.

We do have laws separating church and state, yet the influence of the twin goddesses is so insidious and pervasive that our very Census Bureau calls houses without indoor bath and toilet facilities "substandard," a perjorative term that could be applied to the palaces of all the kings, possibly excepting Knossos in Crete (if we can trust the findings of Sir Arthur Evans). Since to be below the standard in an affluent society is a form of heresy, increasingly the aim is to have more than one such room in order to be on the safe side. Thus we have the fulfillment of a 1954 prophecy called *A Bathroom of 1979*. According to this text, "There will be more bathrooms generally, perhaps as many as one for each bedroom, plus a powder room off the kitchen. There will be more fixtures also (twin lavatories, a dental lavatory, a bidet)." A statement of faith, but only the echo of the deed of an earlier priest, Ellsworth Statler, who in the year 1908 created a slogan for his new hotel in Buffalo, New York—"a room and a bath for a dollar and a half."

As the bathroom proliferated, economy suggested more compact layouts with the fixtures arranged in a row to simplify plumbing. The tub 5'0" long established the minimum width of the room, and the usual three fixtures tub, toilet, and basin set a length of at least 7'0". Designs of this sort were offered as early as 1908 and, excepting for the built-in as contrasted with the claw-footed bathtub, look much like those of today. Such rooms with their furnishings are complicated and expensive. Even after the space has been built and the fixtures fabricated, to complete the work requires the skills of seven trades—plumbers, tinsmiths, electricians, tile setters, plasterers, painters, glaziers. Considering the cost of field labor and the great demand for a product having standard dimensions and composed of elements individually mass-produced, it is not surprising that architects, engineers, and popular mechanics designed and patented notions for prefabricating bathrooms as complete units delivered to the job site like refrigerators, needing only a couple of screw turns to connect the pipes. No new idea, as the Pullman Company had devised ingenious washing and toilet arrangements which were built into their sleeping cars before 1914.

It is a classic case of technological lag in the construction industry that even at this late date only mobile homes have prefab plumbing as part of their equipment. This, as we mention elsewhere, because mobile homes are considered vehicles so not accountable to labor unions, building codes, and other restrictions that affect brick-and-mortar construction.

The compact, claustrophobic, mechanically ventilated and windowless cells are the sanctuaries in which, behind closed doors, we carry out the secret rites of bathing and excretion, activities previously separate but now linked for technical convenience rather than functional desirability. Thanks to ample water supplies and adequate pumping mechanisms, the cells may be placed where we please. Such a possibility was available to the well-to-do by the turn of the century as was the complete bathroom, although only one such room served an entire household (at separate times, of course!). Quite a change from the street fountains of history or even 1850, when water pipes were first brought into the basements of houses in better-class neighborhoods.

Who can say what led to the juxtaposition of ablution and waste removal? Was it simply technical convenience as we've just said or was it that prudery found it useful—"I must wash my hands" (for we call it *the bathroom*). If the unmentionable loo and john, W.C., crapper, shitter, or the older jakes (in German and Israeli hotels, the room is marked cryptically o-o) is located in the same place as the bath, it's another plus for the prude. The bath, by association, also becomes a secret activity. The washbasin, in the house of means, once part of the dressing room or bedroom, takes its place beside the tub, and the triumvirate is complete—body care, like the genitals, is concealed.

For the city's poor in the earlier part of the twentieth century, the pattern was slightly different. First a privy in the yard for the entire tenement, then a toilet in the public hall, one on each floor, serving as many as four apartments (they were called flats). All washing—people, clothes, pots, dishes—occurred in or at the kitchen sink and attached washtub. There were also public baths sometimes privately operated. Your author still remembers with pleasure his visits to *les bains publiques* in Fontainebleau. One entered through a Pompeian-style courtyard and after collecting soap and towels luxuriated in zinc tubs having huge brass faucets in the form of swan heads from whose beaks hot and cold water gushed, all under the supervision of neat little old women. But in general, the worship of Hygeia today is far from the ways of our ancestors in every country and every age.

George Bernard Shaw once said that hygiene was 10 per cent sanitation and 90 per cent aesthetics. We would add that through the ages bathing was 10 per cent hygiene and 90 per cent socializing. The remains of the Roman baths are proof enough suggesting a lavishness of size, structure, and ornament obviously unnecessary for a mere bathhouse. These buildings were huge; the Baths of Diocletian over seven hundred feet long containing theaters, a library, discussion rooms, exercise courts, and the like, in addition to elaborate bathing facilities with a sequence of body oiling, exercise, dry heat, steam, massage, warm and cold plunges—a sensuous dream all taking place in marbled

halls whose floors were kept warm with underground
heating ducts and whose air was perfumed with myrtle
and roses. Those who remember the waiting room of
the old Pennsylvania Station in New York have some
idea of the size and elaboration of these baths, for that
hall was copied from the tepidarium of the Thermae of
Caracalla in Rome.

At different periods in the Empire's history such establishments were used by men only, or men and
women separately, or promiscuously. Naturally, when
the pagan gods were banned, the church fathers also
banned the baths—one should bathe, if at all, through
necessity, not for pleasure.

The architectural historian Viollet-le-Duc tells us "no
one is unaware of the care given by the Romans to
their public and private baths. The ancients not only
considered hot and cold baths as one of the best means
to maintain health but in addition it suited their customs and was a pleasure. One went to the baths not
only to bathe but to socialize, get the day's news, discuss business and pleasures. These uses, which belong
to an advanced civilization, must have been consid-
erably changed by the barbarian invasions. However, if
we can trust Tacitus, the Germans got up late and
often bathed in warm water, after which they had
breakfast. Charlemagne seemed to have adopted the
Roman customs in this respect. Eginhard said that the
Prince very much liked thermal baths 'in love with
swimming, Charles became so skilled that none could
compare. He therefore built a palace at Aix-La Cha-
pelle where he lived during the last years of his life
and where he died. He invited to bathe with him not
only his sons, but also his friends, the court nobles and
sometimes even his soldiers and palace guard, often
100 or more people bathed together.' No question that
Charlemagne in this as in other things took up the an-
tique Roman ways. We don't find," Viollet-le-Duc continues, "such large installations after the 10th century,
and baths from the 12th century on are but estab-

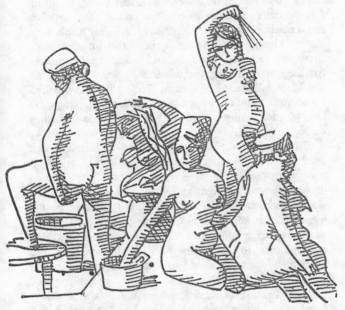

The women's bath (after Dürer, 1496).

lishments analogous to those we have today [1899] though much more commodious. During the XIII century, it was common usage for the sexes to bathe together in the same tub. Bath houses were often found as witness the number of old towns with their Rue des Étuves."

Let us add that many medieval illuminated manuscripts show naked men and women eating, drinking, and in general appearing to have a good time in the bath. No wonder such institutions ultimately came to be known as "stews" and "bagnio" became a synonym for whorehouse.

The so-called Turkish bath (now called health club) is found in many American cities and on the whole is but a poor parody of those remarkable and beautiful Islamic bathing places such as the one at the Alhambra in Granada or the seventeenth-century Yeni Kaplioja in Bursa. Though not huge like those the Romans built, they were equally luxurious and made up in number for their smaller size, spread as they were through all the lands influenced by Islam: Persia, Egypt, the Balkans, Asia Minor. In just one tenth-century Spanish city—Córdoba—there were at least nine hundred such baths.

The regimen was somewhat similar to Rome, a hall used for dressing and relaxation (*Maslak*), a hot-air room where massages were given, a steam room, a soap massage, a cool plunge, and then back to the *Maslak*.

The baths in Arab lands, according to Hassan Fathy, were for rich and poor a "gathering place where men could exchange news, gossip, conduct business and discuss politics in an atmosphere of luxury. For the women the *hamman* would provide an excuse to escape the restrictions of the house." Here was the place where a bride was chosen, where before the wedding day she would be "combed, scented and depilated and made ready for the ceremony."[1]

In Japan it is told that a Japanese emperor aimed to introduce modesty to his people along with other Western imports. He decreed that all persons bathing in the sea change their habit by wearing some minimum of clothing. His people obeyed in their usual literal fashion, playing naked on the beach until ready for the briny, at which time they slipped on their bathing costumes.

"There are some 800 public baths in Tokyo in which it is calculated that 300,000 bathe daily—other cities and villages are similarly provided. Where there are neither bathing establishments nor private bathrooms the people take their bath out-of-doors, unless a policeman charged with carrying out the new regulations

[1] *Architecture for the Poor.*

happens to be prowling about the neighborhood; for cleanliness is more esteemed by the Japanese than artificial Western prudery" (1891).

"In all Japanese baths, public and private, there is no attempt to achieve privacy. Public baths for instance will have large unprotected openings through which people in the street can watch the bathers" (1928).

Thanks to the recent popularity of the sauna, we are all familiar with the Russian or Finnish bath, an institution whose origins date back to pre-Christian times. Here we have nothing luxurious: a wooden hut, inside are some benches in raised tiers, a pile of red-hot stones on which water is thrown. In the steamy air your neighbor slapped you with a wisp of leaves and you slapped him. After a while out for a roll in the snow or a douse of cold water. Such baths were used by men and women alike. "Plank partitions separate the sexes but since both sexes leave the bath naked, they see one another in this condition and stand conversing upon the most indifferent matters." At least that's how it was in Siberia in 1761, according to M. l'abbé Jean Chappe d'Auteroche.

There are still some of us who go on camping trips without trailers attached to our cars, or who remember living in country farmhouses with the privy (outhouse) out in back, or who remember the honey buckets of the army. It was city crowding that made the toilet bowl we use and its pipes and sewers a necessity once we'd discovered germs. Up to modern times most of our cities stank and some still do. Louis XIV built Versailles because the Louvre, surrounded by its shit-filled moats, stank, and at Versailles, as we've all been told, there was neither bath nor privy; the courtiers deposited their droppings behind the draperies, though the Grand Monarque himself held audiences sitting on his *chaise percée*. Samuel Pepys, as well as Samuel Johnson's Boswell, tells the same story of streets—chamber pots emptied out of upper windows, the passer-by counting himself fortunate if he had only the stink to endure and not a wet hat as well.

The privy has had many forms, from the "thunder board" described in the *Decameron* (the narrow Florentine alley, a board on sawhorses, excrement in piles, buzzing blue bottles); to that monstrous invention of a madman spread through Europe by sadists, where on two raised pedestals, islands in the form of footprints, we stand like some Colossus of Rhodes; below, instead of clear and sparkling water, is (if you're lucky and not in Turkey) the partially washed away excrement of the last dozen comfort seekers; to the clever and quite different privy of Japan. "The privy generally has two compartments—the first one having a wooden or porcelain urinal, the latter being called *asagawa*, as it is supposed to resemble the flower of a morning glory (the word literally means 'morning face'). The wooden ones are often filled with branches of spruce which are frequently replenished. The inner compartment has a rectangular opening cut in the floor,

A privy in Asakusa, Japan (after E. S. Morse, 1886).

and in the better class of privies this is provided with a cover having a long wooden handle. The woodwork about this opening is often lacquered. Straw sandals or wooden clogs are often provided to be worn in this place" (Edward Morse). Over this opening one squats, arms extended holding a horizontal bar more or less in the position of a seven-day bike racer.

To the late nineteenth century belongs the change from the ice-cold visits to outdoor privies or noisome chamber pots to the luxury of a toilet bowl that could be flushed. The ultimate luxury of such a fixture for one's very own is real mid-century American.

CONCLUSIONS FROM THIS HISTORY

We may assume several things from this brief history. First, that the most admired and civilized of societies got along very well without the "bathroom" we use. Therefore, it is no improved survival tool but simply a utility of comparatively recent origin developed to suit certain attitudes toward bodily functions.

Second, that bathrooms such as ours are not the only way to keep up a reasonably acceptable aesthetic appearance, an adequate state of olfactory neutrality, and the maintenance of reasonable cleanliness required to remain physically healthy and attractive.

Third, that the bath as we know it does not provide the variety of temperatures, dry airs, wet vapors, and the like best suited to invigorate and clean the body.

Fourth, that the private bathroom like so many of our modern devices has effectively destroyed what must have been one of the most pleasant ways of socializing known to our forebears.

Finally, as the cost in nonreplaceable resources for providing these modern facilities is large and there is a reasonable doubt as to whether their present form is the most efficacious and their present quantity strictly necessary for good health or high culture, we may conclude that a re-examination of the twentieth-century bathroom is in order.

Great oaks from little acorns grow. In our Deep South a black woman whose feet hurt sat down in the "white" section of a bus and almost a century after the Civil War, started a movement to complete it. In the late 1920s at the Bauhaus in Germany a girl who had a stomach-ache found the women's toilet door jammed and went into the men's, inspiring the students to tear down the *Frauen* and *Herren* signs, and so promiscuous use of plumbing became the school's custom. This may, fifty years later, come to pass everywhere, for what used to be called the private parts are no longer so private. It appears the time is near when the door will be ripped off the bathroom. Once this happens, once the mania for concealment of natural acts is cured, then a more communal use of bathing and toilet facilities becomes psychologically acceptable, good news to the conservationist, for the saving, in materials and energy use would be great. Just as an example, consider the New York City Building Code which requires a school dormitory to have a minimum of one shower or tub for every eight occupants and one lavatory for every twelve, while the minimum for a dwelling unit (on the average, fewer than three people) is one of each kind of fixture.

We are interested in such savings but more interested in the potential of the bathing place—yes, and water closet place as well—as social spaces. Once taken in this context, they become strong elements in the plan organization of the dwelling unit, since instead of being minimum-sized elements tucked away as adjuncts to bedrooms they take on a public role, so should be commodious in size and pleasant to be in.

An interesting matter in this connection is frequency of use. For the bowels and bladder, convenience of a facility is (often) imperative. This recommends a relatively close proximity to the user. Perhaps one hundred feet is a desirable maximum, though it might be increased if we returned to the chamber pot (a clear possibility in places where water shortages may occur and the climate is chill). May we not in time return to an ancient Roman way shown by the ruins in Timgad, where twenty-five pierced stone seats each separated by a carved dolphin were grouped around three sides of a large stone-floored room in the middle of which a fountain once played?

The proximity of a bath is not so essential except for invalids as these (perhaps true) anecdotes suggest: It is said of Queen Bess that she bathed once a month "whether she needed it or not." At a famous college in Cambridge the master argued against the expense of installing baths remarking that "these young men are only with us for eight weeks at a time." And some of us have heard that the founding mother of that essentially American religious denomination, Christian Science, considered the daily bathing of the whole body unnecessary and the daily ablutions of children no more natural and necessary than daily taking a fish out of water and covering it with dirt.

It does seem true that much oil is sold to make up for the grease we boil out of our bodies in our daily tub or shower. It does seem we burn a lot of fuel to heat the water, and it does seem the burning dirties the air, thus dirtying us as well as our clothes, requiring the daily bath for us and much use of the washing machine for them. Both requiring fuel which dirties the air, thus dirtying us, etc.

If a reduction in energy will do anything, it will surely clean the air and it seems certain that if there is less energy used there will be fewer products made and fewer vehicles needed to deliver them. There will then be less need for building and for paved areas, all positive ways of reducing summer temperatures and air-conditioning loads. In short there are synergistic effects.

Bathing in time may become not the daily necessity it is but a pleasure, opening the possibility of bathing establishments perhaps not as lavish as those in ancient Rome, since we are a democratic people, our means are limited, and there are many of us.

CHAPTER XII

Land

The United States has over 3,500,000 square miles of land, and in 1970 a population of 203,212,000 people; an average density of 56.5 people to the square mile. Almost three quarters of the people (149.3 million) lived on about 1½ per cent of the land (some 54,000 square miles), an area roughly equivalent to the state of Florida.

Since World War II there have been two opposite characteristics in the movement of people on the land: a marked trend toward concentration in a few areas and a dispersed pattern of settlement within the areas. Thus between 1960 and 1970 our urban areas grew 34.5 per cent (12,865 square miles) while the number

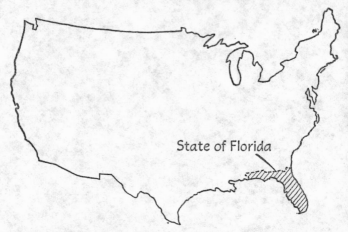

State of Florida

Almost all the "urbanized" land in the United States could be placed in the state of Florida, leaving the balance in farm and wilderness.

of urban dwellers increased only 19.2 per cent. The use
of the word "urban" in the context of these statistics
must not conjure up visions of Paris, London, or Tokyo,
but the definition by the Bureau of the Census. In their
usage an "urban area" is a city of at least 50,000 people and its built-up suburbs, and an "urban dweller"
may be someone living in a place with as few as 2,500
inhabitants.

Nationally the average urban population density is
2,800 persons to the square mile, fewer than 4.5 to the
acre! This is not even garden city concentration but
spacious suburb, since even Los Angeles, that spread
city, has about 6,000 people to the square mile.

We conclude that even in those areas called *urban*
there is ample space, and since they use but a small
fraction of the available land there can be no scarcity
in any foreseeable future, so no reason for crowding.
This should be good news as it suggests we, unlike
many countries, can plan well because we have the
space to do it in. But it is not good news since our history is a record of land used for the wildest speculation, of land ravaged in the using.

From the earliest days land in America was considered a commodity, not only by kings, adventurers,
and trading companies but by the settlers as well, for
this soil had no past to which one was attached, no
parish church or family graveyard; only untraveled
wastes inhabited by Indian tribes and other wildlife to
be hunted down for food, sport, or survival. The land
was mapped into easily salable strips: four-square, 640-
acre "sections" and then into rectangular lots except
where oddities like waterways or mountains interfered
with the symmetry.

There was nothing novel in using the quadrilateral in
planning; it was already ancient when Hippodamus
brought it to Piraeus in Pericles' time and it became
the stamp of Roman towns. What was novel was the
laying out of a vast territory on such a pattern as
Thomas Jefferson did when he originated the "national

grid," a plan resulting in the Land Ordinance of 1785 devised for the disposal of western lands. Townships were laid out called the Hundreds, each ten by ten miles with boundaries due north and south crossing each other at right angles, each in turn divided into mile squares. Into these, willy-nilly, towns were to be built, and if there were no takers then cattle would be grazed or corn planted. A writer recalled that in 1855 so many people had come to Nebraska to found cities that a bill had to be introduced "reserving every tenth section for farming purposes"!

In 1936 the National Resources Committee summarized the problems of American land use in a historic description:

> The fact is that most of the territory occupied by the United States is not naturally suited for a permanent civilization. It is like the land of the Mayas of Yucatan or the land of Babylon—a rich country where a civilization can flash into a blaze of glory and then collapse in a few generations into ruin. Our soil is not enriched by the usual methods of cultivation, but impoverished. By the normal processes of our farming, our mining, and our lumbering we create a desert. Americans need to realize that all other national hopes and aspirations are secondary to the question whether we can continue to eat. Without a fertile soil and self-renewing forests, the splendor of our bankrupt cities will become a ghastly joke. Armies and navies cannot defend a nation against the scourge of wind and flood; constitutions and courts have no authority over natural law. Any nation whose land naturally tends to turn into desert must take measures to preserve the land or it will surely die.
>
> Nations in other parts of the world have prospered for hundreds or thousands of years because either by luck or good management they were able to preserve their soil. In the Orient some of the flat lands have been preserved by careful fer-

tilization. In Peru the land was terraced at a staggering public cost, creating a stable civilization
which endured until it was conquered by the
Spanish invasion. The cost of survival depends on
the density of population and on the extent to
which it is forced to use poor or sloping land. If
the population is small enough to afford land for
grazing rather than for plow crops, the problem of
preserving the land is far simpler and the necessary discipline is less severe. In America, with our
present population and our present knowledge of
agricultural technology, we can easily support ourselves by plowing only the flat lands or the lands
that can be terraced without great expense. We
have land enough to afford to raise cattle without
overgrazing, and we can afford to turn our moun-
tainsides into forest without overcrowding ourselves in the valleys. America, therefore, does not
need to submit to the drastic antlike discipline by
which Egypt and Peru held back the desert. But
America cannot escape the necessity of controlling
the present ominous wastage of the land.

What has happened in the second half of the twentieth century is but a continuation of our historical irre-
sponsibility. Unrestrained avarice and a reckless dis-
regard for consequences has "urbanized" (sub-
urbanized?) the countryside around and between
selected groups of cities all but emptying the small
towns and rural areas, settling the burgeoning populations in ecologically destructive patterns which the
affluent economy favored, perhaps almost unconsciously, because such environments demand a maximum of intermediary services and mechanical energy
to make them habitable.

* * *

Despite a laisser-faire economy in which private
ownership of land plays an important part, governmental intervention in land use has been customary

whether through financial inducements such as urban renewal and mortgage insurance, by zoning regulations to safeguard "health, safety, and the general welfare," or by the right of eminent domain[1] established under the Fifth Amendment to the Constitution.

As far back as 1790 Jefferson wrote in his *Opinion On (The) Capital,* "In Paris it is forbidden to build a house beyond a given height and it is admitted to be a good restriction. It keeps down the price of grounds, keeps the houses low and convenient, and the streets light and airy. . . ." In 1791 George Washington endorsed a zoning resolution for the Capital: "Walls of any house to be no higher than 40' to the roof in any part of the city: nor shall they be any lower than 35' on any of the Avenues." In this century the 1922

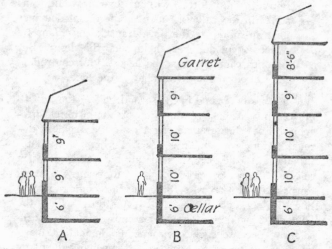

"*A new set of guiding controls.*" The rebuilding act after the Great Fire (London, 1667). Houses fronting on: (A) streets and lanes, (B) streets and lanes of note and along the River Thames, (C) high and principal streets.

[1] The right of the government to take what is needed for works in the public interest provided the owner is justly compensated.

Standard State Zoning Enabling Act of the United
States Department of Commerce has served as a model
for all state zoning laws, and since the 1930s governmental controls and interventions in land use have multiplied.

The New York State Urban Development Corporation is an example. Organized in 1968 it was given
state-wide powers to acquire land by purchase, lease,
or condemnation and to plan and develop it as it saw
fit and at any scale, including entire communities. Another example is the Louisiana Community Development Act of 1972 authorized to acquire land "to promote the sound growth of parishes and municipalities
by enabling them to undertake the correction of deficient conditions . . . through comprehensive and co-
ordinated community development. . . ." These things
to be accomplished by "the encouragement of maximum
participation by the private sector of the economy"
meaning, alas, the entrepreneurial interests usually devoted not to these good ends but to the quick buck.

The alternative to this free enterprise approach is the
equally unsatisfactory prospect of bureaucracy planning
where we live, whom we live with, and how we live.
This was one of the objections of the local citizenry
to the Urban Development Corporation whose original
charter included the power to pre-empt local zoning and
building regulations as they related to its developments.[2]

Being land rich we have squandered some of our best,
the orchard lands of Santa Clara Valley in California
being one heartbreaking instance among hundreds. Here
between 1947 and 1965, two hundred square miles of
fruit land were turned into suburbs when with a modi-
cum of controls the same number of people could have
been better planned for in a fifth the space.

[2] As a result of a five-year-long suit, the charter was
changed; approval by local governing bodies is required before projects are erected within their territorial jurisdictions.
A victory for local autonomy but not necessarily for enlight-
ened planning.

There are signs that such rapes may not happen again as we are beginning to discover that a bookkeeper's profit-and-loss sheet is not the sole criterion for establishing land use, nor does agreement between a willing buyer and a willing seller establish its value. The National Environmental Policy Act of 1970 reflects this new attitude: "We declare a national policy which will encourage productive and enjoyable harmony between man and his environment; to promote efforts which will prevent or eliminate damage to the environment and biosphere and stimulate the health and welfare of man: to enrich the understanding of the ecological system and natural resources important to the nation, and to establish a Council on Environmental Quality." The act sounds sweeping but in fact is limited in scope, for its provisions apply *only* to projects funded wholly or in part by federal funds.[3] Nonetheless, it is a beginning. California wrote a similar law in 1972 and other states are writing their versions. Such laws are, of course, pains in the neck—another bureaucracy, more forms, lawyers, and red tape. Yet if there is no self-control and controls are needed, must not controls be imposed? The answer, I fear, is yes.

Any rule, regulation, or law hobbles someone's liberty and liberty is not to be abridged lightly. In accepting the need for controls, we can only speak (somewhat vaguely) of the greatest good for the greatest number and trust that the greatest number can know, or even agree on, what is their greatest good. At the same time, we mutter under our breath, "Nobody ever said consensus proves a thing right."

[3] For such projects a statement is required, which assesses in detail the potential impact on the environment of the proposal: social, economic, and ecological. The assessment of natural conditions is extensive: geology, soils, vegetation, hydrology, ground water, climate, wildlife, are considered. Among man-made elements to be assessed are: present uses of the land, transportation systems, recreation facilities, agriculture, utilities, historic factors, etc.

The direct way for a nation to control land use is to own the land and there have been cogent arguments favoring it from Plato to Karl Marx. In England Herbert Spencer suggested that if landowners had a valid right to the land "landless man might equitably be expelled from the earth altogether." In the United States Henry George found private ownership of land had "no more foundation in morality or reason than private ownership of air or sunlight," but unlike other radical nineteenth-century theoreticians he found "private occupancy and use of land as right and indispensable." In many European countries the taking of selected land for public use is common; since the beginning of this century the city of Stockholm, for instance, has been acquiring large amounts of land on its peripheries, holding it for development, in some cases for as many as twenty-five years. Control is kept by the municipality as the land is not sold but leased. Or closer to home: Puerto Rico in 1962 created the Puerto Rican Land Administration empowered to "acquire real property which may be kept in reserve . . . for public work, social and economic programs . . . including but not limited to housing and industrial development programs. . . ." Predictably as the act placed few restraints on land use there was a vast increase in the pollution caused by the acceleration of heavy industry on this small, densely populated tropical island. As a result environmental and public health problems became so grave that in 1970 an environmental law was passed which has succeeded in alleviating conditions but only in areas not in conflict with the interests of the large industries.

* * *

As a nation, we are not accustomed to public ownership of land except for roads, parks, military reservations, and the like, so government land banking on any large scale may not be for us, not now, not yet. The simpler and more acceptable route is "a changed atti-

tude toward land—a separation of ownership of land itself from ownership of urbanization rights. . . ."[4] A
strict zoning of all land may be the answer rather than
public ownership of some. As a corollary a different
view of zoning would be needed, for up to now zoning
laws had an almost single-minded involvement in protecting and enhancing the cash value of land and an
amazing lack of interest in the health, welfare, and
safety of people or the care, feeding, and preservation
of natural resources. Nor does there seem to have been
much common sense used in zoning and planning for
more convenient time- and energy-saving space relationships needed in the carrying out of our quotidian activities. As to aesthetics, one would assume beauty, like
the wild Indian, had to be hunted down and destroyed.

The impact of our technical processes on the land
is pervasive, the wastes dribble down the rivers or float
on the wind poisoning distant places, the chain saws
hack out a thousand years of growth in a week, the
machines of agriculture chew up endless acres, and the
wilderness itself is trashed by snowmobile and jeep. To
contain the devastation and prevent its spread, local
controls are often inadequate. In many situations zoning
must be regional in scope, sometimes national, and, as
in the case of the seas, international.

It is not easy for a decentralist to call for any kind
of centralized authority, yet what other recourse is
there? We have problems that at one extreme call for
the gathering together of sprawling populations and at
the other breaking up vast metropolitan congestions into
more workable units. We have the need to limit the
asphalt spread, preserve our rural and wild lands, taking
into account not only the land surface but its subsurface,
water tables, and waterways. Do we need to say that
land is our primary resource, that on it we produce what

[4] *The Use of Land: A Citizen Policy Guide to Urban
Growth.* Report sponsored by Rockefeller Brothers Fund,
1972.

we eat, from it we dig what we need to warm and shelter us?

Surely, then, the bankers and brokers and their theoreticians are wrong when they say, "The controlling factor in determining land use is economic rent."

CHAPTER XIII

The Building Trades and Housing

Though the construction industry in the United States represents about 10 per cent of the gross national product and employs almost 15 per cent of our labor force, building technology has barely changed since the end of World War II, and, with few exceptions, there have been no changes of consequence since the nineteenth-century development of reinforced concrete, the steel-framed structure, and the elevator. This is surprising since improvements in manufacturing processes of building materials have kept pace with all other manufacturing, and, as wages paid building construction workers are among the highest in the country, management should have strong desires to automate. It is an anomaly, true not only of the United States but of Europe as well, that, generally speaking, the cheapest way to build a fireproof wall remains old-fashioned brick or block and the residential type in the United States is still the wood-framed home on its separate lot familiar to our grandfathers.

One would have believed, and many did, that given the mechanization in all other industry, and the huge demand for new housing generated by the shelter requirement of the American Standard of Living, a prefabricated housing industry, comparable to automobile or aircraft, would have been created.[1] No such industry happened, although from the twenties through the fifties, there was vast interest, many proposals, endless discussions, and even some pilot plants were built. In-

[1] Especially in the light of our history: "With the application of machinery, the labor of house building has been greatly lessened, and the western prairies are dotted over with houses which have been shipped there all made and the various pieces numbered" (1872).

explicably, no industry resulted. Today, prefabrication as a way of providing housing is a dead letter with the exception of the "mobile home," which is not mobile and considering the cramped accommodations, ugliness, and impersonality, not much in the way of a home.

Although building construction is very like what it was in former times, somewhat less work is done at the job site—gypsum board put up in large sheets replaces the plastered partition, concrete beams and wall panels are shipped from the yard in finished form, there are glass and metal curtain wall assemblies. It is hard to think of something really innovative other than the proliferation and elaboration of mechanical devices first designed to satisfy our taste for comfort and convenience, later (as architectural common sense became perverted) required to keep the buildings habitable.

What has really changed in the building trade is organization and worker skill. The size and scope of each building operation has increased, as have all enterprises in the centralizing economy: All is geared to the large-scale operation. Since a project whether large or small must go through the same accounting methods and same bureaucratic procedures, how *can* a modern organization, private or public, afford the smaller scale even if it were more efficient? Craftsmanship diminishes, in part because there is a general disdain for the hand worker and in part because large organizations cannot accept individual initiative, the essence of the craftsman's involvement and so his skill.

Building enterprises have become larger and larger. In a city such as New York, an office building in 1925 would be built on a 100' x 100' site and perhaps rise as high as sixteen stories. In the 1960s nothing less than a block (200' x 400' or 600') and fifty stories was considered suitable. From the Woolworth to the Empire State buildings was almost twenty years, and they were landmarks. By the late sixties, very tall buildings were relatively common and very, very tall buildings no cause for excitement. Similarly, when suburban developers first built on speculation, twenty houses at a clip was considered a good-sized enterprise. After World War II, this became five hundred or even whole developments (e.g., Levittown).

The increase in project size was not, as we've said, motivated by improved building techniques or new materials, although cranes, earth movers, and other builder's equipment increased in size and power; the main motivation was money and its management. Developers quickly discovered that money from big institutions, including government, meant dealing with the endless paper work and time-wasting procedures inevitable in bureaucracies. It was clear that it took the same trouble to get a lot of money as a small amount, and as it turned out the man with the small project couldn't afford the time and effort, nor did he have the "connections." Soon there were lots of big projects all in the hands of large corporations, joint ventures and conglomerates, all, or almost all, depending on the kind of government financing and guarantees born in the

Depression, developed to meet the demands of World War II, crystallized in the fifties, and reaching maturity as old-style capitalism fades.

Building used to be in the hands of firms whose owners had often started with trowel or saw in hand, who owned equipment, hired men, and supervised the work, who were in part businessmen but essentially master craftsmen. The organization of the large-scale venture called for managerial, marketing, and cost accounting skills such men did not possess. Big business did. Into the cumbersome, creaking tradition-bound machinery of the old craft of building was introduced not a new technology, but a new management and a new scale more suited to a society that equates growth with progress, size with quality, central control with efficiency, and efficiency with the good life.

On the whole, the product of this new management does not provide the Vitruvian virtues of *convenience, firmness,* or *delight* of earlier buildings, nor have we seen any economies, at least economies passed on to users.

GADGETS AND MECHANICAL DEVICES

A gadget could be defined as a mechanical device that is not strictly necessary. Not all mechanical devices are gadgets although misuse can make them so. The major mechanical devices that have shaped and styled our urban buildings are the high-speed elevator, forced ventilation (which includes heating and cooling), and high-level lighting. These have made buildings usable that were designed without the slightest consideration of climate, economics, or common sense. Such buildings are now found in every city, and even suburb, with any pretense to modernity, from New York to Timbuktu, and are the ultimate example of the Victorian fondness for gadgetry applied to building. These sealed glass boxes are surprisingly alike: in plan a center core containing elevators, toilets, and emergency stairs, often with parking garages incorporated below ground, shops and, of course, a branch bank at street level, steam rising from the rooftop cooling towers. They stand four square, brightly lit night and day—symbols of our belief in the inexhaustible sum of our natural resources.

An Office Building

The World Trade Center in New York, because it's so big and brash, is not so much an example as an archetype; one billion dollars' worth of development including twin towers, each 110 stories high, faced with aluminum (a material requiring fifteen times more energy in its making than steel). The external glazing is symmetrical on all sides as suits the platonic climate of skyscraper builders. No window can be opened by any occupant, nor can he turn off his lights or control his ventilation, for these central systems require that entire floors be turned on at once. No matter if it is sunny outside or the air balmy, the lights brightly glare so that 50 per cent of all energy used goes to provide that often unneeded light, which in turn throws off heat, which must be mechanically cooled. The elevators rush 1,100 feet up their rails in hardly more than a minute, the pumps pump and the turbines turn, all burning up each day 80,000 kilowatts of generating capacity, the equal of Schenectady, New York, a city with a population of about 80,000. Yet these towers are probably occupied not more than other office buildings—eight hours (or is it seven?) a day, five days a week with, we trust, time off for good behavior.

Such buildings might be considered monuments to the U.S. economic model which demands increasing the GNP by 4 per cent a year (equals doubling goods and services in seventeen years, quadrupling in thirty-four, etc.). It seems almost symbolic that the 7,000 toilets in this building dumped their untreated excrement into the waters of New York Bay.

An American Home

Most Americans live in separate little houses on separate little plots of land. These homes aspire to the ideal of the TV commercial—the house as a repository of cleaning fluids and devices, deodorants, fizzy drinks in the refrigerator, motor-driven everythings from can openers to curtains, mixers, and toothbrushes. In these houses, there are electric blankets, clocks, and irons, electric stoves, rotisseries, toasters, waffle makers, egg beaters, and though the block of food, just out of the refrigerator or freezer, is precooked, the oven is self-cleaning. The windows are kept closed winter and summer to keep the dust out and the conditioned air in. In the winter the air is dried by heated blasts and dampened by humidifiers. The clothes washer and dishwasher swish and clack away in phase with the harsh tone of the garbage being ground. Through the sound of country music from the stereo, the vacuum cleaners groan across the wall-to-wall nylon carpeting. The aerator in the tropical fish tank bubbles, the bathroom exhaust fan competes with the kitchen exhaust; unexpectedly, the oil burner adds its pop as the telephone rings. The doorbell chimes over the static from a radio and an untended television bellows, bright-colored face shining in the well-lit ambiance of the uninhabited room. There are sun lamps and night lights, security lights and floodlights, fluorescent and incandescent. Switches and thermostats, rheostats, thermometers and barometers, pumps and compressors, fans and registers, all designed to keep things going or directing where they should go, with an electric burglar alarm system to guard it all.

All these extraordinary objects, sights, sounds, and functions are typically contained in houses quite like those of fifty years ago, except not as well built or as roomy, although the bathrooms do have floor-to-ceiling plastic laminate glued to composition board, the kitchen "genuine" vinyl tile floors and the windows are made of aluminum, as are the venetian blinds. The windows are also draped with fiberglass, the furniture upholstered in Naugahyde (will the Nauga become an endangered species?), and the imitation beams made of imitation wood give a rustic air to the ceiling of the "family room" in keeping with its "provincial style" portable bar.

Outside there are variations in type, "ranch" and "salt box" being prevalent. The walls may be faced with wood siding or what looks like wood, for it may be "maintenance-free" aluminum. The brick or stone may be what it appears but maybe not; the shingled roof looks somewhat like slate but is made of asphalt-impregnated cardboard. Set on its "estate-sized" quarter acre with its foundation planting and the car in the driveway, the style is national, and why should it not be—it is based on prophetically self-fulfilling market research.

We give this inventory not to make fun of people who labor away to possess these things. They, like all of us, are creatures of our time; conned by the well-trained agencies who plan selling campaigns and subject to the impact made when fantastic sums of money buy all ways of delivering the message.[2]

Our purpose in listing these "gadgets" (possessions, many of which fit our definition of gadgetry) is to

---

[2] What does happen over the long run to the minds of the average American family when, so we are told, they spent during 1972 over six hours a day watching television? Since a four-minute slot out of every half hour is set aside for commercials (say three quarters of an hour out of the TV day), it is astonishing that we are not more brainwashed than we are. Perhaps the ad men are not so skilled after all?

remind us how much energy and how many nonreplaceable resources they all require to make, how much
mechanical energy to operate, and what a surprising
number are duplicates in function, or are so highly specialized that they can be used only occasionally. These
oddments and fitments are often cheaply put together,
get out of order quickly, and are either not repairable,
not worth repairing, or very costly to repair. We all
joke about whether the repairman will make house
calls and whether his service is less or more expensive
than the doctor's. So the motto is "If in doubt, throw it
out," which explains in part why the average American
uses up to 874,000 British thermal units each day, and
each day has to dispose of five pounds of debris.

Some Special Structures

We've said elsewhere that almost all the mechanical inventions that make the late twentieth century what it is
were known in Queen Victoria's time. We find this also
true in building technology. The last seventy-five years
have been not much more than a period of refinement
and elaboration, despite the unprecedented volume of
building. Not even such an apparent latecomer to the
scene as the inflatable structure is new, for patents
were granted in 1917 to an English engineer named
William Lanchester for pneumatic structures; the geo-
desic dome generally accredited to Buckminster Fuller
was invented by Walter Bauerfeld as an armature for a
planetarium erected in 1922 on the roof of the Zeiss
Optical plant in Jena, Germany; and even our com-
munications satellite has its structural ancestor in a hydrogen container with a copper skin made by the famous Frenchman Marey-Monge in 1844.

The fascinating webs, nets, and membranes of the
tensile structures of Buckminster Fuller and Frei Otto
are but enchanting and sophisticated developments of

ancient engineering principles used in tents, suspension bridges, balloons, baskets, and even fish traps. What has led to practical modern applications of these principles is in some part due to the computerized ease of calculating the probable action of such structures, but the major impetus is given by the durable membranes developed by polymer chemistry.

Comparatively few such structures have been built, as they have basic limitations: Although spaces of great size without internal supports can be economically spanned, in any practical application the structures are limited to a single story. Their use therefore is most suited to special-purpose buildings such as gymnasiums, arenas, and exhibition halls or as in the case of Fuller's small geodesics, as living space, popular especially among the young. Nevertheless, systems such as these which concentrate on using minimum materials, time, and energy to create maximum shelter are bound to be of increasing interest and importance.

HOUSING

Everyone must have sufficient food and a decent shelter, before the dwelling of anyone else is made ornate. Everyone must be dressed comfortably and warmly before anyone else should be permitted to dress ornately. In order to achieve this, and until this is achieved, the available goods must be delivered equally and planfully among all.

—J. G. Fichte (1800)

In the lexicons of architecture, city planning, and sociology, the word "housing" is a synonym for sheltering the poor. Others have homes, the poor live in "projects."

Since Franklin Roosevelt's New Deal days, it has been an article of liberal faith to say that a third of the nation is ill housed. Statistics are brought out to prove the need for massive destruction and rebuilding; the former to get rid of bad housing and called slum clearance, the latter in the name of urban renewal. As things have gone both terms are in disfavor, for the beneficiaries have not been the poor but the entrepreneurs (which accounts for the support given public housing programs by persons otherwise not exactly known for their generous feelings). On the other hand, from generation to generation, there have been individuals, groups, and organizations of reformers convinced that the panacea for poverty was to be found in rehousing the poor.

In 1890 Jacob Riis reported, "Today three-quarters of its [New York's] people live in the tenements and the 19th century drift of the population to the cities is sending ever increasing multitudes to crowd them. The 15,000 tenement houses that were the despair of the sanitarian in the past generation have swelled to 37,000. . . ."

To solve such problems, the New York City Tenement House Law of 1901 was passed. "This new law," wrote a delighted philanthropist, "is the best that can be hoped for, being equal to the model tenement in its essential particulars of adequate light and ventilation, proper sanitary conveniences, reasonable protection against fire and opportunities for privacy." Within seven years of the passage of the act, one quarter of the city's population were housed in the new tenements. Most popular was the "dumbbell" plan which forty years later housing experts such as Catherine Bauer deplored: "As for New York," she wrote, "I defy anyone unacquainted with the history of model tenements before the war (1914–18) to distinguish between them and any average speculative slum." Presi-

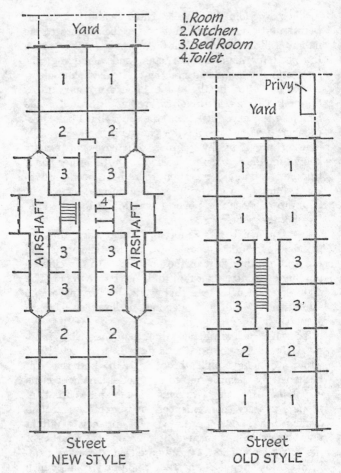

1. *Room*
2. *Kitchen*
3. *Bed Room*
4. *Toilet*

Yard

AIRSHAFT

AIRSHAFT

Street
NEW STYLE

Privy

Yard

Street
OLD STYLE

New York tenements.

dent Herbert Hoover's Conference on Home Building reported in 1932, "It is an anomaly that during the period of our nation's greatest advance in national wealth —the past twenty years—the housing of 70% of our population has progressively deteriorated."

In 1949 the Federal Housing Act became law because "one third of the population was ill housed"— "the general welfare and security of the nation and the health and living standards of the people requires producing housing and related community development sufficient to remedy the housing shortage and get rid of substandard housing . . . to provide decent housing and a suitable living environment for every American family."

In 1969 the National Commission on Urban Affairs repeated the old refrain, "A third of the nation cannot afford adequate non-subsidized housing."

To "solve" the housing problem thousands of buildings, good, mediocre, and bad, were demolished, and in their place, sometimes, but not always, vast housing projects (as they are called) were erected. From the viewpoint of physical planning, all had equal utility, hundreds and thousands of dwelling units (as they are called) stacked up in multilevels or few, ranged in varied geometries of equal monotony. Storage spaces for people.

Some, unaccountably, were found acceptable by the people living in them; some, unaccountably, have been disasters. Among the latter kind, suggesting a gross fallacy in housing theory (though no lesson seems to have been learned from it) was Pruitt-Igoe in St. Louis built in the late 1950s. In the late '60s it was abandoned and later demolished, considered uninhabitable by those it was designed to serve. Amazing! Light, air, white walls, plenty of plumbing, solidly constructed, acclaimed by housing experts and architects. Such an example suggests that the least important part of housing may be in the brick and mortar, the plumbing, or even the architectural design.

No tangible thing, not even that it is "public" housing, makes some buildings unbearable since in many of
our large cities we find privately owned buildings of
all types abandoned, vandalized, burned out. In New
York City, especially in the Bronx and Brooklyn, there
are blocks of these three- and four-story wrecks. Dr.
Frank Kristof estimated there were 105,000 apartments
in such buildings abandoned between 1960 and 1970,
of which 90,000 were still standing and wholly vacant,
this count excluding cleared buildings waiting demoli-
tion and an undetermined number of owner-abandoned
buildings still partially occupied. A New York *Times*
survey indicated that between 1970 and 1975, 30,000
to 60,000 apartment units were abandoned.

In Detroit the federal government was forced to fore-
close over 5,000 single homes in the inner city all
structurally sound but "caught in the ravages of central
city decay, the greed of some real estate operators and
laxity of the FHA which made appraisals at prices
inflated by the speculators. Most of this property lies
vacant and vandalized, abandoned by its owners."[3]
Three years later the Detroit *Free Press* reported,
"Today many major streets are nothing but strips of
abandoned buildings. The United States Department of
Housing and Urban Development owns some 9,000
abandoned homes in Detroit—more homes than there
are in Midland, Michigan, a city of 35,000 people. . . ." The size of the problem varies but is no
different in kind in Newark, Philadelphia, Cleveland,
Chicago, Dallas. It is axiomatic that as cities' economic
and social troubles grow, tax delinquencies and foreclo-
sures will grow exponentially as will the destruction of
habitable space.

At the same time the migration to the large metropolitan areas continues, suggesting substantial abandonment of housing in small towns and rural areas.

If we couple housing abandonment with the slowing
down in population growth, we must assume there is

[3] New York *Times*, 1972.

no shortage of housing, but a shortage of houses that people (even poor people) are willing to live in. Must we not then ask what is meant by livable housing, for surely it is something more than a simple desire for sanitary and convenient shelter.

The Joint Center for Housing Studies of Harvard/MIT once defined a physically inadequate housing unit as "one that lacks complete indoor plumbing facilities, or has all the plumbing, but the heating is inadequate for the local climate, or that has all the plumbing and adequate heating but is in a dilapidated condition." Obviously all but the last of this definition would seem odd to Louis XIV at Versailles or almost anyone living in the nineteenth-century world (including Queen Victoria at Windsor) as a description of inadequate housing.

So when we hear as a conservative estimate that 13 million U.S. families in 1970 were "housing deprived" we might ask whether the housing standard on which such estimates are based is a reasonable one. Could it be that housing agencies, builders, material suppliers, and even architects support such figures because of self-interest and not interest in shelter, community, and a more reasonable allocation of world resources?

* * *

In the cause of conservation of natural (including human) resources, three points can be made on the current housing situation. First, like everything else in our society, bigger, more, and new has been the slogan. Second, in all probability, we have enough housing for all, if it is kept in repair and efficiently used. Third, it's not the housing, it's the environs that need the work. Let me briefly look at each of these.

More. In Brooklyn in the 1890s A. T. White built a "model tenement" block. Each apartment contained four rooms, a kitchen alcove, and a toilet, all in 650 square feet. "The plan . . . may be justly considered as the *beau idéal* of the model tenement. . . . They

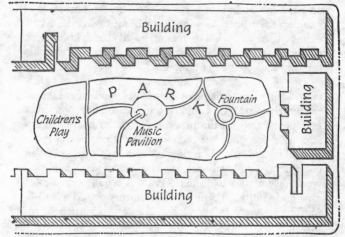

SITE PLAN

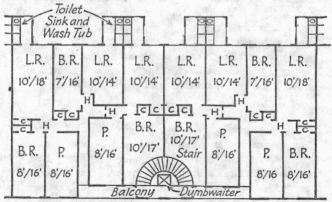

L.R.= Living Room B.R.= Bed Room
P.= Parlor C.= Closet H.= Hall

FLOOR PLAN
showing six flats

A. T. White's Riverside buildings in Brooklyn, New York (1890s). "The *beau idéal* of the model tenement in a great city."

[the tenants] live in peace with one another because they have elbow room" (Jacob Riis). These apartments of course had neither central heating, bath, nor elevators. In the 1930s in New York City, Knickerbocker Village was built. It had central heating, bathrooms, and being high-rise, had to have elevators. The average apartment size was 700 square feet.

As one would expect in a society where the economy depends on selling more and more, we find this sequence. After World War II the basic shell of the average suburban speculative builder's house was 800 square feet. By the time of the Korean War, the average house insured by the FHA was 1,100 square feet and by 1970 had increased to 1,600 square feet, while the families got smaller (there was a 25 per cent drop in family size during this period). As the conventional house got larger (and more expensive) the mobile home market expanded from 112,000 units in 1955 to over 450,000 in 1971 accounting for more than half of all single-family houses bought and for 95 per cent of those costing under $15,000.

The mobile home, often only 300 square feet in area, is claimed by the manufacturers to be designed for "comfortable, convenient, and attractive living." Unfortunately these good things are in the sales pitch rather than the reality. What is real, however, is a smaller initial investment. Mobile homes are cheap but are not bargains—their life span is usually ten to twelve years; inadequate insulation and skimpy construction result in high heat and repair bills; shoddy plumbing, electrical deficiencies, warped doors and floors are among the complaints. It's amazing! A technology which brings forth the elegance of the Caravel can do no better with "machines for living" than these badly made metal containers. Set on concrete blocks in what used to be called trailer camps and are now called mobile home parks (parks as in parking) they produce made-to-order slums, perhaps the ugliest settlements ever devised by man.

Nevertheless, the mobile home provides shelter for many and, unplanned though it was, performs another service of lasting importance: The mobile home manufacturers have demonstrated that shelter can be provided without satisfying the demands of craft unions, building codes, or real estate mortgages since the mobile home is portable hence a vehicle, not a building, not a real estate improvement. Another unplanned result has been the use of the mobile home as utility core. It is suggestive: Standardization of mechanical devices such as cooking and toilet facilities (even sleeping space) is provided; sooner or later, one can attach to it living rooms, small or spacious, modest or luxurious, rational or fanciful as temperament dictates or means allow.

In 1968 the Federal Housing Administration described a mini-house for low-income families as requiring 720 square feet, so it is astonishing to some that a couple, often with a child, can live in the confines of the average mobile home. The secret is that people are adaptable and compressible unlike, say, automobiles—a 4,000-pound automobile will *not* fit into a ten-foot-long garage. In Hong Kong five or six people share cubicles measuring 40 square feet although the local law in its generous way allocates 35 square feet to each occupant. In Guatemala the average number of people is three to a small room while "in a single shop house in Singapore, I saw families of 6 to 8 people facing life in airless, windowless rooms 7 x 10' with as many as 5 children sleeping on the roach-ridden floor beneath the bed" (Charles Abrams, 1964).

Enough. "One thing is certain: there are already in existence sufficient buildings for dwellings in the big towns to remedy immediately any real 'housing shortage,' given national utilization of them. This can naturally only take place by the expropriation of the present owners and by quartering in their houses the homeless or those workers excessively overcrowded in their former houses."[4]

Expropriation is an alternative we don't recommend, yet it may be more equitable to expropriate dwelling space used little or not at all than to expropriate a portion of every citizen's income to subsidize new houses which (a) may not be needed, or (b) if needed should not be built as they often are in isolation from work place, schools, shops, and recreation, or (c) built at densities that suit inflated land costs but not the human need, or (d) designed in the so familiar drab institutional and inhuman way or in the elegant institutional, inhuman way.

It would also seem that if housing is to be subsidized it should provide the maximum benefits at minimum costs. Building huge-scaled, multistoried municipal tenements in the great cities seems a perverse answer. Whenever and wherever built, they have been more costly to construct and maintain while providing inferior accommodations than found in the two- or three-storied garden apartment, row house, or even detached dwelling types. This was true in former times and today, in Europe as well as America. In Vienna of the 1920s workers' apartments of 519 square feet cost 14,400 shillings to build while suburban cottages containing 40 per cent more space as well as a garden plot, more sunlight and better air, cost the same money. In New York in the 1930s the city housing project called Williamsburg Houses cost $7,866 a dwelling unit while a suburban unit of the same size cost $5,000.

The recent (1974) housing in New York is called subsidizing of upper income households: "38% of the apartments aided by tax exemption programs are ex-

[4] Frederick Engels, *The Housing Question*, 1872. Not different a hundred years later: "Around Rome is a belt of squalid shanty towns housing 70,000 people. At the same time 50,000 apartments in new buildings officially classified as deluxe are vacant for want of buyers or tenants." (1975)

pected to have monthly rentals of $140. or more a room, requiring a family income of more than $30,000. a year to afford a 2 bedroom unit. Another 41% will rent for $100. to $139. a room, requiring a $23,000. income for a 2 bedroom unit."

It used to be said that less than 5 per cent of New York's population could afford new housing built without governmental subsidies. This is probably an optimistic figure. If our aim is to conserve resources, then recycling is the word that applies to buildings as well as cans and bottles.

Rehabilitation and repair of older buildings seems in order (let's not forget that in a city like New York 75 per cent of its buildings are *less* than seventy-five years old!) and while making these older buildings habitable, let's also not forget the newer ones. Perhaps now is the time to think of changing the occupancy of redundant office buildings, "for in New York—and Chicago, Pittsburgh, Dallas, Denver, Minneapolis, St. Louis, Houston and Los Angeles—there is more office space available than tenants care to rent. In a number of cities, new buildings stand half empty while construction is being completed on others that will add even more space."[5]

It's not the housing. "40% of the distress among the poor, said a recent official report, is due to drunkenness —and it recommended the prevention of drunkenness by providing for every man a clean and comfortable home" (Jacob Riis, 1890).

It should be clear that after generations of agitation for housing reform and over forty years of government-aided housing for poor people, we should recognize that bad housing is not the only or even the major cause of crime, drunkenness, and disease. Or that slum conditions will be wiped out simply by improving the housing.

The slum reflects the misery of its inhabitants, and if the physical surroundings are "improved" it is evident

[5] *Wall Street Journal,* 1974.

they will soon, and even violently, be brought to their former state.[6] If this is so then was Pruitt-Igoe found unsuitable by the tenants because its white walls blandly announced all was well when all was unhappiness and despair? How else shall we explain the nationwide vandalizing of newly built housing? How shall we explain Talbert Mall in Buffalo or the Stella Wright Houses, the Scudder and Hayes Homes in Newark?

Talbert Mall is a low-density garden apartment development, similar to hundreds found in middle-class areas throughout the country. Publicly subsidized and tax-exempt, it was built in 1959 at a cost of $9.7 million with rents adjusted to the tenants' income range. In 1974 nearly 50 per cent of the families living in Talbert Mall were on welfare and 9 per cent more had incomes low enough to qualify for welfare supplements. The average family had more than three children, and 45 per cent of the families were headed by parents who were separated, divorced, widowed, or unmarried. Vandalism was as common as terror. The local police captain said few crimes were solved "because people are simply fearful of singling out persons as being responsible for a crime. They are afraid for their own well being," noting there were fifteen arrests for every one hundred crimes at the Mall with many more unreported.

At Stella Wright the story is similar. Here are seven thirteen-story buildings built in 1960. Fifteen years later there are only 430 tenants in this 1,200-apartment complex. Like Talbert Mall the rents are proportioned to income; like the Scudder and Hayes Homes it is a wasteland of broken glass and defaced walls set in a no man's land of razed buildings, empty lots, and garbage. In the middle of 1975 the Newark Housing Authority proposed to start "full scale renovation work. We have $5.8 million for that purpose and approximately $1.3

[6] No different in fact than the luckier who do the reverse, clearing out of *their* neighborhoods the ramshackle or unsightly as unsuitable.

million for the development of a tenant management corporation."

So it goes. It is no satisfaction for an architect and physical planner to report that there is little evidence showing new housing to be a prime requirement for the safety, health, and welfare of poor people, adequate evidence that the housing the poor spurn would be considered superior by their parents and luxurious by their grandparents, and all kinds of evidence showing it is not new houses but a better kind of home life that is needed. Similarly the need is not for better school buildings but better schooling, not new community centers but in people finding a sense of purpose. None of these things can come about as long as there are people who feel themselves redundant, whose sole social function is to consume but who don't have the money to buy the tempting goods nor the wit to escape the life-draining situations the welfare state supports.

An affluent, energy-intensive society has many problems. A major one is finding the answer to *what a man does when he has nothing to do* (except make a general nuisance of himself), since it is simply not enough to provide food and shelter as to an animal in a zoo. The products of society's work may be given him, but they are virtually meaningless for it is not the product that engages people, but their involvement in the production of the product. The zucchinis that grow from the seed planted, watered, and tended taste not merely fresher than the store-bought kind but have a further dimension—involvement in their existence.

In high technology the do-it-yourself movement, peripheral to the "work" day, often offers the only genuine work satisfaction. (Such work does not enter into calculations of the gross national product, yet providing the tools, parts, and materials is a $6-billion-a-year industry.) If the small satisfactions of occasional carpentry, sewing, painting, and gardening are so important, let us try to imagine the pleasure of a life in which every effort was expended to create the necessary and the pleasant, in which involvement in the production was the norm, not the exception.

Our productivity per man-hour has trebled since 1900; an unexpected by-product is the permanently unemployed. If Erich Fromm is right in saying "the mode of work is itself an essential in forming a person's character," then what do we say to the destruction of character implicit in an evaluation of the United States by Gunnar Myrdal: "nearly 6% of workers in the civilian labor force are unemployed, and still worse, the unemployed are becoming a homogenous, depressed class, such as is not supposed to exist in America—unskilled, uneducated, demoralized and inarticulate. Our unemployed are largely unemployable."

These are not the jolly workers emancipated by the machine, celebrated in *A Nous la Liberté* of René Clair, nor the slaves of the assembly line in Chaplin's *Modern Times*, but human beings turned into pollutants by what hindsight shows to have been sheer indifference and the inability to weigh cause and effect. To have destroyed the possibility of people earning a livelihood on farms and in small towns, forcing mass migrations to the cities, was an act of unparalleled stupidity. In the United States we see the result in the pathos of our welfare cases, our hoodlums, our lost souls, and we are not alone: "In Paris, Honoré Gévaudan, a senior officer in the criminal police, characterized the typical holdup man this way: 'generally he quits school at age 14, he comes from a broken family, he lives in a housing project, he wants to get his hands on money easily . . . hard luck kids—but real bastards.'"

Contrary to all common sense, many of the unskilled, semiskilled, and blue-collar workers have been concentrated in the core of our cities exactly where meaningful or even possible employment is not, exactly where the living and housing costs are greatest.

It is not with bricks and sticks that we'll solve such problems.

For the time being the architects' and planners' practical job is a humble one: to make do with what we have, squeezing the last useful bit from our housing stock partly to teach ourselves the disciplines of conservation, partly because there are scarcities, and partly because time is needed to find our way without haste or waste forward (and perhaps with more than one backward glance). It would be a boring program for an architect if it were not apparent that no matter how cleverly we patch, our existing buildings, streets, and towns will not do in any long-range view. How could they? As fuel sources diminish, we will again have to place our buildings so they relate to sun and breeze, plan our homes, work, and play places in more compact and convenient ways. Still more important will be the effect on our planning of the changing household structure caused by the decline of the nuclear family, the general acceptance of sexual equality, and the widespread yearning for more communal social arrangements. And then, we may presume, our future clients will not be anonymous users, passively accepting or brutally rejecting, but partners adding their sense and experience to the enterprise.

As in everything else a new style in the architecture of buildings and towns results from a new way of looking at things, from new demands, a new understanding, a new mode of solving problems. In a way designers of the human habitat now have a simpler theoretical problem than those of the past when changes both in culture and in technology had to be reckoned with. Since we have more than enough technology, we can concentrate on a single aim—to find the expressive form for the postindustrial society.

Index